Jackass on a Camel

Fossils, Freaks and Mayhem
in the
Cradle of Humanity

www.jackassonacamel.com

Foreword

A friend of mine, Ric Barbera had been decent enough to read the first few chapters of this book. He said he liked it. Said it was funny and had a good style. Then he suggested I'd better clarify what it was all about in the first chapter, thinking that readers who made their way through the beginning might find themselves confused as all living hell by the advent of my rambles on *paleoanthropology*. Ric's a keenly insightful, hilarious and gifted writer. Although I am sure he's right on this account I certainly wasn't going to change the flavor of my first chapter on that silly prick's advice. Well, that's not exactly true; I did make some changes in the first part just as instructed. And suddenly paranoid that I still wasn't getting it right I decided to throw in this intro to boot.

Paleoanthropology. Now how's that for a mouthful? It's the word that covers the study of human evolution in its fossilized form. It's got eight syllables, is unacceptable to MS Word's spell-check and it lies at the heart of this book. Or it was at least the idea which led me to the places and events that would provide the material to write a book. As an aspiring writer I wasn't coming up with much to say from a purely creative sense. My forays into East Africa and dabblings in paleoanthropology, however, offered me enough material to make a cheap and easy start. Besides, it almost had already been written. My field journals were crammed with the odd tales, opinions and observations that follow. Not much more to do than make it legible and throw in a million commas.

In 1994 I had enrolled in the Koobi Fora Field School, a joint venture of Harvard University and Kenya National Museums. Before I'd even set foot in Africa the notion of a book was already in my head. Originally the idea was to write another popularized account of human evolutionary study: the thrill of discovery; the riddles posed by thrilling discoveries; the frustrations of discovers over the failure of academia or the public to be thrilled. The Field School didn't actually make any incredible finds but after the first couple of months in the program it was apparent that it could provide enough offbeat and lively material to make an interesting read.

If you were to pick up this book with the intention of gleaning a little insight into the paleoanthropological world you'd find yourself reading a while before you came across any. Somehow the paleontological stuff lost its prominence as the overarching theme of the book. Instead it became something like a jigged long-line which snagged and dragged a whole mess of other crap on board. There were clashes of culture, happy interminglings of disparate people, fucked up crazy animal encounters, organizational politics, backbiting, sabotage, bigotry, intra-racial racism, desperate poverty, bottomless wells of hospitality, fat people, sex and alcohol abuse and engine trouble. By the time I quit writing it had mutated into something other than what I had initially intended. What emerged was something I no longer knew how to categorize.

I only had to reread and edit the ugly monster a half dozen times before coming to any conclusions on the nature of the book. There are musings on evolution and diatribes over some of the hypotheses about our ancestors. There are dirty little passages, philosophic interludes, tales of terror from the animal kingdom and treatises on intestinal distress. Throughout one will find a cavalcade of decent people and downright jerks. The less likable characters help put meat on the bones of the tale and it's the frustrations, not only with them but how close my own character often aligns with them which often drive the narrative. Looking back over it all it's still tough to say if I was among the good guys or just another one of the jackasses. I went to a rather extreme place to study human evolution and possibly saw the advent of my own, for better or worse. So, whether we call this an autobiographical novel or a cheap little memoir it's still just a story. But it's one I had a blast living though and writing about later.

Back to paleoanthropology as it remains an important theme here. What we did in the Field School is covered. The research of some notables is touched upon. I also try to make plain what I've believe are serious flaws in the discipline – and not always in a nice way. I'm pathologically enchanted by the study of evolution. I love the search for our ancestors and get utterly pissed off about the behavior, biases, and overblown personalities which have directed the course of research and discovery to this day. Just mention to me the recent rash of very ancient, two-legged ape-people things unearthed in East Africa and you're in for an earful about the irresponsibility of discoverers proclaiming new species and genera on the basis of mashed jaws and squished fossil heads. Bring it up after I've had my tequila and your brain will warp wondering what the hell you ever did to deserve such a ranting, spitty lecture. I get very passionate about things like this; paleoanthropology can be a fucking frustrating science. As in many other fields there are prominent participants who seem less interested in piecing together the puzzle than in claiming large parts of it as their own. Whether we're trying to see why and when an ape took to two feet, or attempting to create a vaccine for HIV, or seeking to understand global warming, when individuals place the race for glory – or grant money – over the search for honest solutions then it just sucks all over for everybody. I muse about these things and make fun of some of it. You might even get the impression that I'm rabidly attacking some icons and their precious ideas. And that's okay, because I am.

With that in mind, here's a note about the names of characters in the book. It is a true story for the most part; there are some screwball exaggerations and psychotic interludes but they ought to be obvious to most. I should also make clear that the book was fully written a few years after its events. Though working from detailed journals and field notes some fleshing out of the information did rely on recall. Our memories are fairly flawed instruments so there may be some gaffes here and there. There are no outright fabrications but I have may have flubbed the chronology at times or attributed some minor detail to the wrong people (along the idea of saying Dick got devoured by termites when it was really Jane who has the exact haircut as the effeminate Dick...) To that end I have changed almost everybody's name. I don't want too many people getting upset...

There are some actual names I felt needed to keep, particularly those of the famed (relatively speaking) researchers who had some relation to the field school or gave us the theories and hypotheses we had to deal with. This won't matter much to some since I'm just a guy writing a wild, pulpy travel tale about his time in the fossil beds of Kenya. As for the prehistoric archaeologists, geologists, anthropologists who might be offended? Well, they're out publishing and trumpeting their roles in amazing discoveries so screw 'em if they can't weather a little unflattering light.

This is self-published, by the way – there are going to be typos.

One more thing: Writing a story is one thing but seeing it through to becoming a book requires a little help. For that I'd like to thank a couple or three people: Megan Murphy, the book doctor who patiently dealt with my disregard for tense through three drafts of the manuscript; Dr. Harry V. Merrick, the most generous and effectual mentor in the field of East African Paleoanthropology; and especially my wife, Elisa, who's had to suffer my inertia, hopes, gloom and revisions for way too long.

FHR

Further acknowledgements, slander, caveats, expurgated material and pictures might be found at www.jackassonacamel.com

For Elisa

Straight White Anthropology Student Seeks Arousing Adventure

Half past seven in the morning and half asleep on a runway in Holland. Not even halfway to where I need to be. About 3,500 miles from Boston, it's as far east as I've ever been though nothing looks any more Chinese here than it does at home. There is still some more west to put behind me but it's going to involve a steep drop in latitude which will land me in East Africa. That translates into individual hash marks in southerliness as well – The Dark Continent, the Equator, Kenya. So, from stretching the cardinal directions of my horizons and longer slides down longitude lines to new continents with countries this trip is lousy with personal firsts.

There'll be a few more places on a map to puncture with thumbtacks to be sure, but that's not quite what this trip is all about. It's not going to be a dream holiday riding busses to the Savanna to watch prides of lions licking each other. This ain't no vacation as there is something greater lying beyond this string of airports. An inception waiting for me to ingest and let it drive me in new directions. What's ahead is an education. The couple grand Harvard charged me for it really made that clear…

The next sky bus would dump me in Nairobi. Some other sort of vehicle would drop me off way up in Kenya's northern desert where huge Lake Turkana snuggles its salty self into 180 miles of sand and rock. *Going to the Jade Sea to go to school!* A field school, that is, and human evolution is going to be the curriculum. Studentship, for me at least, in that sort of gig is akin to a fresh baptism, like getting a dunk in the River Jordan. With significantly less focus on Jesus, of course, and a better promise of intellectual exhilaration. Rather than a pamphlet summary of God's first work week this ritual comes with heaping brainfuls of our own deep history on Earth. I guess to that end the religious analogy blows. Perhaps I need to think of a season with the Koobi Fora Field School as being a raw dumpling soaking up flavor in a stony chowder of geology, ancient ecology, the archaeology of really old stuff, the evolutionary study of animals and people with an emphasis on people animals. In a nutshell, it's off to a heck of a big lake in a hot, rocky place to learn *paleoanthropology*. After years of just talking about these things, only half reaching towards the dreams, it makes me feel like I'm finally getting my shit together and doing something.

Some extended taxiing on Schiphol's non-captivating runways had me drifting back to onset of all this. *Paleoanthropology... How come?* Part of it came from the thrill of having friends' eyelids droop whenever the word clunks out of my mouth. Mostly it's just where I've finally felt I needed go in life. Until a few years ago the term which would have fit me snuggliest was *directionless*. Granted, there has been some direction to my adult life: I am frequently propelled straight towards excessive drinking. There has also been some assertive drug use which was quite nearly the same direction, say more of a scenic route which always merged again with boozing. And sex, of course. Cheap, unlovely fornicating. It was usually on the same route as the liquor or the narcotics, just on the other side of the guardrail. Come the early 90's some reprioritization appeared to be necessary.

It began when I was twenty-two, with an awakening in the archaeology courses at Boston University and the realization that it was indeed possible to have a job where one could play in the dirt with the bones and broken toys of dead people. BU included a crushing financial education as well and I was ultimately expelled as impoverished. During a winter exile from Boston ambition was rekindled at a freezing bayside shanty in Jamestown, RI and in some courses at URI. Human Evolution was the bee's freaking knees to me by the time I strolled past a yellow flyer on the bulletin board in the Anthro department. I was defrosting my fingers in some searing cafeteria coffee when the silhouette of a *Homo erectus* skull snared my gaze. It was superimposed over a gnarled, black, infected appendix-looking thing (turned out to be a graphic of Lake Turkana.) *Learn Paleoanthropology in Kenya,* the little poster pitched. *Spend a Summer at Lake Turkana and the Koobi Fora Field School,* it proclaimed. Boy howdy! If that didn't just sound nice to me; time to get myself to a plane.

After seven hours of sleep in four days I had a daisy of a snooze on the plane to Holland and still woke with ample time to flirt with two bewitching black stewardesses. Lingering and laughing over coffee refills they had me feeling a little better than a ragged animal just off his bon voyage bender. Not that it could have led anywhere, mind you. It never does. Women might loiter and smile during initial chatter but short-notice engagements aren't within my abilities. No matter what closing suggestion I make - a cup of coffee, a ride to church, help move a refrigerator - women suddenly react as though filthy litter boxes were getting tossed at their heads. Something in my tone must make *I'd love talk a while longer* sound like *I've got some unusual ideas for your vagina* or *I can't control my bowels, please help me to the potty.* Entanglements with beautiful women only come with larger swaths of time or via drunken nihilism. A bartending job had helped immensely with the latter; as though having immediate access to vermouth adds sheen to your aura, symmetry to your nose and a touch of intelligence to the lecherous walnut throbbing in your skull. So no matter what fantasies these flight attendants inspired, I wasn't shaking martinis in coach and there was simply no time. I shifted thoughts toward more virtuous playgrounds ahead, to hop rocks and trip sober into gullies in the hunt for fossils. Hoping the sleaze will cake up and slough off me on the dusty prairies of Lake Turkana, I quit batting my eyelashes at the jet girls while they were still smiling. Putting the brakes to the skates before reaching weak ice is my *hagakure* these days.

There's an intriguing sensation to landing in a new country in the early daylight. The air comes at you differently, as if there's something exotic about jet fumes, ozone and wind when you find them in Europe. I had a hangover like clam shells and gum tangled from the midbrain to the landing gear but the decidedly unoriginal air slipping up my nostrils felt zesty, aerating a sense of possibility along the basal contour of a dehydrated brain. I thought about leaving Schiphol Luchthaven, or however the fuck the Dutch say it, and going to Amsterdam proper. I churned the desire to slurp sludge coffee with cheesewiches on a canal or suck beer from a tulip vase but didn't get further than that. The terminal's wide panes didn't reveal vistas of anything cosmopolish so whatever Amsterdam looked like, or wherever the hell it actually lay, it wasn't close by. The panorama was a tarmac lake lapping at horizons fringed with green fuzz and an occasional white or gray chunk of building which might be used to homogenize milk, mill soap or stamp out little squares of Soylent Green. Nothing struck as an Impressionist museum, a hash house, or a boutique where one could buy something swank in latex. This trip was big for me and with barely two hours between planes I didn't feel up to risks, small as they might be. Wasn't flush with money either and that also bleached the sense of possibility. Didn't need to blow guilders on a bus to a town where I might drop my wallet in a canal and return too late to leave. Instead, I trekked the airport's halls, imagining the concourses would be Amsterdam itself some day. And when I'd had a half-hour fill of the tacky travel mall I kicked back on a putty-hued banquette to stare at some fat Germans eating breakfast two tables over.

Adhesive to the eyeballs, I'd been utterly transfixed by one of them: middle aged and extra burly with the outfit and skin tone of a sun-faded Hummel. Little more than field observations were ticking off in my head...*Mustache*: coarse and thick. *Teeth*: thick and ridged. *Sausages*: pale, shiny, skinny. A chin crushing a twin brother, momentarily revealing a slight ribbon of neck before burying it again with a swallow. *Mustache, mustache, mustache.* Teeth freckled with pork. Greasewurst with biscuit crumbs licked back from lip bristles, a *fettmensch* dancing his face gracefully like a thresher plowing through barley and chopping up rabbits. Yet it didn't lull me to sleep the way you'd think it ought to. I zoned with a cigarette down-cocked in my teeth and a glazed leer which stratospheric fatigue and overall inconsideration prevented me from breaking off. Inside the gullies of thought I shrank into a cultural anthropologist, the sort which might otherwise study the elusive tribes of Amazonian rainforests... *Fascinating to observe the feeding habits of these Germans. Warriors unique in modes of violence they nonetheless exude unbridled homosexuality around the breakfast table; the subcurrents of dirty love bathing me like scented sunbeams. An inherent blood lust for eastern real estate is balanced, it would seem, by an appreciation for shapely, khaki field shorts, which I wear daily. I'd recently demonstrated their cornerstone belligerence by giving two robust, mustachioed males each a Glock pistol; informing either that the other had been naughty with his frau. Experience anticipated the sight of the vanquished impaled rectally on a Kaiser helmet and I offered the victor a stein of deutschemarks and a sousaphone – precious commodities among Teutonic clans. Gaining his trust in such a manner he allowed me, as an objective observer, to document his ancestry and suck the mustard off his sauerbraten...*

I don't appreciate anthropologists so much, particularly those of the cultural bent. It's especially funny, when you consider that what's ahead in Kenya for me falls under the anthropology umbrella. *Paleoanthropology* could use a more definitive term like *Human Paleontology* to suggest its focus on elucidating our origins based on concrete evidence. That would set it apart from the perverse whimsy and fiction of cultural anthropology. That's a world of spadefoot twits weaned on paint chips and soy substitute inconsequence, painting other worlds in weird colors to match their lousy outfits; screeching that we accept their truths without inquiry. Considering that culture has been part and parcel of our environment for eons, exerting selective pressures on us as we've evolved, it's a low down shame the cultural theorists haven't brought anything to the table in terms of grasping how we developed from social animals to urbane vermin. The advent of culture as a self-reinforcing influence in the human niche is better grasped by biology anyway. We don't need to know if Kalahari people prefer nuts over meerkats to get a handle on the ramifications of language and ritual in the course of hominid history. Fat monographs on the *Yanomamo* aren't going to explain much more about humanity as a whole than a glossy magazine piece on the tribe.

The noodles in the talent sump of anthropology are miserable, half-sized, plus-sized, stuttering and emotionally gimped. Thumbsuckers. Loveless, vestigial humans aching for woodsy places where better beings might overlook the lisps and compulsive booger-eating. Dreaming that near-naked primitives, blessed with such mystical insight as our Maker bestows only on retard and savage, would recognize their greatness and make them a princess. Or simply the receiver of weed tiaras and many, many, many sexual offerings. That's what it comes down to with anthrostooges: *Sex; how to watch* and *where to get it.* Or *Sex and Violence.* Or the ethnographic trifecta: a culture deeply immersed in *wicked sleazy sex, ultra nasty violence and far-out, fuck-you-up-funny narcotics.* Having missed the boat on all the fun as tykes and teens they seek out obscure bands of bark and root eating, Death & Fuck-crazed brown people and invite themselves to the party. If all they can do is embed themselves among peaceful aboriginals to score handjobs for trinkets, they'll still document their hosts with slathers of gore and psychotic dream states punctuated by the shamanistic spilling of semen. Shove 'em in closets with their equally useless philosopher kin; let them swap vapid tracts and finger diddles but let's have no more reports from these hobbled dribblers of primitive, dirty fantasy.

Nothing nice to say about anybody.

As for my own cultural depravities, escaping Amsterdam came not a moment too soon. I couldn't handle another Dutch woman walking past with The Breasts of Archimedes and whistling, elf-spun hair. Those stern, martial postures and squadrons of seraphic hineys! Expressionless angels, legs like buttermilk lightning shot into sensible shoes from heavenly arcs of Edam cheese (cupped in what must surely be navy blue cotton panties). *Oh, Mommy!* People go to Holland for hash and South American call girls? I can get a Columbian hooker anywhere and the chance to get baked socially seems a waste of airfare. I believe I'd go back just for the debilitating erections attendant to unconsummated gawking at the indigenous daughters.

We skidded into a lightless Tanzanian airport near 8:15 on either the day I left or the one after it. The pilot had explained the time change before launching into an ode on how stunning Mt. Kilimanjaro would be if it weren't invisible in the night ink outside. Meantime, my liquor had been metabolizing too quickly. I felt weird, excessively awake, and the mountain tease had me thinking they were hiding better things out there than giant rock hemorrhoids on East Africa's Great Rift Valley. Bug-eyed alert but dreaming of licorice dragons, twin-engine bats and gliding giraffes picking off hyenas in the dark. Seriously, something crazy had to be going on outside since there were jittery people bouncing up and off the escape ladders, harried as cats with centipedes in their ears. We were supposedly delayed for a late flight from Johannesburg, though the hubbub implied something more urgent or terrifying out on the tarmac. Or one would hope. Simpler explanations generally prevail and the commotion merely involved corralling dummies back on when they shouldn't have gotten off and others getting chased out for flailing aboard the wrong plane. Terrifically disappointing. Finally the correct Jo'burg bunch scrambled on, sweating thickly as though the giraffes had been dropping burning scat from the sky. We re-launched and the jet shuddered through the flak and griffins all the way to Nairobi

With a little algebra I calculated the time it took to get from Boston to Tarzanland as improbably large. Apparently I'd been traveling longer than I'd been alive. I monkeyed with the math a little more, subtracting the anthropology delays in Holland, and arrived at fifteen hours. That's just too much time to be at the mercy of machines and altitude. I could whine, paw my eyes and say *Oh my, what a horrible flight.* But I'd had, overall effect aside, a whole mess of booze for free. Nothing hellacious about that at all.

Saying *Boy, that flight was hell* is a knee-jerk summary anyway. One which travelers expectorate after any journey longer than a half hour. The hangover dragging scrap metal through my head at departure had been infernal but it was not the worst I've had to survive. In the end we touched down in Nairobi, pleasantly surprised to be alive. My suspicions have cemented that airlines choose their oldest, rattliest planes for African routes; figuring that if they crash they won't take out anything expensive. Hell of a flight...

Hello, My Name Is _____

Considering I'd never forwarded flight details to the field school, hadn't the foggiest idea of where to stay in Nairobi or how to get there, I guess I got lucky with my arrival. There was a pewter-bearded, four-eyed gent holding a *Koobi Fora* sign. I introduced myself and got his name: Dr. H, the guy in charge! When speaking with him on the phone the friendly, alto slant to his voice suggested a pint sized geek with fine, fawn hair in the ballpark of thirty years old. But I'd also been reading *Earliest Man and Environments in the Lake Rudolf Basin*, compiled from work such as Dr. H's way back in the 70's. So he was certainly more than a bit older than me, unless he did fieldwork when he was six and suffers from *progeria*. But I hadn't gotten around to switching the youthful pipsqueak image to that of a middle-aged half-pint, an adjustment which still would've fallen short. The guy was tall and lean with shortish salt and pepper hair of wavy, indiscriminate partings. I'd gotten the glasses right. There's simply no recreating accurate faces from disembodied voices; it's the principal behind lumpy, carbuncled porpoises staffing sex phones. He was surprised by me too, but smiled brightly. Told me that he'd never received my flight plans and that he guessed I'd gotten lucky…

I squeezed in on his ride, a late model Land Rover the color of sun dried mayo. A steel haggis overstuffed with four well-luggaged students and one unexpected dummy with his huge black duffel. It probably sang something about my coming relationship with the program. Dr. H liveried us over bunches of miles and kilometers of spectacular African vistas drenched in deep darkness until we sped into Nairobi's spare illumination. For a city of millions it cut less light into the night than Woonsocket,

Rhode Island. I was inclined to think the impenetrable pitch had to do with the road's fringe course or trees obscuring city lights. But even the sky revealed more stars than you'd expect to find glinting above a twentieth century metropolis. Pulling up on the narrow parking hill of the Chiromo Garden Hotel drove home how fortunate I'd been to run into Dr. H. The odds I would have made it to this inn were even with a cabbie misdriving me back to Kilimanjaro and the searing guano rain of Tanzanian dragons.

Dr. H signed us in. As a bunk mate I drew Lorenzo Lujurio. At the airport he dove into the Rover's shotgun seat like it was a platter of Ramadan kebabs at sundown. I was too tired to figure him out but what I did gather, before my ears fell asleep, was that he's Italian in the Argentine exile manner and that he'd had some dealings in France, the military, or the French Military. He also had deep issues with Italy's phone service and was bug-eyed emphatic about his quest to find an *"Ustrallapeethacoooze"* skull in the fossil sediments of Koobi Fora.

I can be shy around strangers, especially when holed up with one who looks like a stock actor from a Sergio Leone flick. Umber hair and shiny skin moderately pitted under a scrubby beard, he's what Italian directors pass off as Mexican; *El Cascarón, not a mang to cross weeth only one boolet een jor pistola…* Usually I pull out a clutch of halting small talk to keep polite among goons but Enzo had an extra strange air about him. Very excited to be here yet quite cranky about it all anyway. When telling him I was going out for a cigarette I had expected to hear hissed behind me,

"Een ten meenoots jool be smokeeng een Hell!" Instead he just looked puzzled.

"Ay? What? Noooo! You smoking in here, okay?" And with that he shook me out a fag from his own pack of Gauloises.

The hombre was a puzzle. But I was fatigued beyond reason and the night was not for giving a crap about strangers in the room. I yanked out *Earliest Man and Environments,* pretending to read as Lujurio kneaded his mattress for a spell, cooed adoringly about the lumps and fell into a snooze before I finally fell off into a dream about the redheaded Wordsworth's girl who'd sold me the book on my chest.

Almost identical to days of the last year or so, the dream was even more a vision of perfection in that there weren't any jackasses playing banjos opposite the Harvard Square doors of Wordsworth's Books. But most of it was the same, shopping because I needed books or excuses to look at the red haired clerk. She'd been responsible for most of my recent literary acumen. Seriously, I'd been tearing through books just to go back and buy another one from her. One might call it obsessive, but then I spend far more money drinking and listening to music than on the volumes her flawless hands had placed in mine. It's possible I'd even dated other women since first salivating at her cash register though peripheral recall hazes when this angelic wonder lies across memory.

The wind would whisper the song of her copper spirals along the Charles River, across the harbor into my hovel in Eastie. I could resist until at least a third of the way through the latest book. Then it was back to Cambridge in the most normal of manners, no trench coat and very little hunching over, to locate her within the store, strolling through the first or second level, right side, left side, Reference or Cooking or Pet Care and always playing helpless and dumb. *Are the social science books alphabetical by author like the math ones? Do you know if the humor section has any titles that are funny?* Well, not that stupid. But awfully close and I would buy a book from whatever section she was gracing even after grabbing something elsewhere that I'd actually needed. The extraneous reading kept me broad and I'd be ready to discuss anything with her if I could ever get past am asphyxiated *hello*.

Nothing was as intense as the moments when she was at check-out or the computers of the help desk. The opportunity to speak to the angel with alabaster skin was the stuff of my subway daydreams. Each encounter with her gingery hair was a scene stolen from a fairy tale. I'd expectorate *hi* from a throat of soup and bones, stutter a book request four times until it came out in English or pay while mashing up a broken *thanks* before slinking out with change clenched in a sweaty palm. Charlie Brown and the little red-headed girl, though I doubt Chuck's deepest desire had b-sized breasts which pitched and brushed lightly within an always sheer blouse. One look at the faint spray of freckles across her nose and I couldn't say who my mommy was or where I'd lost her. Scrambled through and through, absolutely paralyzed in her presence. I had built up such a myth of this girl that I could no longer reach to her. Then again, the overwhelming inertia in her presence might have had something to do with the way she never seemed to remember me; just one of a thousand slugs trying to parade an erudite, store-bought taste in literature.

Once, while cutting through Boston's Public Garden I spotted her. My heart jumped into my throat to get beaten senseless by esophageal gremlins. *At last, a chance to say hi on neutral turf,* thunk I. Or at least a way to find out where she lived until a future day when I might actually develop the guts to try talking to her. I followed her through the Garden and the Commons all the way to Tremont Street, begging my ego at each step to get up just a little fucking nerve to introduce myself. It wouldn't and I couldn't cross Tremont behind her either. Tandem park meanderings are one thing but sidewalk trailings change you from a customer with a crush to a creep in need of a restraining order. I turned off and went to work. There'd be more books to buy that week. Sawdust about paleoclimates, B. Kliban cartoon collections or riveting tomes on stringing beads. I was learning to stare from the very edge of my eye, dreaming of nothing more than her cool forearm finding its way to my burning cheek. Never knew her name. But thanks in part to her I come across as very well-read for a stalker.

Days Two, Three and Maybe Four

Nairobi is quite an okay place. A spectacular city of filth stuffed with a billion people, most of who seem to be loitering. A sprawling toilet choked with shiny toys towering from a dust-frosted muck of garbage and feculence. That was only the first impression, though an improved version doesn't seem promising. As for the folks I would meet here and remain with beyond the city limits? The still arriving field/classmates are proving themselves ninety percent fine enough. All assert a readiness to brave our primeval homeland, giddy as ducks for the impending digging and scorpion ambushes. The bulk of them have been easy enough to get along with in the scant hours we've been together. These first impressions are sure to change. I've been a forgiving judge of character in people here because, apart from one or two cuties, they'd only just entered the periphery of my concern. Kenya stomps in the spotlight and I'm still stupefied by what a rat hole its main metropolis is. I'd only taken a quick walk downtown during the first morning but each step away from Uhuru Park made the view one meter uglier.

Lodging at the Chiromo Garden Hotel, near the National Museum and a little ways off from the urban decay, helped with the image problem. While the hotel has its own sense of decomposition it's more representative of what I'd imagined an African city to be: lots of greenery, smiling African people, the light smell of stuff burning and lots of big, loud fucking bugs. A few students from the previous field school session had stuck around the hotel, reclining like lightly seasoned ex-pats around tables of beer and spinning sagas of weeks spent in the wild sands. Kids taking in a little R&R while waiting for home-bound jets or buses to the beaches of Mombasa. One of them proved to be a pretty, sweetly sarcastic, hard-drinking freak. Nice, nice, nice for me. A haywire Vancouveradian of strong bum, latte skin, Mongolian eyes, and an upward arching mouth with the most decadent of lips. I dug her, and not simply for the wee bit of extraneous ballast in her ass. And she dug me. I know this because she'd told me exactly that – a few minutes before getting in a car pointed at the airport.

"I've really dug you since the night you arrived, Frank."

Crap! Crap! Crap! I'd harbored an erection for her for almost a day and a half and a little frolic in a lowbrow Kenyan hotel would have been just dandy. That is how it goes with me; no game because my only speed is "wait and see." At good-bye she slammed the full magic of her bottom lip against my tongue, dulling an urge to garrote her for even bringing up this attraction. It's awfully impolite to suggest passions for a guy only to leave him at a hotel with a boner crimped in an awkward crease of his jeans. And teeth gouged through his tongue. Not nice at all.

There was some high-speed babble as we tried cementing the now mutual passion like two pheasants outlining a verbal contract; her hopes for an autumnal escape to the East Coast and my promises to guide her through the birthplace of the American Revolution. Maybe get her a roast beef at Buzzy's, right on the spot where John Adams slew the Scythian horde. At least we'd see if this moment's lust could turn into a distant weekend's infatuation complete with a soup bowl full of screw juice. That's right, I'm buying into the daydream wholesale with whatever funds I can spare. Cheap fantasies aside, the girl said she'd be returning to Koobi Fora next summer as a teaching assistant. Apparently this can be done if you're smart and toe the line. I'll probably start sniffing about for the correct fannies to smooch and see if I can't do the same. Which doesn't seem like I'm moving away from gimcrack daydreams at all.

Getting to know some Kenyans with any depth had a slower start, but after some short forays into the city I came across Michael, the guy from Turkana. *Howdy now!* I was soon to be at a Lake Turkana! As I think about it now I can't recall if he volunteered his homeland before or after I'd declared my destination. But as it was my first encounter with the more congenial and erudite contingent of the Nairobi moochers I hadn't felt concerned about picking over a stranger's story. I'd been on a jaunt around Nairobi with some of the other students when this young man stopped in mid-saunter to say, "*Jambo.*"

"*Jambo sana,*" said I, which he countered with a remark about the resemblance between me and Jesus Christ. *The* Nazarene?! Our Holy Lord and Savior!? Well, certainly the way to get me to give up all my extra pin cash was to make me feel akin to the Messiah. *My stars, what a nice thing to say! Here, dude - take all the worldly hindrance out of my crappy nylon travel wallet.* Polite and conversant or no, this guy had no idea what he was up against. It was going to be some work to get a disbeliever with a little patience for healthy, clean panhandlers to part with much for a silly compliment. Already uneasy about having enough funds to get me from July to September, my dear old ma would have a rough task prying a buck or two out of my fist. Anyhow, Michael, as a *Samburu (Turkana? Samburu?* Now it was obvious he was polishing and straightening his schtick as we went) dropout of the U of Nairobi, knew the town and decided to take us anywhere we wanted to go. He talked politics, talked culture, talked shit and just kept flapping right up to the moment he asked us for a little cash to get him back up north. Drained us all of twenty shillings and a candy bar, an incredibly modest handout, but it was all he was asking. Small price even for an obvious situation. Obscenely small, as a matter of fact, and it was almost something to feel guilty about. Like a freelance concierge he had revealed a fair swath of the city to us and the tour had been richly informative. There was history involved and the current state of the economy and how an Indian holy man owned one of the brightest, shiniest skyscrapers in the village. That real estate info wasn't all too astonishing – Indians don't seem to see any conflict with being pious and conspicuously consumptive, there are yogis and Krishna CEO's out there living like Hugh Hefner on the sale of enlightenment. It hit me only minutes after Michael departed for his country bus to wherever the heck he was really from that we'd cheaped out on the kid. Sure we gave him exactly what he'd requested but nobody thought to tip him. I didn't even get the jabbering ambassador a soda pop. But having been remiss about gratuities lay in just what actually had astonished me on the tour and it wasn't far from the shadow of the Holy Hindi High Rise. Something Mike had said at that point pulverized the capacity to think in terms as small as a lagniappe for some eloquent, stray prick tour guide.

The poverty doesn't hide on the gravel and tar conduits of Nairobi - the *Place of Cool Waters* in the tongue of the Maasai. It's all over the joint. It's there wherever you look. From a hotel doorman swimming in a clean uniform he might be sharing with three other regular Joe's to a woman balancing a bale of clean laundry on her head and walking cautiously; not to maintain the balance of the wash but to ensure her worn out, busted sandal doesn't ditch her. Even Michael, neat as a pin and well spoken, worked hard for his sixty cents and chocolate bar. But I'd harbored an expectation for all of it. This is a developing nation so the two or three million people in town couldn't possibly all be doing well. Nearly everybody begs for something: a few shining coins to put a shine on your hiking boots; for you to buy one of their ebony rhinos carved from white acacia and blackened with boot black. A quick assessment suggests an economy based on shoe polish. There's just not enough to go around and all struggle for what they need. A few mendicants made my notice here and there; the bare feet and shredded shirts pressed on my heart and some got what I had in change. You have to elbow some of the periphery out of your perspective and squint past the destitution in front of you or you'll quickly collapse into a lake of tears and slick, dusty mud. So it has to be eyes down and save the blunt words for the bastards with smudgy, knock-off carvings and shitty bangles.

It was an easy habit to maintain. Until, that is, we rounded a corner in this purgatorial city right into an oasis straight outta Hades. The sun was still high, strained only by some gauzy clouds. Daylight crushed the sight of a shadowless lot, almost empty except for the garbage in flattened, lonely hummocks protruding off the scaly ground like infected scabs. That and the kids. The sight of the kids in that block of contusion put my toes in a vice and wrenched me to a stop. They weren't doing much of anything. They sat, crawled, stood, knelt and squatted without a purpose among the clumps of trash. Rail-width children draped with ribbons of clothes in colors no different from their skin of slate, old steel and tarnished silver. Not one was rummaging for a scrap of food and a few looked up toward us with eyes filled with pus and vermillion webbing. The air felt like cement as I turned my head to find anything else though it became plain that the city behind had fallen away towards Gehenna. A boy and his withered left leg hanging lifeless above his only knee dragged my attention back to the plot. Polio had eaten some of the other limbs before us and paralysis crept painfully through me as my eyes landed on a sidewalk at the north of the lot. Chipped plaster, a low row of voided shops selling nothing and spilling despair and affliction. Beneath an overhang men loitered. Skeletal bodies embanked along the wall or leaning on posts, half asleep in vigilance against daydreams. *Where were the women? Couldn't women be robbed of life the way these men and boys had? If men make the realm of power a gender exclusive club do they keep it just as restricted at the vacuum depths of that game?* The questions tore at me because I knew women had one last thing to sell when men had lost all earning ability. That's why there were boys there. *Then where were the girls?*

More shriveled limbs became visible among the men. The aching soared along my nerves as I felt the muscles petrify in my face. One man almost escaped my despondent stares along the ground because he was nearly not there to be seen. From a wad of ragging on the pocked concrete he wasn't more than his crooked arms and the head which slumped above a crumpled torso barely inches high. Between that and the cement were only questions for a horrible imagination. That tiny, human example of the Creator's antipathy towards humanity directed his wet glare into mine and burned through it. Rounding a single corner had stepped us past the street hustle and panhandle base of the Kenyan economy right onto the viscid scar tissue which formed around it and for the first time this day not a single man asked for a single thing from us. This scene expressed more than anything I ever thought about hopelessness. These were men who left hope long behind and children who had never lived anywhere near it. Michael pulled at me to move.

"…let's leave here. This is not a good place…"

As we moved back into the more acceptable exiguity of the streets we came from I asked more about those people, the sting still strong in my flesh from horror, shame or guilt or some other sensation that I have no word for.

"They are not people. Children, men who sniff glue. They are nobody."

It was the savage strapping to the coat of needles which had enrobed me in the square. The paralysis drained and swelled my feet with bile as I squared towards Michael and considered ripping an arm off him.

It was too much to hear that he thinks of his fellow men in such a reprehensible way. Didn't that fucker notice that some of them were children? Forget that they inhaled solvents to destroy hunger pangs because what the hell would any of us do when the trash heaps ran out of breakfast? Disregard the way each day flayed and filled their souls with glass shards and corroded saw teeth...and it suddenly seized me. I wanted to hope that Michael was right in what his cruel assertion. If these children had been created within that malevolent niche and born soulless then it was possible that they weren't suffering any sense of loss. They had all which had ever been promised and profound despair could not devour them. I wished that to be the truth because I hoped like hell not to have just encountered the saddest state of being alive. One way or another they were nobody. The most deeply forgotten of the *unthought-of's*. These were not the children of the charitable missions seen on television back home. No fat actresses or burly do-gooders would stroll across those lots – it was too much for even those in that business to see or bear. It's easier to push a mug of rice and muddy water at some near-dead tyke in the desert than to have the worst of our urban sins reflected in the mucosal eyeballs of gray wraiths hiding in the dead corners of Third World's cities. Everyone else has left that place and those people behind. Just as I was doing as I cowered off with Michael and it stole meaning from everything in me and voided all other desire. I no longer gave a fuck for catching sight of shingled pangolins rooting for greasy worms in tropical undergrowth or for coming within charging range of a rutting rhinoceros blasting urine backwards from its crotch. I no longer cared to see any awesome feature of the East African Rift System. Paleoanthropology seemed about as fruitful an endeavor as its cultural kin. Was I going to spend the next two or three decades trying to examine how we all got here when it would only make clear that the evolutionary impetus propelled us beyond *kill or be killed* into shoving each other into sewers of ongoing suffering?

Welcome to the Koobi Fora Field School.

Near as I can tell, no one among this gathering squad of Darwinian partisans has been risking wild adventures too far from the Chiromo. The hotel bears little resemblance to a resort but most students treat it like a self-contained holiday nexus; daytrips and guided museum tours if you want them but little other reason to leave. You see, spending hours on end drinking cheaply in the garden bar is far more exotic than chugging pitchers in a university beer pit stateside. And within the confines of this markdown compound there's little danger of getting eaten by elephants, army ants or headhunters. For those seized by the call of the wild or intrepid recklessness there are buses and roomy British taxis to buggy them out to Nairobi's feral suburbs. Some of the kids had finally put on the courageous pants and took a joyride out to the Karen Blixen House. I had no interest in finding out what Isak Dinesen or Meryl Streep really looked like but there were reports of petting giraffes and getting licked in the face by them. That stirred jealousy in my chest since giraffes are the second to the last things I'd eat before starving. Amphibians, frogs in particular, would probably outlive me and I'd be dining on people before turning a ravenous glare on gentle Geoffrey. And he'd still need to die of natural causes after signing a statement making it crystal clear that he wished for me to live off his remains. But even then, I mean, *geeez, how could you?* Giraffes are really fucking neat animals.

For my own morning safaris I'm drawn to the monkey fossil peep-shows of the Museum or back to the streets of Nairobi, mesmerized by each little facet of this urban calamity. Entirely dusty but it hasn't turned out as all that forsaken or sad as I'd first assessed it. School-attired children play in grass lots between buildings; skipping, kicking soccer balls and laughing their merry little asses off. Men swing and catcall for passengers from garishly painted vans which hum and twang to onboard radios while careening down boulevards, grazing sidewalks without heed for oncoming vehicles. Or for pedestrians. *Semi-public transportation in developing economies* – now that just may be a worthwhile thesis for a cultural anthropology grad. And whether it's the Doppler pulses of minibus tunes underscoring your stroll, or you're standing in a throng revivalin' to a preacher with a bloomping bass guitar, there's music everywhere. I run into all sorts of melody-charged sandlot ministries as I walk off my white eggs, bacon and jelly toast.

Those fried eggs with the fucked-up pale yolks stick with you in thick burps straight through the afternoon introductory lectures. Sour Nescafe and sunnyside gas build-up harass me during three hour overviews of the school, the paleontological significance of Kenya overall and the upcoming hardship and hazards we'll get to enjoy. The *coma ovum* was suffocating my consciousness all the way through the last discourse. When it wrapped up I got myself another mean, ugly cup of instant coffee to wake me up for supper. And for drinking more insistent beverages - in the weeks ahead we might encounter the immediate heartbreak of snakebites or snails as the slow avatars of death. But we wouldn't see many bars; time to binge while the taps were open.

The evening was a mambo rattling to a duet of Tusker beer bottles and tables tipping off kilter on the patio. The gobbles and brays of people getting to know each other and repeated requests for my roommate to repeat whatever the hell it was he'd just muttered. I came with a functional grasp of Spanish so I translated as necessary and kept my mouth shut as discretion dictated. Lorenzo spoke English well enough, but a little alcohol tended to lock him into an Italo-Iberio crass mode, the merged linguals featuring steady streams of derogatory observations on women. It'd only been a couple of nights but the faces opposite mine had been shifting frequently. Promising buddies failed, rotating to other table ends or to other tables all together. Idiosyncrasies would debut and fester speedily in some cat I thought was cool as some chick's luster dulled in a vapid ramble. One girl, already fit for transfer back home, perpetually swatted the air ahead of her nose with metronomic regularity as though plagued by phantom spiders that wouldn't scram. Or she perhaps was only trying fan away the rotten stench of Enzo's words. The hombre's multilingual small talk was tightly focused on vaginas, snarling at the kid who never stops touching his face or calling the Virginia girl a *porca putana*. That's "Pig-whore" in Spatalian. It was hard to sympathize for her as she had her own disagreeable manner, incessantly pealing off lists of everything wrong with the lodgings and service in our host country. All that in a Dixie drawl twanging through her nose like K-Mart's finest banjo. There were times when various nitwits continued addressing me as I gloved my beer and shoved off, Enzo and his slander shadowing me like bodyguards. There are a few still worth the company and I'd settled in with Kalle McInnis for the rounds this evening. Something about Kalle inhaled me into an empty seat across from her. Librarianesque, in the finest way, and a sterling flash in her irises when tilting lager to lips, taking in the youthful group with *been there done that* disconcern. She'd also been indifferent to Lorenzo's convoluted rambles on *Homo erectus* in Aragon peppered with Spanish asides about tits. I'm in no hurry to give up a stool near her in the beer garden.

I did slide over to accommodate some new friends, Sgt. George Kabu and pals, UN soldiers from Ghana taking some shore leave before heading to Rwanda. They were excellent guys and so good natured it was hard to imagine them headed for the heart of the continent's greatest nightmare. Not sure how many arteries they could stanch in that bloodbath and with awful inklings as to what they'd see, we kept the talk far away from genocide. It was cheery banter, laughter, passed cigarettes and drinks for the dudes whose next working shifts would be hazardous as all Hell and far more important than anything my own defender-of-the-free-world government has even thought about doing.

As the night wound down and I headed back to bed I smiled to myself over the straight up wonder of these first few days in Kenya. Wonders all around and unforeseen connections. Now it's always pleasant to drink and carouse and stretch hands across borders to laugh with soldiers. But it's even pleasanter to knead the luxurious flesh of ravishing Kenyan twins. Lorenzo, though all crank and testicle and as unbalanced as anybody I'd met recently, brought an identical pair a beautiful locals back to our suite. That was thoughtful. I convinced myself they were cocktail waitresses hired to encourage pasty, fat Euros to spend money on booze...not hookers. Because why the hell would I sell myself on that idea? Bar employees are not allowed at the rooms so Enzo slipped the night manager two hundred skins to scan the floor for lint as the girls tiptoed through the lobby. He brought two as providing extra sluts for new friends is the natural hospitality of Tuscan gauchos on the Pampas. I guess that's how it works. Why shouldn't it work that way? Not that it mattered why; the two of them were awfully nice to look at. Since they were duplicates of each other there was none of the anxiety involved when drawing for the short straw to get the bowlegged troll.

The second hand barely clicked thrice before we had a mocha tornado of nakedness in our tiny room. Believe it or don't, I was actually hesitant about the situation and initially wanted no part of it. This was a Third World city and, smoking hot or not, who knew what sort of tropical microbes the wet membranes of these women could be hosting. Maybe even European viral transplants donated by some perverse Swiss louts. That in itself might be worse since the last thing I want in life is a touch of Continental syphilis to kick off aging in a very unlovely manner; lumpy and greasy with wet lips and snot strung eyes. *No thank you, guvnah!* I'll just take my good ol' American age spots and a timely heart attack.

A cardiac arrest was precisely what one sibling was aggressively trying to give me. She looked delicious and felt heavenly but yielding to her advance couldn't be all that great an idea. Still, she was fiercely seductive and when Jane shed her undies, squeezed her bare length along the clothed stretch of mine and began to gnaw at my carotid artery...well, I lost the battle. Losing also meant rationalizing up some crap about having a little faith in the condom I'd convinced Enzo to fork over. It was a boatload of confidence, you see, since the rubber wasn't exactly fresh from the wrapper. It was pre-owned, so to speak, having already been filled with Italian semen. So...I, umm...*washed it*. Excusing myself from the spectacular strumpet, I moseyed on over to the sink to give the prophylactic a thorough drain and soaping. The thought occurred that Irish Spring suds might have absolutely no detergent effect at the microbial level and there were tiny cartoon rubbers jumping frantically on the sink, whining out warnings in the tones of effeminate, Gallic midgets.

"Arrêt! Non! Non! Pas de savon! Nuit, nuit gravement pour la crapaud!"

I barely understand French so I just stared briefly at the dancing mirages, smiled, nodded, muttered *Toot-sweet to you two Nancies!* Then kept on scrubbing and wringing the skin; ignoring the hopping jimmy hats as they pleaded and tripped over each other. It was a judgment call but I squeaked the thing down where required and off to the fuck side-show went Frankie. Gracious me if it didn't turn out to be a lovely time.

The circus flavor never left the atmosphere, however. *Lights on. Lights off. Lights on again.* Enzo, playing with the main room switch, must have been searching for a scrap of carpet to replace the donated rubber or was so drunk he needed streetlamps to his target. *Lights out.* Then he was off doing odd things in the bathroom; running the tub, flushing, grunting, cursing and laughing. His date, far from alarmed, grew bored with his madness and decided to saunter on over to my slab for a visit. Both twins were climbing on me for a pace. Though it was nifty to have them both batting my weenie around I surely could not let it wander into the woman the slimy lunatic in the bathroom had just screwed. Although the latex had seen her innards once there was some concern regarding regional Enzo residues, as if anything mattered by that point, and I didn't have the energy to put her in the sink for a rinse. But she thoughtfully scratched my back while I got back into Jane. And that was a kind and considerate thing for her to do. Going to need a blood screen in a month or so, I'll bet.

When the coupling was drawing to a close Jane said, "I feel I must warn you about something…"

Wonderful, here it comes – she just got some bad news from the clinic…

"What's that?" I asked, ready to pass out.

"I am a nymphomaniac!" she exclaimed. With all the pride of someone who'd just won gold in the long jump.

"Hmm? Oh, well, no shit…"

"What? What did you just say?"

"I said *no* shit. It wasn't hard to figure out since we've just screwed and I have no idea who you are…"

It stung her. She called me a terrible person and I instantly regretted talking to her like that. I can't be taking swipes at any trollop's dignity because I do love nymphomaniacs, whores, tramps, polyamorous women or whatever the hell one wishes to label them. And it's not simply for the fun stuff. Regardless of benefits to my own visceral sleaze there's just a wonderful honesty in them. Often very comfortable with how they see themselves and well tuned to their natural desires they seem to embrace themselves, flaws and all. Be great if we all could get that kind of grip rather than painting wonderfully colored balloons gassed over our true natures. Jane was a nice woman as so many easy girls are. She was deeply affectionate, speaking softly and sweetly throughout our brief tryst. The confession was simply a way of making cute small talk, a joke at herself to break the ice *post coitum*. You don't find that in the legions of women who hold their vaginas as ridiculously priceless as Fabergé eggs; demanding windy hymns of flattery, feats of wallet and stumbling gauntlet runs before allowing access to their precious gift.

The prize, on the other hand, is rarely commensurate to the effort. We are all animal in bed; oozing internal fluids and smearing mucous across our skin in the name of starting families or just having a blast. But some animals preen for weeks only to disappoint miserably in that ultimate slippery, sloppy moment. Carnival prizes, dollar upon dollar thrown away to batter milk bottles with bean bags or to toss rings over chipped plaster clowns only to discover the big purple bunny isn't cuddly at all. It's coarse, inflexible and smells strangely for something fresh off the shelf and to which you had the first privilege of handling. Perhaps musty for having been rarely let out for air. Find the sluts, or life-term lesbians for Platonism if you need it, and you'll discover lives without lies and friends without duplicity.

I wish I'd taken a second to think before acting like a dick to Jane so I apologized. She accepted and we settled in for a warm cuddle. But it didn't last too long, the vibe went weird soon enough, about being in a strange country in a college program of unclear moral codes, in a hotel with two strange women and paired with an increasingly unhinged roommate. I seriously doubted the faculty would appreciate seeing them exit the room come daylight. I terribly wanted her to stay the night but the anxiety over program propriety took precedence. It had to end too soon so I apologized to Jane with a disclaimer in tune with my overall tact of the evening.

"Alright, Janie. I gotta be a terrible person again," I said putting the jerk shirt back on, "but you girls need to scoot. This might get us in dutch with the chiefs"

She was mildly disappointed this time but seemed to understand. She whispered for her sister but Lorenzo had remounted and was barking up a storm.

"Enzo?"

"Enzo…"

"Christ…Lorenzo! Excuse me buddy, but you have gotta let your friend go"

He muttered something in three languages and went right on making more plumbing noises on Jane's sister. Then he seemed to fall asleep.

"*Enzo!!!* Dammit, wake up, man!"

"Eh? *¿Que?* What?"

"We can't have these girls here in the morning. Probably not cool with H"

"What? Oooh. Yes sir, man! Okay, girls! Time for go home now! Go. Go!"

Any tact I'd tried to recover with Jane was smudged out as Lorenzo corralled and hustled them out with a boner still flapping at his thighs. It was a done night at two when the sorority, panties literally in a bundle, scurried back to the bar. Maybe to get drunk, maybe to fuck somebody else. The realization that I may indeed be a terrible person wasn't all that disheartening. I'm over it all, settling into a complacency about my bad behaviors. With a little luck all the rotten things I've done will come back soon in a karmic blitzkrieg and lay me to waste. *A communal rubber?* That really can't be good. Madness like that is going to catch up with me one day. But after the field school, I hope, since I'm into this deal for about five grand.

Goes to Olorgesailie, Molested by Small Devils

The get-up knock hit our door at seven a.m. I snapped awake, then immediately felt impelled to cower from myself. Somewhere in the night my brain had been cruelly pulled through a shag rug and now it was all burny and hurty. There was also the pushy reek of ripened fuck battering my olfactory bulbs. The stink of stale beer, cigarettes and smegma would take days to fully wash out of my nose. Smoke and booze working its way out of the pores can horribly sour the sweetest, metallic flavored glaze left on you by the most immaculate labia. Small-change karma and I suppose it was unequivocally deserved. There are worse things to live with. But when the mirror introduced me to the fresh bite-mark on my throat I collapsed into a vile monologue on whores and hemophilia.

I wrapped it up in a few seconds, though. It wasn't Jane's fault. How could she imagine that a living, straight boy would try resisting her silken onslaught? Usually not prone to hickeys I suspected a lack of iron in my beer and the sudden Indian lunch diet. I sought remedy in a breakfast plate of wet, white eggs, limp toast and granular bowel acid coffee. The vat of venom and terror simmered down to a controlled level and Jane was no longer a barroom *malaya*; just a sweet lady kind enough to straddle me last night. I refocused the negative neckbite energy into trying to understand why the yellow part of eggs here are white.

Olorgesailie. The word of the day and it's uttered 'elgrl-uhlglerh-selllglegurl' with a Polish accent. Jesus, that isn't even funny to me. It's "*oh-lor-geh-SAI-lee,*" which is almost exactly the way it's spelled, and refers to a dead volcano in southwest Kenya, the dead lake basin in the mount's vicinity, as well as a death ditch archaeologists have been gouging at since the forties. It means *Place of the Giselik People* in the *Maa* tongue but don't bother looking them up. Rick Potts, chief landscaper of the site, has stated that nobody knows who the *Giselik* are or ever were. An intuitive guess is that Giselik was a renowned *Maasai* guy from the way, way back who held the real estate with his entourage until the neighborhood went to hell and it became fashionable to live in Tanzania.

Olorgesailie lies on the floor of the Great Rift Valley about two or another number of hours southwest of Nairobi. It probably wouldn't be the average anyone's first choice for a day trip but it's quite famous among folk with a Stone Age mindset. For everyone else the name is as familiar as Lucy's left foot – *and just who the fuck is Lucy to the rest of the unanthropological population?* In a hot, semi-desert scrubbed by acacia trees Olorgesailie isn't necessarily spectacular. The *Maasai*, however, appear fond of it as do their stubble-grass and sand gobbling cows. And thus concludes the backstory to the geography.

If paleolithics are your game then Olorgesailie is a gotta-see place; the mangy land is positively infested with prehistoric stone tools. *Acheulean* hand-axes are all over the place, meaning cave men way back when were pretty busy in what was once a thriving woodland and lake basin. *Homo erectuses*, conventionally presumed, left their chopping rocks all over the place for maybe 300,000 years; from a bit less than a million years before present (*1Myr BP*) to a bit more than a half a million years ago (*ABMTAHAMYA*).

Let's float an idea here: If hominids had only dropped a single hand-axe per year as they trespassed here over the course of just 100,000 years it would still amount to a boatload of tools for us to find. Tons of litter, which would no longer be necessarily indicative of *intensive* hominid activity. It might mean hardly any activity at all. There are factors which do suggest Olorgesailie was indeed a bustling area at one time, but it'd be nice to keep this concept of *incremental* changes over large swaths of time in your head.

As a matter of fact there's no need to keep it in your head for very long as it's time to get some thoughts on evolution, time and our ancestry out of the way. So here's the deal: While the accumulation of small changes over time is a central concept of Darwinian evolution it's one that gets neglected by many prominent people who deal with human evolution. Particularly where it pertains to the migration of early hominids - things like the presence of *Homo erectus* in Asia and Africa during the same time period have really put hairs across the asses of paleoanthropologists.

Trouble starts with bones like those of the *Nariokotome Boy* from the western shores of Lake Turkana and skulls like *Sangiran 17 (Pithecanthropus VIII* to yer professor grandpappy) from Java. They're both widely considered to be *Homo erectus*. The African fossil is 1.8Myr old, give or take, and the Indonesian head lived 1.7Myr back with a similar deviation in dating accuracy. It's the 0.1Myr difference which bugs researchers; simply not enough time for *H. erectus* to get from Africa to Southeast Asia in their eyes. Some pull hokey tricks to make facts accommodate the *way things should be* and end up in rabid aging disputes and argue that the Asian fossils are so primitive they must be descended from a different ancestor altogether. Thus African erectuses just gotta be more advanced and thence in need of a more progressive name like *Homo ergaster*. The reactions and reasoning get baffling considering that these geographically distanced beings look an awful lot like each other.

So how in tarnation did those primitive *Homos* get from Africa to Java, about 8000 miles walking or 4800 breaststroking, in *only* 0.1 million years? First off, it's *Homo erectus* and not a tree sloth. It walked and ran and hunted and made tools and eventually used fire. Secondly, 0.1 Myr, which looks small when written digitally, actually means *one hundred thousand years*. That's a damn big chunk of time, enough even for a sloth to go from Brazil to Bangkok for a massage from an *orangutranny*. If *H. erectus* had moved its pillow only one mile per year it would have gotten to Java in 0.008 million years! Even if it was a touch slothful, shifting camp a mile every 12.5 years it still makes the trip in a hundred millennia. I'm a city boy who uses mostly footpower to get around. I used to walk four miles a day to get to high school and back, did five mile runs out of shame at my figure and once strolled twenty miles in a day for charity. I've even skipped along for six or so miles on LSD because the guy driving the dune buggy in my head pined for fresh scenery. All that strolling in life might've already taken me as far as Jakarta and I live without any primitive compulsion to trail migrating food animals or run when the climate shifts.

So there's no real problem, see? Baboons could do it, though the weather in Kashmir might have paddled their leathery asses, and Macaques had long ago filled the range of *H. erectus*. Those monkeys infest more earth than any primate except us. Maybe *erectus* ate them and simply followed supper out into the world. Essentially any creature that isn't biologically restricted, like penguins, to specific environments can do wonders with a little wanderlust. *Homo erectus* just needed an open road, a song in its heart, and a sharp rock to bash the living fuck out of anything that got in its way.

Think about this: The cane toad was introduced into Australia in 1935 and a bit over half a century later it is poised to complete its conquest of Oz. A fucking frog overrunning a continent in sixty years and 100,000 might not be enough time for *Homo erectus* to get to Indonesia? My, my, my…how's about a little faith in our ancestors?

So having *Homo erectus* in Africa and Asia so close in time makes fine sense. Except, of course, when you throw in the *erectuses* up in the former USSR. Georgia, I mean, and those folks are 1.8 Myr old too. *What? Are you fucking kidding me?* What's worse now is that these Central European boys and girls seem even more primitive than the average *erectus* so there's the temptation to say that *Homo erectus* evolved *outside* of Africa and migrated back. And of course nobody wants to say that. Well, some do and there's nothing wrong with thinking that way. Evolution works pretty darn well when a species splinters up and later reconvenes to mingle its slightly differentiated genes. It works well for the evolution of all types of organisms except ours, simply because we don't like the regular rules to apply to us. Our slant is to employ whatever rules we choose as we make them up. It has long been decided that *erectus* emerged as an African animal and no amount of evidence to the contrary is going to change, or even slightly modify, that fact. Overall it seems we've been hell bent on keeping *all* hominids in Africa until they have developed into distinct species, meaning any that left the Dark Continent had finished evolving, sort of making them dead-enders.

What many researchers wish for is an unbroken line of African evolution - no side trips to backward places like Eastern Europe or Asia - until arriving at us. Once *sapienated* into the quite-nearly-us in Africa they were free to leave but not allowed to return. There is a somewhat racist subtext to this idea in that African *Homo sapiens* became *Homo sapiens sapiens* (a slicker, smarter version) in Europe and Western Asia(a chunk of the world which could also be called "Cauc-Asia".) Thus the old fossils from Dmanisi, Georgia freaked out the anthro community for being there in the first place. Even if it was a more primitive *erectus* or even an earlier species, say *Homo habilis*, we're still talking about a walking *Homo something* and getting one from Addis Ababa to Barcelona or any other place way back whenever isn't that big a conundrum. Lots of animals migrate and while that's seen as freaking spectacular for lots of animals to do, so many paleoanthropologists still tend to view our immediate and slightly removed ancestors as clumsy dingbats. Seriously, no matter what the concrete evidence before us – stone tools, million-year old fire hearths, or full skeletons of early hominids – there is a tendency among paleoanthropologists to develop as many extra ideas as they can to justify beliefs that early members of the *Homo* line could do anything at all. They examine and reexamine *Homo erectus* finger bones, then scan the interiors of *erectus* skull for the telltale dents and creases of the brain's dexterity lobes, just to get some extra lines of support to the idea that these hominids *could* have made their own tools. If we can't exhaust all the proofs that *erectus* could bust a regular rock into a chopping rock then we might have to fall back on the hypothesis that a long time ago, in a galaxy far, far away space robots began a mission to travel to the third planet of a distant yellow dwarf star to impart their superior pebble-shaping ability to a race of dancing apes who were no smarter than sea otters.

We know hominids could walk upright as far back as 3.0 Myr at the very least, and we've got a nearly complete *Homo erectus* (or *H. ergaster*, depending on who's sniveling) which definitively asserts that these boys and girls could walk, run and jump. Nevertheless some highly regarded researchers got their paws on a CT scanner, went tomography crazy on fossil inner ear holes, and declared they now had evidence that *Homo erectus* could walk, run and jump. They had the frame of a running biped right in front of them yet there was a compulsion to check the ear anatomy to make sure the skeleton could do what it was built for. Always second guessing Nature, these dipshits. Was there ever a possibility that the *erectus* inner ear was not designed in tandem with its skeleton? That these were people who had to wait millennia for their ear evolution to catch up as they shuffled along cave walls, hugged trees or crawled for fear of getting dizzy, falling down and throwing up all the time? Well at least the CAT-Scan brainiacs settled the issue. All the heaps of evidence they can pile up on the ingenuity or aptitude of the ancestors yet they still get befuddled to discover that Corky and Schlitzie Erectusson stumbled off into different continents early on in the game.

But the fossils are here, there, everywhere and after all the harrumphing and head-shaking nobody really denies that the *Homo erectus* skeletons actually were where we found them. But the knee-jerk disbelief that follows the discovery of things is symptomatic of the pandemic mindset which hobbles this field. Evolutionary anthropology's European (read: *white*) pedigree runs thick as bad lymph in the field. It's how it's presented to the world and how we're taught. Aborigines reaching transcendent dream states in Australia and tickling wallabies under billabongs even *before* Cro-Magnon got to Europe and ate all the Neandertals? No fucking way. We don't like our ancestors doing bright things unless, or at least until, they've already been blanched and polished in southern France. Ignore the Macaques and frogs, to the gentry of paleoanthropology our evolution ran like this: gifted monkey, ape, ape, ape, somewhat better ape, colored folk, smart *Caucasian* human.

An ugly, abscessed issue in the study of our evolution lies with researchers who find problems where there are none and inflate the hell out of tiny riddles. The biggest anchor to progress is not the paucity of fossilized protohumans, it's all the egos gone batshit, each gripped with the need to be the one-and-only to claim the Holy Grail – the species which split off from the line we shared with chimps. Or any direct descendant species from that point which led straight to us. But that's a topic for another day. There's still Olorgesailie to badmouth…

The excavations at Olorgesailie consist of acres and acres of pits and ditches infested with people-processed animal bones and stone tools. But with one little hitch – *no hominid bones*. Not even a lousy *Homo erectus* tooth splinter.

The hominid absence somehow screws with a researcher's ability to make sense of the collection of cutting, chopping and bashing instruments. Scientists, well archaeologists anyway, have gotten bunched undies over this boondoggle. Caches of hand-axes, ninety baboons chopped up in a pit, a maimed hippo fossil - but the perps have split the scene. *Homo somethingorother* may have made the mess but they didn't leave any bodies clutching hand axes to make that clear. No stony mandibles which might elaborate on who did what where… *Now over in that gully we used to make most of our tools. Betty Lou Ergaster was especially handy with percussion flaking. If you take a gander across this dead stream bed you'll notice the deli… Have you tried corned baboon? It's to die for…"*

We've found the tool shed but not the handyman and therein lies the rub. Maybe. As far as explaining away what could be intentionally heaped piles of *bifaces* we might say *Surely hominids piled these spiffy cobbles up for a rainy day* or *No, they're just heaps of tools somebody chucked in the creek* (surface wear suggests the stone axes spent considerable time submerged and tumbling in the drink) *which piled up by wave or river action*. Or, *The layers of doohickeys in the ground, however the hell they got there, eroded into each other in geologically recent times*. One way or another the dumps don't offer an excess of hints as to what business the hominids actually had going on here. Did they live here or was it simply a nice spot to visit and kill things for a few hundred thousand years?

The mass grave of baboons is indicative of hominid capacity for hunting, butchering and sticking around a while to eat. The bones are notched, scratched and gashed like somebody had cut the meat off them. Barring an *Erectus* NRA convention, ninety is a lot of big monkeys to slaughter and dine on in a brief occupation of the site.

So why should anyone expect there to be any hominids at the site? If river hydrodynamics (pushy water) caused the accumulations of stonework then the less dense corpses of hominids *should not* be expected in the same heaps. Water flow strong enough to move heavy cobbles would have sent tumbling body parts further downstream. If a hominid did wind up in the same formation as the hand-axes it's likely that the same erosional factors which brought tools back to daylight would have disintegrated a fossil long before Louis Leakey found the exposed caches of rock tools. The baboon bones, on the other hand, had been discovered buried.

Think about the baboon dump as the local hominid butcher shop. It implies hominids did indeed live or hang out in the hood. But why would any critter with a functional nose let bodies of its own kind decay in its dining room, sleeping pit, billiard room or what not. Rotting people stink. If *H. erectus* was sharp enough to make its own tool supply then they knew the perks gained by dragging a pal's cadaver out of the functional areas to someplace where the stench wouldn't piss anybody off. And it just wouldn't be couth to toss an uncle in with the monkey bones. We can't just dig everywhere so it becomes a matter of taking better guesses at where hominids might actually lie based on places we've found them before. Then do a lot of digging. But until that comes to pass[1], or until the current crews do dig up a body, this particular scientific community oughta quit complicating the scenarios and shut the hell up for a while.

On the way back from Olorgesailie my Land Rover gang was quizzed, Latinly, about animals we'd seen. Mostly farm animals - donkeys, goats, sheep, cows and camels – as well as giant wasps from outer space and bees the size of kneecaps. The most thrilling part of the day came as our pilot forced an oncoming car off the edge of an asphalt escarpment. Turning to face questions from the back of the Land Rover and scanning the land for vermin, his eyes wandered towards some giraffes and the truck roamed to the other side of the road. A car of oncoming, white safari crackers opted against being killed head-on and drove for the gravel below the pavement. Good thing Kenya doesn't take much stock in guardrails. There were splendid noises in the wake of their escape, shockingly loud sounds not unlike snapping axles and bashed oil pans. It was the audio track to a good fucking

[1] And come to pass it sort of did! A team led Rick Potts found a *Homo erectus* cranium in 2003 about 1.5km from the handaxe accumulations

because it ain't like there was a gas station just back down the road a ways. The poor bastards rolled to a stop in the dirt while we drove off and I chuckled to think that they'd be spending an afternoon in their own personal Olorgesailie on the side of the highway.

The day beat me up. Dust, heat, a smidgen of ennui and horst blocks of frustration over the stasis and regression in paleoanthropology. Throw in the previous night's fornicative indiscretion and whatever the fuck is in Kenya's beer that makes one feel truly horrible at breakfast and you might say I came to East Africa for the poison, tread-worn lectures and self-destructive behavior. Just like home with more monkeys, cheaper cigarettes and I burn off the hangovers in Land Rovers whizzing through the shadows of volcanoes rather than inching through urban canyons with cabbies trying to catch every red light between my bed and the next bar.

In the Olorgesailie morning I'd felt like an old diaper. By evening I was wondering if mommy was ever going to change me. Dinner blew like you wouldn't believe. For a clammy, beige meatloaf with Salisbury sludge sauce it amazed the senses with just how much it sucked. Like the cold, damp testicle of an elderly carcass scented by a yeast infection. Marvelous. My thoughts skipped like a record player on a rotting barge. Should I be eating mixed meats from a cut-rate hotel kitchen? *In Africa?* Considering how I'm able to rethink conventional condom use the worries over food quality were superfluous. I must be begging for an ignominious death and to prove just that I got three more half liters of Kenya's chemically disinfected Tusker Lager and drank 'em all in the shower. With a body free from dust and the fugazi shellac of a dirty night, I fell into a deeply disturbed sleep. Plump white babies cut in half, looking like cartoon mutton roasts, not bleeding themselves but rather wading, flipping and kicking through an office five inches deep in slick, liquid plastic blood. Two blue ducks wearing sombreros slapped their fannies in the sangré and gleefully barked out a Mexican barroom cantinela. *Yessir! The medication is wearing on for sure now!*

No Class

What I'm supposed to be doing here has finally been taking precedence over things I shouldn't have done since arriving. The snazzy fuck stories have been prepped for memory with layers of packing peanuts and the slanted observations on the city are sent to asphyxiate under sawdust for now. The de facto daily mechanics of prehistoric catechism is in full gear now. Stone Tool Lecture at the nine before noon: *How hominids chipped rocks; Why hominids chipped rocks; How you can chip rocks in the privacy of your own living room.* Can you feel me? Because some of this has just got to be mundane, am I right? One William Anyonege, a Kenyan dude and grad student at UCLA, spoke paleontology to the group at 11:15 a.m. A solid lecture which sponged off the residual glitz of jetting across continents and clenching drinks with sticky eyes locked on flight attendant ass.

Anyonege is a saber-tooth specialist/fanatic and that's refreshing in a herd with upstraight apes freckling our brains like psoriasis. But it is saber-toothed cats after all and you have to wonder if that's the only alternative to dinosaurs in animal paleontology. It's obvious that people have been busy packing textbooks with the lore of interglacial gophers and Carboniferous millipedes but you just don't ever meet these folks. The coolest of the paleonerds get assigned to the Ultrasaurs, Super Crocs and Mega Cats. The rest must get stuffed away in institutional caves, working with pencil nubs by candlelight to reconstruct nightmare bugs from the squished imprints of the Burgess Shale; monks airbrushing roan coats and speckled hocks on three-toed horses for the pretty color-plates in the literature. And Anyonege did have some slick picture books as well as posters of big pussies dappled in the shadows of trees, leaping with velveteen testicles at angora hippos or paring their kitty lips to show off cesium fangs in three-quarter profile. It was that sort of colorful junk that put bark on my elementary prick as a kid. His books were even better, with updated animals from an even weirder and wilder post-Cretaceous planet than was available in my youth. Massive horn-lipped *deinotheriums* tall as cartwheeling buses and hell bent on violating of the Second Law of Thermodynamics; flipper-legged cheetahs with compound eyes and frilled antennae; pigeon-toed hyaenoids calved from cedars like pine cones. *Caffeine, caffeine, caffeine.* If only there was such a thing as caffeine in the awful, fucked up coffee they provide at the Chiromo. Four cups in and I'm alert only until the stomach ache wears off. I lost most of Anyonege's spiel to the plasma blisters and sinkholes in my failing consciousness.

William's fossil jabberwocks had only opened for the main event: A frumpy, four-eyed monkey woman. A Buckeye? Groater? I can't recall what the hell you call ladies from Indiana. Her prattle was Miocene apes and other simians. She spoke of monkeys from deep in the eons but they were just dull myths without stunning color glossies of lava monkeys or oceanic gorillas to back her claims. Mere flow charts mimeographed with branching diagrams, underlines and italics don't prove anything to the semiconscious. Will's nifty, graphic monsters had barely kept me awake and her primates only existed in a few vandalized mineral jaws, an arid speech and some handout screeds written in the lost tongue of Ugric-Banshee. Throughout her scholarly desiccations my lids were clamping painfully over asphalt eyeballs, solely for the honeyed tingle of ripping them open again. Each time they scraped ajar they caught the monkey nun glaring at my rude, wobbling head as it came to on an upswing.

They cut us loose for recess. With no further need to impress the faculty with a respectfully riveted attention, a short wander to Nairobi's Westlands was due. It was a back alley trot from the Chiromo because there was a need to take note of banana trees standing sentry in smoky negligees spun from smoldering trash heaps and the beautiful hornbills and massive rooks in wife-beaters prodding the rotten garbage for recyclables. A stroll over pulverized gravel amid crests of rubbish to the nearby shopping district for tobacco reserves, hard candy and all the sneering the Indian shopkeeps could deliver. That is now the glamorous caesura to the educational story as the jungle fever of previous nights slinks into history to become the garbage wrap for half eaten fish.

The slam dance of scholarship resumed at 2:15 p.m. with a Paleontology Lab in the museum's warehouse of skeletons. Thousands of bones in thousands of boxes. Bony, boxy and unequivocally thousandy. Nearly depleted on adjectives and running on fumes all I have left is a nod to the most super fossilized thing I've ever seen or touched: a *Hyaenodontid* mandible. It was a big boy among the extinct *Creodonta,* an order of meat-gobbling early mammals. Now tyrannosaurus choppers and the dentition of *Megalodon* sharks are awe inspiring biological weapons. But rows, or even rows upon rows, of dental work where every tooth resembles the one ahead of it can't hold a candle to the crown and crevice diversity seen in the frightening teeth of the *hyaenodonts.* The National Museum is filled with all makes of fabulous fossils which lie unidentified, inspecifically labeled or of negligible intrigue as the winds of paleontological fashion gust elsewhere. They remain as such until the climate shifts toward revisitations or rookie researchers get stuck cleaning the attic. Anyonege had pulled out a few creodont pieces in the lab where we visited replica heads of hominids from a nearby vault. There was a mandible which resembled a dog's to a certain, gargantuan extent. The remainder of the extent held crazy, shredding carnassial teeth fully back to the beast's fucking ears. Molars crowned by sockets of interlocking daggers engineered to scissor the crap out of meat. All of a size which would make lions go wee-wee in fear of getting pulped by one of these monsters. Good lord, it was all so neat to look at. But to close the *Rhapsody Hyaenodontidae* in deplorably dull fashion there's this: they're not all particularly enormous and terrifying. Just a taxonomic group, much as the *Canidae* which encompasses both wolves and Chihuahuas. The bones in my hand were at the awfully big end of things. If I'd only handled some weasel-weight creodontid thingy we'd all be asleep at this point.

Extinct, giant critter-eating varmints make a nice segue into dinner at The Carnivore, where a few of us went for dinner. A sprawling, jungle motif joint with a big central fire pit roasting all sorts of game spitted on *Maasai* swords. A fanciful mess hall where you go to gobble slabs of zebra, eland, hartebeest, crocodile and chickens. Big, feral, baby-eating chickens, mind you. The shack drives for the delicately adventurous Ameropeans; folks who like Africa's wildlife dead and barbecued but get squeamish on the actual killing. Or for Great White Hunters who long to kill, don't want the fines or African jail time but still feel hungry. Disappointingly, most of the mammalian fare tasted no different than supermarket beef. Nary a thing had much flavor distinguishable from a Safeway rump steak except for the zebra. Better tasting than most beef, it was brow-raisingly tender and awfully nice all around. Means I must like eating ponies too, which is nice to know in case they start showing up at Stop & Shop. We were informed that the gluttonized animals had all been farm raised. Maybe even shot through the gills with hormones and reared in plastic bags. But it's hard to give a flying fuck in a rolling donut about the birth-to-market history of dinner in the face of endless meat sliced off pikes; bloody liquids greasing your chin as you knock back one *Dawa* after another.

A *Dawa*, since someone's bound to ask, is a lovely cocktail of limes smushed with ice, honey, and what the morning will likely reveal as the cheapest vodka on earth. It was a familiar beverage – the *caipirinha* in Brazil, right? Nope, different booze base in that – *cachaça*. Vodka means a *caipiroska, da?* But on a different continent than this though here it's still delicious and tailor made for washing antelope through your belly.

As the fat tumblers of hooch swelled my blood stream the tongue got loose and I gave my dining classmates an ugly, ethylated monologue on the blight brought to human evolution by the Leakey family and all their sycophants. Research drones who suckle at Richard Leakey's nuts for a chance to work towards proving that all pertinent fossil hominids in the line leading directly to the highest life form on Earth, the *British Colonial Male*, are only found in Kenya. And maybe in Tanzania where his Mum and Old Cocker Louis discovered some famous rocky crap. It's a paleoanthropological monopoly the Leakeys run here, quite Republican in style. Toe the ideological line or get shouted the fuck out of the museum and find yourself banned for life as heretical and unpatriotic.

Back at the Chiromo's beer hall the normal jabber swerved from the abusive amount of ABBA in the jukebox as the spit and gnash evening of trashing Richard Leakey carried on. It could be that some things I'd said at the Carnivore struck notes with the kids and they'd taken it to heart. Maybe they'd come here with Leakey rancor already rooted and after a few beers the mob just goes with the loudest jackass. And that jackass was me, as far as the most famous white family in Kenya was concerned, and the students were all aboard. Blood Leakeys were the marks, with ambivalent grumbles for the arguably competent lasses who married Leakey boys. Arrogant Anglojerks with unbounded opinions on *their* lineage of humanity. Louts with lazy DNA who oughta reconsider their own placement, if possible, among modern *Homo sapiens*. Screw 'em all. Even the better trained spouses and whoever weds their ugly kids.

Everybody fighting them for the missing link limelight could go straight to hell too, as far as we were concerned. This battle of egos and inflated claims based on fractured samples of strutting chimps is doing nothing for the field. Decades of pigeon-chest beating by Don Johansons, Christopher Stringers, Milford Wolpoffs, and Alan Walkers has done dick to advance man's knowledge of where he came from. Like coots hunting beach nickels with metal detectors they'd only have to pool their finds, buy a better machine and look deeper in the sand to make everybody rich. Yet it remains every man for himself with the loudest dipshit getting his or her half-assed allegations published. A new generation of thinkers is pulling up to the curb. At least I hope it is. More dudes like Tim White, who manage to keep lids on fossil discoveries until they've been studied enough to label. Or not label; if it isn't definitively this or that then let it be nothing. Not all clues in a puzzle are useful. Paleoanthropology may then seem to move ahead in a pained, slower manner but moving it will be. Then we can shut down the loudly carousel and let it rust properly. The bastards have screeched their cracked ponies under busted bulbs in the same circle for just long enough.

Dragon Fresh

It was finally time to go. We hit the road for Koobi Fora around 8:30 a.m., later than planned but far earlier than expected. All big trips are doomed to delay: for supply double-checks; for relocations of freight; and above all for engine trouble. And occasionally for missing people - we'd suddenly come up shy one Kenyan student. Frederick Odede, who'd been slurring clues for days as to possible drinking issues, had gone AWOL. Not for long, however, as he was located in the first place we looked: the bar. I had no idea you could drink there whenever you'd like. Maybe you couldn't and the guy behind the bar stuck around in case the kid with his face stuck on a table came to thirsty and larcenous. It took a slap or two but we roused him, neon-eyed and smelling like a stinkfoot sock soaked in Napalm. Our boy was still, as we say, wicked freakin' tanked and somebody was about to get stuck in a seat next to an aromatic drunk who was going to be that way for a while yet. There were two lorries and three Land Rovers. I got into the open-air cabin over the cockpit of the cargo Mercedes along with four others who needed a ride to smoke in. Management decided that bobblehead Fred ought to be with us. *Glory be! We shall lie with our brother though he breathe pestilence and stinketh with the taint of Judas.* Good grief. There have been few times in life which saw me hurtling for a good seat yet it always bites me in the ass. Tripping to get there or screeched at by pricks who wanted it more. When I do score an optimal perch I get babysitting duties for flat-out plastered dudes reeking like garlic, sulfur and cheap home perms. Keep them trucks a-rollin', we need the air!

My Olympus OM-10 snapped up a storm of photos in the afternoon. National Geographic quality pics of zebra herds, baboon troops, elephant herds, camel herds, mountain herds, volcano flocks and at least one other thing. So I hope the camera had been working since I get pretty pictures when it does. But the shutter release sticks like a bastard. Why? The *why* is an answer not even the picture school experts at Ferranti-Dege could produce. A lumpy fuck in the Cambridge shop offered me condescension when I needed solutions. Since the shutter seemed to release correctly after twenty or so tries the gourd-shaped douche bag suggested I do just that. My suggestion to him was to pack the camera and ship it to somebody who could fix it and keep his fucking mouth shut until he had advice that made sense. I'm supposed to waste almost entire rolls of film just to get one accurate snap? Jackass. He might have gotten the last word on me, however, since the shutter still stays open for seconds on end. I'm thinking he fucked me over and never sent the camera anywhere. Whenever I'd spotted something neat to capture on film it took a score of snaps of my riding crew to loosen the shutter up enough to capture the arresting beauty of a shepherd driving flocks through tin neighborhoods now a half-mile behind or the awe-inspiring flick of the last elephant's tail as the entire herd disappeared back into a forest. My visual documentary of Kenya will include many, many overexposed portraits of Freddie and that's just swell. Doubt he wants to be reminded of how ghastly he'd been looking.

Apart from two delays, lunch and a busted radiator hose, we made it to the generously environed Maralal by evening. The area has groovy outdoor things like trees and grass and hills and what have you. A frontier town, three hundred something kilometers from Capital City and civilization, and it gave us our first real exposure to African natives strutting in their jungle savage regalia: sneakers, polo shirts, pants and witchdoctor shit like ballpoint pens in their pockets. They ignored us intensely before disappearing as gauzy phantasms into the forest or into buildings.

Not so much to say beyond all that. We arrived at dusk, pitched tents in twilight, ate in the dark and slept until we woke up. And we woke up to campfire-fried French Toast and tropical fruits. So far, camping in Africa does not suck.

Narcoleptic Excellence

Twelve hours a day pitting our skeletons against potholes and installing stretch marks on our bladders. Nairobi to Koobi Fora is 746 km; even more than half that figure in miles. On Day Three we were far up the eastern shore of Lake Turkana when daylight quit about two hours shy of the final destination, the sun shooting off the greasy equatorial horizon like a grape on a hot buttered helmet. It was a scramble to pitch tents in a sandy *laga* near Allia Bay while trying not to be murdered by puff adders in the twilight. All was peachy. Skeeter bane was misted on my veiny parts while jackals croaked the lullabies of strangled tykes.

The day itself had blurred into trees, rocks, lake views, rocks, dirt and rocks. I had a turn to ramble with Dr. H in his fat ride. The "White Rover" was a treat after a couple of days crammed in the overhead cab of the lorry. On Day Two the ferociously hungover Fred Odede was sent to plague one of the Rover groups and two girls took his place, taking up enough extra space in the cab to ensure that somebody else's parts were always in contact with mine. And that always hatches snakes in my skin.

The new seat was a candy deal, a chance to kick back, spread my thighs an extra inch and kiss up for merit points. All businesses require a measure of knee-scuffing and this one is no different. It never hurts to thumb and mollycoddle the top boys' testicles if you want a seat in the game room. Not that this should be assumed of Dr. H. He does seem to be about brains, will and integrity but I haven't sucked up to enough betters in life to know when I should or shouldn't. And to go right on kicking this corpse, what say I add this: If the human evolution gig revolved around ability and toil - as opposed to bihominid politics, fellatial sycophancy and luck - the riddles of our kind might've been wrapped up ages ago. At least that means jobs are still available. Time to pucker up.

This opportune shot at paleoanthropologic advancement went along the usual modes. My first crack at making a big impression was to fall into a deep sleep as Dr. H addressed the landmarks and ecology along the road to Koobi Fora. It burns my ass that I can't catch ten minutes of shuteye while drinking heavy on all-night plane rides when all it takes for a deep snooze here is to merely start off awake in the presence of one of the top cats. It's not that I find any of them dull, it's just the contrary - I'd have drank in every last syllable from even the monkey lady's mouth if I had a say in the matter. It must be something hidden, a dickhead gremlin in the aural clockwork of this school which makes the dignitaries come at me like horseshoes swung in a lead bag dusted with Benadryl.

They could've written me off as merely narcoleptic, but it gets even better. During the trip my spine went slack, dropping my head into the crotch of David Kipkebut, a *Kalinjin* kitchen guru. He was too polite to shove my noggin aside as my eyes popped open an inch from his pants, wondering what the hell I'd been dreaming about. *Denim gopher dens?* I figured it out quick enough to catch the rope of drool spiraling towards his thigh and straightened up. Though seated next to me I hadn't really had the pleasure of making David's acquaintance by that point. He's awfully underspoken, as is the other *Kalinjin* man on staff, our head cook Willy Chesire. He nodded, smiling my gushed apology aside which left me with little else to do but wonder what I could do to get a little attention.

Get a mouthful of water to help recover, swallow it wrong and choke on some dust before expectorating like a nauseous camel at Dr. H and his extra-butch assistant, Georgette? *Check*. Did it in style too, spraying saliva glaze in a wide scatter towards the front of the Rover. Spritzing necks shiny with mucous is a good shortcut to making anybody hate you. You become a pariah into perpetuity for that kind of transgression. Could there be more? How might I sear my name in their memory for ages to come? Unable to come up with anything immediately I slipped back into the coma to get swallowed in a stress nightmare. I was horking great volumes of spitty air at a brass band and trying to warn a brunette that she was entering my hack range, screaming at her to back off, it wasn't safe. Crawling things were dragging dewclaws in my trachea and I had a ferocious cough to get to. She rebutted my manic warnings with a sultry Latin tongue. I was floundering in my caveats. *What the hell's the word for cough in Spanish?*

"*Tos!*"

I shouted it to nobody in particular but bursting back into consciousness I'd lunged halfway into the front seat to scream the Spanish term right in Georgette's ear. I'd no idea how to apologize for me anymore.

Sidelong glances of disquiet and suspicious revulsion joined me for the rest of the ride. Apart from giving up on giving a fuck I could only fall back into my slot and admire the lush oasis we were approaching. Everything else on this prairie was near dead, withered balls of varicose shrubbery dangling up from a mantle of dirt powder. But we also came upon a rich tangle of palm and weeds and acacia, *with leaves,* getting a sweet coat of dazzle from the afternoon sun. Good water saturation in this dirt and a fine place for all to piss or wipe themselves off in. We'd have lingered longer had I not pointed out the giant piles of feces; elephant crud and it was fresh. Everybody was hustled back to the van before the pachyderms came back in a kicking mood.

Last night needs an airing. About twenty minutes north of a shack village called South Horr is a vast space of wood, hill, and desert of the same name. A stronghold of the mystical *Samburu* people-eaters and a glitzy place to camp. It was an exquisite dirt circle surrounded by hills, sand plantations and gnarled acacia shrubs. With explosive gusts repositioning my scalp over my face it also seemed to be a tornado lane. Cement tent foundations were poured and sleeping bags were stuffed with boulders to keep us from getting sucked out of the flaps and off to an East African Yellow Brick Road.

As though the Land Of Oz weather system wasn't disturbing enough the darkening terrain began to seethe with pocket-sized instruments of woe. Squatting over some camel bones in the dirt, *when in Rome,* I shined my flashlight on an unhappy carpet viper rasping a death ballad with its scales. By scratching its coils against itself it does a dead-on rattlesnake impersonation and it's a pretty cute serpent for something lethal. I'd say my instincts were still wet as I was just about to swing my ass over its face when the thought of lighting up the ground occurred to me. No harm, no whatever, so he made his hissing caveat, gave me the hairy eyeball then beat it. His spot was repopulated with a little freak parade of scorpions, spiders, and crawling cargo wasps showcasing the evening's choices for screaming spasms of agony. One could not deny how nifty the dangers were in Africa. Life was good. And it was suppertime.

And what a mother of a feast it was: Spaghetti with Spaghetti Sauce. *Really good spaghetti sauce.* In the goddamned desert of Central Nowhere we had a nice marinara, with garlic toasts no less. After inhaling a couple of helpings I stomped off with Vic Thorne, Jen S. and the little knockout fire whip, Janet Hixon, for a suicide mission into the wasteland. Hyenas, jackals, snake carpeting and lions; who the hell decides that the second night ever spent in East Africa's wild is fine for traipsing into the pitch to poke around for stuff? The howling night air sang the tale of a medieval map of the Atlantic I'd once seen. A little west of Ireland were the words *"Here be Dragons."* I'd rather have dragons than lions since huge monsters are easier to hide from. The authorities didn't notice that we'd ambled off into the realm of fire-mouthed nightmares. But if we ended up on the desert's menu someone was going to regret not leashing us better.

Our idea had been to follow the road about a klik back to some bones we'd seen hanging in an acacia. A string of vertebrae, accented with ribs, and so brightly white they'd looked as real as Halloween props. Leftovers of a leopard kill? Kind of a low rent hood for leopards considering all the trees were merely big bushes. There was a thick green woodland not far south so a suburban cat might go there for takeout. *Maybe the leftovers of an ex-leopard?* Even better, though we'd never know as we never found them. Hanging roadside as we came up, they were now lost. Though my tracking talent is unimpeachable, along the trek it was meshed in Janet's hair wondering if it smelled as nice as it had the morning we left when I kept leaning her way for a little nasal counterbalance to the olfactory assault of Freddy Odede. *Still looks nice*, I chanted as we walked too far into a weird world no one knew a thing about. No fucking sweat, this kind of fun doesn't come around too often.

Janet led the way, scuttling into the scrub at every flashlit twinkle in the dirt. We'd faithfully trail her to give the big cats meal options. *Don't think for a minute that a flashlight beamed at her bum was anything less high minded than bodyguard duty…* Vic and Jen finally got fed up with the chase, or wisely grew terrified, leaving me with Janet on the deranged junket. Fear had pulled its hooks from my heart and the talons of weird excitement took their place in the gouges. We were taking on the unknown night with adrenal glands on the verge of exploding.

The wild night air affects the mind's tissue in manners that are hard to get my head around. It's an experiential issue; the words, they don't work good about this. Got me? In that atmosphere, magnetic over threatening, emotions ignite. I was mystified, in fear, in awe, paranoid, crushed serene, fully erect and ready to scream in laughter until my lungs ruptured. The thought that the sands might coil and sink fangs into my foot in that bruise-toned infinity, or that lions could be divvying up organs as our screams cycloned in echoes around camp, sharpened my awareness until the senses became a gerbera blossom of rainbow razors. Harlequin centipedes tickled my brain, listening to everything when there was little to hear. The smells were light but distinct and blazed unfamiliar images across my mind. As the night goes on you feel your body becoming less isolated. Skin transmutes to ionized gauze for the universe to permeate. The eyes take a little while to catch up, especially with clouds plastering the stars. But they come around, framing the off-road hillscape against the burnt blue skies and the shivering bush-trees in the ashen dirt. We'd killed our flashlights a ways back, walking in thick lightlessness for some time. For just a second my brain shrieked in horror. *What the fuck were we thinking? No lights?* Then it passed. The dark was beautiful, its untainted magic charged my circuits, and I didn't want to scar it with battery illumination.

Going back we felt no need to stay on the artery through the whimsically lethal drape. I underwent a wee philosophical clash - an affinity for the pure ferality of the environment versus the snaking hard-on swelling for the person ahead of me. My normal personality hadn't fallen too far behind. Perhaps it wasn't that much of a conflict. A burning erection for a healthy set of cute-as-heck genes might've been dead-on appropriate for the wild. Naturally I can tell myself anything I want to when no one is listening.

Greasy Monkey

Big rocks in the Turkana basin push maliciously through the road, eating transmissions in stealth even though the sun promised to reveal all hazards. There is a quaint aspect to the roadscape once you reach the splash zones of Lake Turkana – everything becomes the same color. Along some stretches it's all a Martian terrain of burnished boulders in the tones of drying blood. Other parts of the highway are swallowed in the overall yellowy-gray hue of a scorpion. By and large the road is a detectable course of dirt and there is even a whole quarter mile span of concrete pavement north of Loyangalani. There also times when the it is barely distinguishable from the fat stone fields surrounding it, being a mere thinning of the rocks. Under these conditions there is no night driving. Unless the dragons chasing you are coughing enough fire to light the way.

We'd called it quits at a dry river bed, or *laga*, near Allia bay. We'd be back in a few weeks for a dig and it is a super swell place to camp. There's a breezy wood lining the *laga* channeling the soothing *khccuuuuhsh* of Lake Turkana a couple of kliks off. The nighttime slipped away without event. *No it didn't.* There were light diversions. At supper someone spotted a puff adder and the entire contingent of Kenyan staffers leapt together with *pangas* and kitchen utensils to confront the threat. They went after the reptile as a manic knot of legs, dust and weaponry, like a throng of constables waving billy clubs in Benny Hill skits about chasing gap-toothed English dames in big bras. I went to see what a puff adder looks like after our guys kill one. This particular viper looked like wet, pink and purple gravel. The men are thorough.

There is a woman in this class who nuanced the sleepover in memorable fashion. Tubby, and in her mid-thirties, older than most, she'd been scuffing her soles on a quiet fringe as the studentship coalesced and polypped into cliques. This morning, however, she became the center of attention as the first girl to get seriously clobbered by intestinal bugs. I've never been taken so off guard by diarrhea that I couldn't get fifty feet closer to a toilet before losing the clench on my sphincter, so there's no way for me to comprehend what horrible ass calamity had prevented Sheila from escaping her tent. Without even discussing her pants, it's puzzling to wonder how she managed to shit all over the flaps of her tent. Well, not that perplexing; I can picture the whole scene. The real head scratcher is why somebody would wait so long to get untrousered *outside* before disaster struck. Can the trots be that catastrophically sneaky? At any rate her mousy anonymity was destroyed as she bawled and wailed while smearing crap off a tent which she'd unfortunately pitched close to the trucks: In the morning everybody was ultimately destined for the parking lot.

I got to help Sheila through her ordeal as I'd gotten tagged to ride with Dr. H again. After the social atrocities I'd performed in his truck the day before I have no idea why he singled me out again. But it was a sweet ladle of luck offering me the chance to revise the hacking lout impression I gave him the day before. So when the Doc says we're hanging back a couple of hours, maybe more, to help a sick woman clean up then replace a maimed radiator, there will be no jumping ship, no questioning the option. Jiminy, all the options are worth taking these days for me – scholarship is too willing to spin its wheels and leave me choking in the dust. While the convoy moved on to Koobi Fora I stayed back to lend a hand. I used to clean my uncle's unbelievably filthy service station as a kid. When I wasn't rinsing grease off tools with gasoline he had me changing oil and lubing chasses. He was probably charging customers twenty bucks an hour for tires rotated and balanced by a twelve year-old making two-fifty. It was as good a prerequisite for the job as any. I could mount a radiator. I only wondered how much petrol it would take to remove poop from tent fabric.

Forget Paleolithic archaeology, H is a crackerjack mechanic, correcting errant machines without wasting time on pre-planning. Doesn't need the socket wrenches laid out by ascending widths; just tell him where the engine's at and the trouble is half over. I'd heard a truck wheezing like a hot hamster, Dr. H heard a cracked radiator and a loose fan belt. I didn't know when to pitch in until I was sent under the Rover to tension the belt and bolt in a spiffy black radiator. It got gritty when the bottom hose clamp slipped and pissed coolant in my ear as I squirmed in gravel mud trying to get it back on.

My gashed knuckles and muddy hair got me a thanks from the Doctor and I made a better passenger for the final leg, staying bright eyed all the way. Sitting left side shotgun, I got to sell my better self and sucked in even more about H and *paleowhatnots* overall. There's nothing like private tutoring in a barreling Land Rover with the smartest guy in the show. He revealed broken plains of *bioclastic* sandstone – little more than ridges of dark, rusty rock at first take but chock full of ancient ex-gastropods and other shelly stuff when he takes you in for a closer peek. I held a *stromatolite* in my hands for the first time. A squashed muffin formed of unicellular thingies and their petrified calcium mucous which often grew as big as swimming pools. Mine was like a coffee cake, it even looked delicious. But precious rare antiquities aren't the only things which need to remain where they came from. Even the bacterial residues of our living history do not leave their final resting places without a formal assay and a court order. I put my fossil danish back, crossed myself in a Catholic seizure and took a leak.

At the Koobi Fora main camp I felt new cravings and a real sense of place. Things had queered between me and Janet in the few hours I'd been apart from that cute tarzaniac. At the end of that crazy stroll in South Horr she'd turned to me with wild eyes so energized I was sure she was about to mash her mouth against mine and chew my tongue out. Then people had come to welcome us back from the edge and that was that. She seemed indifferent to my arrival at Koobi Fora but there was no need to dwell on it. It's barely more than a potential summer fuck in an isolated place. And, pretty bosom or no, she ain't no crumb cake stromatolite.

Low Riding Goblins

The class had been oriented around the base camp while I was mucking beneath a battle scarred SUV at Allia Bay. They were decompressing so I was on my own once I got to town. I'd been assigned to bunk with Enzo and Vic in the most lakeward of the two student *bandas*. All buildings here are called *bandas* - *Main Banda, Men's Banda, Kitchen Banda* and onward. Various sized huts built from stone to about nose high followed upward by beams, chicken wire windows and thatch roofs. Beyond rummaging among the lab's crates of animal bones and other light exercises no exceptionally taxing feats were expected from us. I hovered a while at each of the bandas; popping in to say *Jambo* to Ben Sila and other guys working at the storage banda or sucking back lake water desalinated in an evaporation banda while watching Gregory and Nyanga giving Rovers seven-point lube jobs from an inverted banda shoved into the ground. Cool as it is, there's not much variation in Koobi Fora architecture. Just a matter of where the banda is on the landscape, who lives in it and whether you stand on the floor or the ceiling.

Once the banda visits lost freshness there was little else to do but saunter through the blonde razor grasses and rock village which define the Koobi Fora spit. It was just a nice freaking day. A collectively fine mood ran through all; even the cranky vegan chick hadn't scowled in hours. I boogied on down to the beach. *Lordy, what a big fucking lake.* Stretching like an infinite slick of blue lime juice seasoned with salt, it was what I thought parts of heaven would be. Desert and papyrus shoving right up to the water where three smoldering volcanoes ran like Godzilla's spine keels. It only needed thirty foot waves, a packie and some teen girls experimenting with bisexuality. But I was truly charmed by it as is. As the air on the spit grew crazy hot I stumped back to my banda, said *jambo* to my bat, an unassigned roommate, and took a nap. Nice bat. Hangs from the thatch and swivels as I whistle at him.

Let's talk *Solifuges*. Or *Solifugids*. *Solifugae?* Curses! This lust for accuracy is a real thistle in the corn pipe, goddammit. Anyhow, *solifuges*, I'll stick with that one, had come up in dinner conversation. Allan Morton, the chief of staff, and Tom the knuckle-sucking teaching assistant, were trading bug stories from last year. I perked up over their scorpion yarns as they are the champagne of arthropods in my book. They had been a preferred prize in my desert forays as a lad in Arizona; something to bring home in a pail and give my mother a seizure. They came as big as your hand in the American Southwest, chockfull of charisma too, and I'd been keeping myself pretty for when I met some of their quarter-pint African kin. When the faculty boys started in on solifuges we were all clueless as to what those might be. The veterans described them as neither spiders nor scorpions but rather scorpion-clawed spiders. That sure sounded fucked up and the spidery half of the descriptive voided my urge to see one. It is silly that a man who finds scorpions as so *neato!* and *whoo-hoo!* can approach psychological collapse at the mere idea of spiders. It has nothing to do with morphology; scorpions are as mean-looking as predators come but somehow they give off an air of sexy slickness. Their eight-footed cousins, on the other hand, have all the horrifying beauty of clumps of hair clipped out of the devil's nostrils. If you were to put one of those tiny, teddy bear jumping spiders within a foot of my face you could irrigate a car battery with my lip sweat and charge it via the tension in my neck. It's all about spirit: scorpions just go about their naturally ordained functions; spiders are densely tangled knots of iniquity, neutron clusters of evil stuffed in a bug shell. Even scorpion pincers couldn't make solifuges sound more enticing; it only suggested that they were compound abominations. Frankenstein spiders. Just had to hope there weren't any scheduled to scuttle into my future.

In the rearview it's plain to see how solifuges were the Devil's sick marionettes juiced on electromagnetic evil. I hadn't seen any of these mutato bugs yet, not even in the night-stroked sands of

South Horr. Then again they'd never come up in chit chat or even the lectures, though I'm ill-qualified to report on the latter. But almost as soon as folks started dishing rumors about them they commenced their infiltration on our village. It was less than an hour after the initial solifuge discourse, while still slapping arachnophantasms off my arms and nicotine-washing the willies out of my nerves, when I spotted the first one. It wasn't part of my paranoia – it was too distinct and scratched its palps too fucking loudly on the concrete of the open air dinner *banda*. I coughed the Winston out of my face, leaping up to scatter my chair and the people sitting too close to me.

"That has got to be a fucking solifuge" I howled trying to distance myself without tripping over anything I'd just knocked over.

The kids at my end of the table saw the fist-sized atrocity quickly enough, launching into a crazy riot which helped beard my own chickenshittery. They shrieked and collided as it turned in place with an abhorrent "*khickk khickk khickk*" on the cement. It wanted out as much as we did and chose to tear off at Vic to escape. He was the largest creature on the patio but with a mere two legs he must have looked a safer bet than the stampeding bipeds near me. Still it was a doomed decision as the big boy took a step aside and brought a sneaker down on it as it whizzed by.

So now we had a solifuge to study. I can't be sure that my first impression, a spidery thing with three or four inches of body propelled by legs of a similar measure, was correct. We did know that it was squishable to the dimensions of the fore sole of Vic's tennis shoe and that's still a substantial bug. It was an ugly mess of gray abdomen, ruddy cephalothorax and waxy yellow legwork. A sump of arachnid snot like crème brûlée with blue and purple streaks. *Betty fuck a bunny*, I was not going to sleep for days.

Later on I wanted some distance from the nightmares Kenya was trying to crack open in my head. Reading in bed was a happy idea. I'd broken into Steven Weinberg's *Dreams of a Final Theory* and was enjoying an off-ramp into a layman's scenic overlook of theoretical physics. We have kerosene(*paraffin* in the colonial tongue) lamps for light and naturally they bring in the bugs. When resting from a thousand laps around the flame, insects alight on shelves, rafters, or the mosquito nets draping the beds.

My pillow lies opposite the lamp so I rest a flashlight on a shoulder to get me brightly through some pages before dozing. This draws them in closer and before you know it there's a bustling arthropod convention with the heaviest floor traffic right by my head. They are on the outside and as long as I don't train my eyes on the peripheral hubbub I'm left with a scuttling galaxy of freckles. A visual lullaby - sweet, soothing, whirling blemishes. Tonight a big henna fuzz ascended in the far quadrant of my right eye. A large blurry bug hovering to make sure I was getting sleepy, to tell me reading in such poor light was bad for my little eyes. That was nice. I turned to thank it and thought it was funny that its presence wasn't obscured like the other insects with all that skeeter gauze ghosting up their forms.

Because, you see, it wasn't looking out for my best interests among the gentle cyclone of bugs outside the net. It was inside my fucking net and it was a fucking solifuge that must have chewed through the goddamn fabric *because it was suddenly at my face and coming to eat my fucking eye!*

The wretched critter, eighteen times as nasty as the hairiest spider and so full of ugly it could melt children, blazed to the top of my net making small pops as it screeched past the sound barrier. I was out of the mesh before that miserable scab of agony moved two legs but looked at it long enough to describe it in exacting detail forty fucking years from now. Those infernal spider resemblers must have been engineered for horrible forms of biopsychological warfare by evil animae back in a day when beings really hated the hell out of each other. Why o why won't history's combatants ever clean up after themselves? Landmines still blow the limbs off Laotian ladies in rice paddies and solifuges now hunt for my organs.

The beast at the top of my worthless canopy paused as I put a big knot in the netting to keep it inside. Vic came to my aid; having already murdered one a blood feud was on - this solifuge might have mistaken me for him. Gloving his hand with a squishing sock he lunged and mashed the little bastard good. That sickly crunch again, the same sonic vomit squeezed under Vic's sneaker a couple hours back. But when he pulled his hand back we found no bug goop on the sock and absolutely no corpse in the net. It had vanished, affirming that the critter was equipped with powers channeled from the guts of Hell itself. We knew what had to be done now. The only way to stop vermin charged with evil magic is to tear apart everything it had been near; to flip, thrash and beat the shit out of the furnishings, maybe set things on fire, until Lorenzo wakes up cursing in three broken languages and the girls next door start giggling at you. You have to keep at it until either the cobra under the bed bites you or you find the satanic arachnid crushed up and dead. Neither of which happened.

As the dust settled to mud on my sweaty flesh we saw the solifuge jerk swinging over the shambles in the very spot where Vic first took a swipe at it. It was *smiling*. Maybe even laughing, but I couldn't hear because Enzo was calling us *pig-faggot babies* in his now intolerable Spic-Dago idiom. That mean greaser creep doesn't use a mosquito net yet never gets bit, which says something about how desirable he is to other living things. Passing up such an easy mark made it clear the solifuge had an axe to grind with me for abetting in the killing of its cousin, with Vic next on the vendetta. Hopefully Enzo will be devoured by dick-eating plants out here. I wanted to take the arachnid alive and tuck it up his fanny but reality doesn't see me handling spiders or Lorenzo's poop chute.

We launched back to the kill in a fury of flying socks and annihilated the monster. Or at least we crushed the hideous shell of the pernicious spirit and tossed the mangled body out of the banda. Its physical residue was no longer with us but the emetic crunching noise of that diabolical varmint's death will be with me forever.

The awful fracas was over. My netting has been re-inspected a dozen times and tucked tightly beneath my mattress. I was committed to bug-eyed sentry duty, clicking away endless seconds thinking I'd be awake forever. But the vigilance collapsed quickly. After I noted the episode in the log book my adrenaline petered out, followed quickly by consciousness. Lulled to sleep as Enzo snored out Latino derision I slept soundly without dreams or urine breaks.

Aharyaraga? Khalarata?

Two women have put the collywobbles in my libido since I got here. The Vancouver tasty who'd insinuated a liking for dirty stuff, though only clearly so about ten minutes before ditching this continent. Then Janet, now a sputtering froth of social and political conviction, lost luster amid her liberal nineteen year-old inability to stop talking once in a while. There was also that Kenyan *malaya* who may have left me with some yet undeveloped Nairobi viral souvenir. So more than two and I won't go too far into how Enzo sometimes drags an eyelid when he falls asleep looking at me.

Now there's Kalle McInnis, the Bangalore Boy. While reading the intro pack's student list back home my eyeballs mashed her name, *Kalem Cinnish was* what I saw, the M/c combo not even clicking in my half Irish mind leading to wincing thoughts of journeys with a cinnamon-toned dink. A Mumbai brat bastard who'd bring along a penchant for annoying me with his annoyances, who'd drive me to seek out the comfort of mosquitoes. It's highly likely I read the student roster on a cross-eyed hangover, mashing and adding letters to her name on top of that for the fun of confusing myself. Boy howdy, it was nice to finally meet him and see that her Finno-Celtic name combo meant "crystal eyes like hot, clean honey and a sucker punch". She's a Canadian from somewhere south of the Yukon, that much I'm solid on. And she's different...

I'm almost sure about that.

That she's quite pretty is incontestable. Blonde in a groovy, cascading ringlet way, with scuffed crystal eyes and a fabulous bum. At least I think it's a great bum. It ought to be, though the extended wear we put on our pants out here doesn't aid a fair outlining of anyone's hind quarters. So one can't say with alacrity that her bum would get a blue ribbon at the fair. What the hell am I saying? In general, my focus factors for female infatuation are sharp tongues and fantastic bums. And a little hygiene in the paint. She's clean, devilishly sarcastic and I'm developing a preoccupation for her. Force the deductions just a bit with all of that and *ergo* Kalle's bum must be right on the money...

She's taken a shine to me too. Or I've been fogged in by great vagina demons singing their flutey hypnosis, a possibility I won't deny as it happens all the time. She passes time at my table off the main banda, a chancel of communion or slab of exile for the nicotine crowd and she doesn't even smoke. Isn't that how you can tell when a chick digs your junk? A penchant for nicknaming me hints at a growing coziness. Last week I was *Boston* and now it's *Gyps*, for "gypsy," though why hasn't been made clear. It could have something to do with the dark curly mop on my head. Or it just might be the somewhat sissy Harley bandana occasionally strapping my dome. It has too much mauve in it for American style machismo, but it might pass as swank among the Romani. At any rate, I own neither earrings nor tambourines so I guess I just won't know Kalle's inspiration until I ask.

It's tough to put this into perspective when I've been bouncing from lust to fuck to crush and back since the moment I boarded the jet in Boston. At least with Kalle I've had a consistent pal and I haven't put much thought into sandy hummocks where we might pop a little Freixenet and exalt in resplendent procreative practice. I just dig this lady. She probably wouldn't do me anyway.

My recall of current dates is disintegrating into a profound inaccuracy. I've got an inkling that we're in the initial days of August. It feels like August as it's pretty fucking hot out. Then again this is Africa and that's usually what you get. Nothing extraordinary has been going on, leaving ample time for paranoia and fueling my suspicion that vengeful polyfooted assassins are keeping low until I drop my guard. Spider eyes fleet from every crevice in every banda and the spit sizzles with bug whispers. Heavens to Murgatroyd, I do so dislike doom. Makes it hard to focus on the business and we are busy, in the throes, or at least in the training aspects, of fieldwork now. I'd spent a hefty chunk of blazing morning daylight assisting foreign students Cyrus (Kenyan, so not so foreign) and Tamrat, (an Ethiopian and thus nearly alien as I). A little help with sight-leveling projects, using zebra sticks and tiny telescopes with vials and bubbles and crosshairs all stuck on a tripod to find how long a walk it is to the lake from a rock in the front yard. Or, if all the dirt in front of said rock was scooped down to lake level, how hard a fall it might be if you got pushed. I've mastered this and it's a feather in my cap for performance. It won't win widespread admiration but Dr. H felt I could pass the know-how on to mates who were struggling with the exercise.

I shouldn't forget that I slammed a Rover door shut on a project coordinator's finger. Yikes! Well that put me right back on the blacklist again with the brass. It happened up at the Museum Banda which is a short drive away up a low ridge from HQ. Sort of a no place in particular in the greater nowhere of here, it has fake plaster hominid heads, turtle and croc fossils all of which probably hide solifuges. It's no bigger than a HoJo's restroom and it's challenging to say why we went there since we have ape-man skulls and fine reptile remnants at the main camp. But consternation over a seeming waste of time wasn't why I assaulted the girl with a car part. It was just an accident. She was in the front passenger seat leaning towards the driver's side window as people piled into the Rover. I jumped in the back seat last from the left, slamming the door out of habit without noticing that she had her hand wrapped around the door frame. *Glunsch!* The funny sound preceded a stutter of *oh*'s and *ouch*'s. Thank Jesus for the belligerent heat of a Koobi Fora afternoon – the pliable door bent over her digit instead of crushing it off as it latched. It left her little worse than deep purple and any fondness developing between her husband, Allan, and me took an ugly slap back to square one. Nothing but the hairy eyeball from him since.

Even though women in distress can suddenly acquire a measure of allure, I have noticed no seminal interest burgeoning over the project coordinator. Certainly cute enough to warrant a second look in a wasteland she is nevertheless married to a dude I find intriguing and likeable even though I find no cuddling cravings over him either. But I sure as hell have been musing a lot on women. Don't that figure? Out in one of Earth's strange, wild places and getting wrapped up by who I'd like to get slippery with and if it will happen any time soon. Janet looked delicious again tonight. The moon was a gleaming razor sickle, the Milky Way pasted so thickly across the sky it threatened to rake your scalp like stucco on a low ceiling. She'd let those ridiculous corn-rows out of her hair and was cute as raspberry jam again. Maybe a dozen notable stars in the city skies of home, billions here and I was only imagining wearing Janet like an ascot. Hearing my inner rambles about fucking again finally left me deeply irritated so I set a camp chair on the lawn, gnawed my inner cheek, chain smoked and searched the heavens for constellations I'd never even heard of.

Once I'd determined the Southern Cross was at least thirteen different star configurations in separate regions of the sky, I went to bed to make notes on the recent paleoanthropologic activities. Identifying random animal bones - lots of *gerenuks* on the frontier but none of their heads were in our collection boxes. *Biostratigraphy*, scaling the eons of dirt via pig fossils. *Microstratigraphy*, mapping ancient mud veneers. I do so want to reference all of it and footnote the crap out of my little diary. Aw, screw that biostratigraphy patooie. If grandkids ever come across my notes in the rubble of my final home all they need to know is that I've touched fossil hogs and it was cooler than living heck.

Some new faces had arrived a couple of days ago. One Wellesley student, hence preprogrammed for lesbianism or becoming a housewife with a bachelor's degree, though she strikes as a little too Tracy Chapman for the latter. Late because Air France had been on strike. She was brave to stick with that airline since *les mechaniques* hadn't touched *les jumbos* all summer.

A screwball archaeologist accompanied her, bringing along the most cynical and diabolical sense of humor yet to the faculty. A goofy hick prick, loveable for an acerbic, albeit museum-quality, wit. Possibly hilarious years back, obsolescence has encroached on his particulars of nonconformity. But no problem. He can become our relic-icon when the new generation takes over the business and does a little house cleaning. It'd be nice to leave an element of Frankenstyle in the field as well; splattering the discipline with my puncturing insights and thick, reverential unorthodoxy until some younger jaded prick with some passion and a journal declares me pathetic and past tense. Bucket of blood, circle of life.

Screaming Blue Omo

This is it. The big It. The eve of my virgin trip into real excavation where I'll trod and scratch and eat bone-bearing dirt like the great discoverers of yore. We're hitting the dust for the Karari; a windy, scrubby desert that's pretty damn liberated from water this time of year. Most times year as well. But what it lacks in swimming holes it makes up for in fossils abundance. There's no great chance of uncovering the next great mineralized hominid – the rock fairies rarely bestow such altruism on passing packs of knuckleheads who plan for a mere week of prospecting. But I'm betting more on the Karma, praying the *Bodhisattva* of human evolution can pat my fanny nine ways towards a pail of mighty paleoanthropologic aptitude.

Preparing for the excursion involved a little laundry in the crocodile pond with my little box of Screaming Blue Omo detergent. Can't seem to stop saying *Screaming Blue* when referring to my soap, which, factually, is only labeled *Omo*. Must be driven to push the product in loud, truck show fashion. Omo must have a decent amount of bleach or color-killing agent in it. Alongside the punishment of drying your clothes under the rasping African sun one Omo cycle will make a new shirt look like grampa wore it at Omaha Beach. All while the *Omo River* flows out of Ethiopia and into Lake Turkana. Omo detergent could suck the brown off a wildebeest yet the vista lakeward includes a long nutmeg stripe of river sediments darkening the midline of the Jade Sea. How's that for irony? Yeah, it's pretty light. I got nothing today.

For others the day bore things more colorful than sudsy dialectics on blue-greens versus brown. For them the irony involved antimalarial drugs and their side effects. Most are on some form of prophylaxis; Aralen(*chloroquine*) and Doxycycline are in some travel kits though the majority of them are on Lariam(*mefloquine*). That not-quite-so-wonderful wonder drug became the hot topic as debate bubbled over as to it being an ineffective elixir, a serum of inconsiderate horrors or an inoculant of sublime joy. Everybody has a take on the drug and so far I'm the only guy touting the pills as fun. War tales abound from the slightly itchy and moderately nauseous to fully agitated and crazed humans (interestingly, only women humans so far) claiming minor seizures and ragged psychotic fractures. Matter of fact, one young Lariam user went batshit just this morning. What began in paranoid whines about the whispers she could hear from all over the compound crescendoed into barks and shrieks of *Get me the hell out of here!!!*

Watching as she ripped her fingernails off on the chicken wire of her banda's window we all wanted to help. I entreated her to shut her fucking face, following it up with cooed threats about splitting her skull asunder with a Samburu war club. Her scooped out brains would reveal her most sacred, bobby-socked thoughts to the general public should she continue with the flaky crackpot horseshit. So she gave up, slumping into a sweat puddle and a mute torpor. Fuck her, by Jiminy! Fresh on a Lariam tablet, I've never felt so together as I do this moment.

Lariam bestows comfort and pleasure. Dreams throb and writhe and the appetite dances with a metallic lust for meat. Only yesterday I stood amid a circle of geologists, students and whatnots twirling a nifty Estwing rock hammer, a flat-faced pteranodon with a chisel backside. A rosy notion burst into bloom within me - *we were very, very, very far away from any serious law enforcement.* Tweren't a doubt in my head that I could drive my hand tool through thirty brains before any of them put together what was coming down. I'd take fair Kalle back to base camp for a little looting and a lot of rutting. Then it would be off into the wilderness with a new bride and a regional cracker homicide record. She'd give birth to my tribe, which would one day conquer Earth. The drug is worse than the cure? Bah! What the fuck do these gnomes and warbling chimps know about it?

Don't Talk to Sheep. Sheep Lie.

Archaeologists and anthropologists, as previously insisted, are by and large thickheaded sorts. Opinionated through their dull eyes and sticky teeth but rarely very smart above the armpits. Established ones are beyond learning, or accepting, anything new and many aspiring pottery dopes are far too willing to lap up soured helpings of slanted knowledge, as if anything spouted from the old guard were adamant truths of biblical permanence. The problem with both disciplines is that they're very vulnerable to the imaginations, or even fantasies, of the practitioners. It's a steep mount to overcome in archaeology since it deals with the physical creations of cultures no longer available for comment. Say an archaeologist finds a 20,000 year old figurine of a fat girl with oversized breasts. Chances are there aren't any 20,000 year old sculptors to explain what he/she was thinking while carving the piece so the archaeologist is left to come up with a plausible hypothesis for the meaning of the figurine. A nice, tidy idea could be that the rock used to make the figure was round to begin with and big boobs are easier to sculpt than the well-defined rack of a Mesolithic Scarlet Johansson. That is plausible, sure, but an even better idea is that it wasn't carved by just anybody looking for a way to keep busy back then. Mightn't it be plausibler that it was carved by an locally important Shaman, whose *precision* etching of the giant tits was intended to confer fertility to whoever handled it and it was obese because said Shaman had mommy issues. That explanation does remain within the scope of possibilities but it wins because it's way more interesting than the first one.

Cultural Anthropology, along with its subdisciplines, works in like fashion. When documenting some tropic island culture with an overall social structure very much like ours, minus the up to date technology, the anthropologist is faced with a dilemma: if the subject culture is like most other cultures who is going to care what's written about them? The researcher can: 1) Dig deeper until something hidden and unique is uncovered; 2) Inflate the heck out of some minor quirk, like reporting that Polynesians wear grass skirts because linen is believed to cause goiters and homosexuality; 3) Make something up altogether. Tell the world that hockey was invented on Easter Island and any islander who scored a hat trick was immediately eaten to spread his potency among the population. How the hell can you publish a thesis or sell a book on them if they're just ordinary humans?

Facts are one thing – you can attach yourself to them or not. But ideas sprouted from one's own mind are hard to escape, almost impossible to disregard. So once an archaeologist or anthropologist, or anybody for that matter, comes up with a pet hypothesis he's going to have a hell of a hard time letting go of it, even in the face of strong evidence against it. If lucky enough to have the idea published far and wide there will be legions of young students reading about it. And young minds, from preschoolers through middle age, are vastly impressionable. If it's in a book then it must be true; flimsy or not, the hypothesis will live on and thrive until it gets annihilated under overwhelming evidence to the contrary or the original theorist gets convicted of statutory rape.

Paleoanthropology ought to be more distinct from the two ologies above. Ideally, it has foundations in biology and geology and thus based on concrete science and not the generally speculative methodology of archaeology and its parent anthropology. Ideally. On the other hand it is still a baby and after three syllables still has 'anthropology' in its name. You could argue that it barely has more than half a century of real progress and to an extent it often operates more like a cult rather than a dynamic system of belief. Leaders, largely non-scientists, are intolerant of questioning. Changes in thought arrive slowly with black eyes and bruised egos mired in the wake of the snail mucous behind. In short, there are too many archaeologists and anthropologists running the show.

Case in point: A new *bovid* skull had been found out in the scrub of the Koobi Fora spit. To clarify that, a "bovid" is a member of the *Bovidae* Family, a group which encompasses over half of the animals belonging to the Order *Artiodactylae*: even-toed ungulates with multiple stomachs and hollow horns. Cutting though the Latin, let's just say that cows, antelopes, sheep and goats are all bovids. Now the new skull's inclusion into the compound's bone collection required a more specific designation than *bovid cranium* so a few of us enthusiastic novitiates were trying to work that out. I was still hoping for a *gerenuk* noggin but its features were looking far more domestic than that and quite comparable to the collection's *Ovis aries*(sheep)skull. So it could have been a sheep, except for the teeth, which found their best match in a similar skull labeled *Capra hircus*: a goat.

Now there isn't a tremendous amount of difference between the dentition of goats and sheep. They are very close relatives who essentially eat the same stuff so their teeth ought to look a lot like each others'. With a bit of variation because, after all, they are still two distinct animals and that's just how it goes. Highly similar nevertheless and their skulls have far more similarities than points of divergence. But when you flip the head over and the teeth of a probable sheep look identical to those of a definite goat, the kernel of a very tedious argument begins to germinate. Georgette elbowed in to show us how gloriously identical the mystery head and the known sheep's skull really were. She pressed the idea of dental wear patterns to proclaim that their respective dental arcades, though no longer any place close to identical, were nonetheless "...*exactly the same.*"

There was no way, unless the unknown bovid had gnashed a diet of granite and lag bolts, that both sets of choppers had ever been identical twins. Pointing that out perturbed her and a curious French accent fizzed through her sibilant litany on cranial congruencies. But that was another issue: our goat cranium was awfully darn similar to this new skull, except for the presence of horn stubs and lack-thereof on the new head. Which brought us, me at least, to a seemingly simple question: Does the goat specie, *Capra hircus*, have *dimorphic* gender variations? That is to ask: *Do boy goats and girl goats both have horns?* Because if some goats go about fashionably unhorned then tagging the new head was going to become a whole lot trickier.

No one among the teaching staff, the astute Dr. H was off overseeing vehicle repairs, could actually answer that simple question. Even our Kenyan "Bone Expert," Jomo, was unwilling to commit to an answer. Goats and sheep are all over the fucking joint and not even a local – one _trained_ to distinguish one bone from the next - could tell me if all goats came with horns. Goshdarnit, you'd think it was a riddle fit for particle physics.

But nothing, a paucity of clear answers or even a lack of basic information, prevents the experts from drawing up sound conclusions. _This was absolutely a sheep._

"Just look at the skull!" I got.

"It has no horns!" they persisted, disregarding the unresolved relevance of horns.

"The teeth do have a lot of differences _but it doesn't mean they're different..._" Yap, yap, yap and then,

"What if the skull had _no_ teeth? Then what would you say it was?"

That trap was laid nice and smugly by the now feverishly pissy Georgette. Some classmates fell in behind me for support or perhaps to shield themselves from the sparks of agitation brought on by my insistence for clarification. Counter arguments were being directed only at me and Georgette's new angle was a through-the-teeth hiss. _How about that, smart guy? Case is closed, you needling pain in the ass._ Well sure, if it had arrived edentate then I'd have to call it a sheep. Unless, of course, I'd already met a hornless female goat.

"Shit on all your eyes," I thought, then said "Okay, that's a fair question. But how about trying on this one: what if the teeth had _no skull?"_

That nifty riposte set fire to their heads and turned their self-righteous bowel fluids to Drano. Steam whistled from the pores on their necks as anger glinted beneath the tattered masks of congenial debate. I was just trying to get some basic questions answered before making a judgment on what that lousy fucking head might be. I was exercising one of my prime bad habits, pushing just a little too far until I dove over the line to point out that paleoanthropologists spend careers creating or assigning species on the basis of rows, or single instances, of fossil teeth alone. A single, unexpected molar can make all the difference between putting a hominid fossil into either the Australopithecine or Homo genus. Some researchers don't even need the rest of skeleton to make important classifications. Just give them an incisor with a slightly uncommon ridge pattern and they'll give you back a brand, spanking-new species!

It was an iron spike to their guts and probably a mistake. Nobody likes to be held to their own double standards and somebody here is going to want revenge for the pain. I was now competing with the vegan student to become the most detested kid in class. Tough cookies. I wasn't demanding cabbages boiled no less than thirty feet from open cans of potted meat and in water never swum in by fish. I don't sneer at people eating ham sandwiches. I was merely asking for a little science. Just a smidgen of rational, deductive argument and I would have backed off.

The matter was finally settled when two other sheep (labeled as such) crania were pulled out of another cobwebbed box. Having teeth matching the ones in question it looked like the animal was a probably a sheep after all. That was fine now that there was more evidence bolstering the conclusion, but the twats had been too content to rest on impetuous assumptions supported by very thin arguments. I was convinced just enough to let it go, but deeply pissed about getting wrapped in the polemics of imbeciles. I still don't know about goats and their horns. My educators are treating it is as a black secret wrapped in a code of silence so I'm on my own in finding the answer. In the end it's just a fucking farm animal. There's only so many testicles to pinch and eyes to spit in before you're tied to a cot and pummeled senseless with soap on a rope..

The victorious team dispersed to savor their ascendancy by gnawing on hangnails and wagging their heads against encroaching doubt. In the meantime I went meandering about the main banda, trying to let it go and having my brain monitor my face to make sure it wasn't muttering audibly about the silly debate. I avoided sheep heads while passing among the osteological shelves, opting to play with lion paws and kitty spines instead. There was a nice line of replica hominid heads in the lab but some odd apprehension kept me from taking a seat and having a good, long look. Each cranium represented a Grail of sorts, having lain hidden for ages only to be uncovered by the diligently devout. Whether I needed to make burnt offerings or ablutions or drink urine I felt as yet unworthy to get intimate with them. The skulls of legend eyed me from the table, *Australopithecus boisei*, *Australopithecus aethiopicus*, *Homo habilis*, *Homo erectus* and *Homo ergaster* – the last two being the same apeman with a cloven sense of identity.

One, however, kept locking me in its gaze - *Homo rudolfensis*, *KNM-ER 1470*. It's quite famous, as this stuff goes, having once blown the collective paleoanthropological mind for its age, brain-size and facial characteristics. The original age of 2.6 Myr had been corrected to 1.9 Myr, making its cranial capacity, around 750 cubic centimeters, not so terribly controversial or surprising anymore. That put it at the upper end of the *Homo habilis* range and for a while that's what people had said it was. It had no teeth, however, so it could easily have been a goat…

Jokes aside it is the most screwed up monkey-man thing I've ever seen. The cranium wasn't too weird at first glance; primitive, frontal bones constricted behind the eye sockets, bumpy, old and smaller than mine. But looking closer some things seemed out of place for any specific kind of hominid. There is a little bulge near the apex of the frontal bones as though it took a ding to the noggin shortly before death. Parietal fragments flare out like bent jigsaw pieces, the chips seemingly misaligned during reconstruction, giving it the look of a raggedy ice cream ball blown from the cone. Taken together it all appeared to inflate the head and thus the actual cranial capacity (which approximates brain size) of the living creature. The flat, squared face struck me as screwy from the get-go. It was less a fossil and more some geek sculptor's idea for an archenemy of Space Ghost.

The queerly nasty Georgette caught me in mid-fuddle to rehash the skull crap.

"You know, when you look at the bovid skulls you *really* see a lot of differences… I, like, mean at the base of the cranium!"

Shoulda brought it up earlier, Butchie, because all I want now is to punch your sub-cranial characteristics through your damn larynx…

"Sounds like you're trying to convince yourself now," I tried to find a balance between outright contempt and classroom civility but couldn't contain the smirk.

"What? No! Of course not," she stammered out, her words smoldering with that creepy *patois Françoise* again. *Didn't she say she was from Rhode Island? Horns and national origins must be things we keep secret at Koobi Fora* "I believed it was a goat all along. I mean a sheep. Yes, it was always a sheep to me. Nevermind, we figured it out anyway, yes?"

Who let that dummy have the job? Oh right, she's an archaeologist - it has nothing to do with qualifications.

But it's time to forget about idiotologists. Gotta pack up and get ready for what I've been aching to experience: The wastelands which were once the wetlands which were among the places where we evolved into what we are now. Off to the Karari in the a.m.!

Who's Better Than Me?

I'd been feeling sort of old. Not in a sense of limping decrepitude or pining for tunes warbled off a Victrola. *Old* isn't the right way to put it... taking a second thought, d*isconnected* should do it. Most of these people are of normal college-age with normal undergrad mindsets. The last time I was age appropriate in school I got the boot for never going, subsequently spending the last eight years developing the perspective of an embittered failure. Paying rent, drinking heavy and tossing salads or pouring liquor to support those two habits. Most of these kids still don the drippy fuzz of lanugo and their naïveté percolates through gleeful tales of dormitory drunkenness or Deadheaded litanies on curing the world's ills through sustainable hemp farms. In the sandy, dead bed of the Karari's *Il Naibar* stream, cutesy Janet had asked if anybody had ever tried *Goldschlager*. Her unbridled enthusiasm was disturbing, nauseating as the cinnamon hooch itself.

"It's got gold leaf in it!" she exclaimed.

That's just what the distillers wanted – the tiny gold flakes to distract drinkers from what 107° sludge of cinnamon sugar would bring: bad behavior and shrunken brains nicked through the temples by shovels. Novices. Hangovers are all they know about real ugliness. Getting in a tipsy slap fight with jocks bears scant semblance to drinking in the wrong bar and having a knife slashed across your arm. Suckling gold-flecked schnapps into unconsciousness and having your boyfriend let his chums fingerdiddle you is a far cry from ending a slightly buzzed walk from the subway as the center of a gang rape. Neat, sterile worlds with a light, vomitty scent. Those of us forced to pay attention a little earlier are going to chuckle when the ignorant are whining over midlife hysterectomies and prostate harvests. We'll giggle and dribble hi-ethyl schnapps into their freshly stitched gashes.

Whoa, Nellie! Let's say we take back the part about feeling old. Looks like I'm a wee bit cranky!

I must have acquired a hair across my ass during the day's doings of geologically important stuff. The *Koobi Fora, Burgi, Lokochot, KBS* and *Moiti Tuffs* were examined. *Tuffs* being fat beds of volcano-spewed ash, while all the tiers of rock, dirt or pyroclastic packing peanuts above a tuff and below the next one are collectively known as its *Member*. I'd gone in a pod with the program's geologist, Melvin Waybill, to track the *Okote* and *Tula Bor* members over several kilometers. Humping over hills and sliding down gullies to keep running into new cuts in the same fat slabs of hardened ash drives home exactly how powerful volcanoes are. And we barely gazed on more than relative slivers of what the ash actually covered. Once upon a time a serious blast could put superheated pink, blue and gray powdered glass from horizon to horizon in depths measurable with one or more yardsticks.

It took morning and late afternoon excursions to cover the ground Waybill wished to map. Saw lots of very old dirt in tiers representing past worldscapes tread by critters of Earth's memory. There were low bluffs where layers had been bent up and down by grievances aired seismically by the planet, warped surfaces where animals must have tripped or fallen on their asses. Some eroded sediment exposures shaded little snakes looking dapper as clams as millipedes, bigger than mechanically segmented penises, skirted curbs in the tuffs. Between hikes was one break for lunch and a lecture in the full shade of our hats or hair. The Karari Escarpment is a heck of a hot place.

Very hot. Even a metal wristwatch exposed to the sun becomes a torture device in the Karari daylight, heating up and searing the arm of whoever it's on. It doesn't seem to get to me, though. Perhaps that's from years of cook work in whatever temperatures badly ventilated restaurant kitchens reach in the summertime. Or maybe it's my rubber-cased Timex that doesn't get much warmer than my skin. Overall, the heat here is inarguably mischievous. You don't sweat. Or sweat doesn't have a chance to exist as water on your skin, sun and sere winds vaporizing it faster than your glands make it. Some people never realize they're dehydrating until salt entombs their eyes and thirsting brains crystallize within brittle, crackling skulls. I drank at least a gallon of water on the first day, possibly more. I only pissed once and it came out like maple syrup.

While freshening up for supper I got a complimentary nature lesson at my tent flaps. There was a tiny, dusty spider having the time of its life murdering an inch-worm. The unfortunate green caterpillar had made the easy error of ambling through an undetectable web in the dry silt of the bank. The sharp predator had laid spiral threads about a tiny hole where it waited until a lunch crawled by to serve itself. This worm had its bum stuck to the sand, writhing in misery. It seemed a sadistic joy for the arachnid, skipping lightly to bite the doomed insect, dancing a reel and jig amid assaults. Then it settled in for business, caudally sucking its victim to liquefy its ass and aggrieve its dying brain.

I'd witnessed an insecticide but my statement would have to wait until after dinner if the authorities stopped me on their inquest. Rice, beans and *chapatis*. Hot Damn! I don't think I've ever been more thrilled over a simpler supper; it's already my favorite. The carbohydrate load helps lock in your internal water for the night and the subsequent starch coma means solifuges could crawl over my face and snip off my nose without disturbing me.

A few of us managed to fight against impending sleep long enough to sit around Lorenzo's fire. None of us had thought to make our own tentside campfires and Lorenzo had a slight smugness over his little blaze. But he also seemed elated to have the company. Matter of fact he's been cheery as all get out since we rolled into the Karari. Must be the vibe of possible hominid fossils. I haven't seen him this bubbly since he got those Kenyan girls to come back to our room.

No, You Can't Get Syphilis from a Sweat Bee.

The midafternoon is a lazy time for reading but the late-evening fire light studying had lost all its magic. All the fucking eyestrain and steel nosed mosquitoes poking through shoe leather to suck the scarlet gush in my fat foot veins mandated a switch to daytime homework. Between lunch and the afternoon's fieldwork there's always an hour or two to do whatever I feel. Since I usually feel like sucking on Dunkies' iced coffee or the privates of nineteen year-olds in turtlenecks there's obvious need for alternatives. Diary doodles often become the Karari surrogates for all that I wish or want to be doing while cooling down in filaments of shade.

There are also occasional heat siestas when I'll simply commune away the hours with sweat bees - cute, tiny, airborne carriers of undocumented disease. I don't have specific knowledge on the contagions, if any, borne aloft on the toes of sweat bees, but in an equatorial region it's safest to accuse everything of packing germs, human-threatening or otherwise. I have my own private squadron of tiny bees which hover like a hundred personal air escorts. The little girls are twice the size of gnats, four times as loud and thoroughly unrivalled in their inconsideration for other folk's right to peace. It's harder to get angry with them, however, as they're adorable midget bees just loitering for whatever moisture they can get to, like the perspiration of a guy trying to rest in the toasty shade. Funny thing is they never appear to land on my skin so I have to guess they're happily sucking in my immediate atmosphere, hydrating themselves on sweat fumes.

This morning we splintered into three groups - people who felt like creating macrostratigraphic maps of blocks of sediment deposits and others moved to walk all over volcanic litter-zones looking for surface fossils. The rest of us were those who believed that sifting through kilotons of eroded outwash for fractions of fossil fragments would be the Karari equivalent of a Union Hall Jamboree sweetened by a hand job from the pastor's wife.

I'd wanted to be in the first group, pining for all the extra learning I could get in geology. But a couple of snatchy tarantuladies showed up in that group to do the same. I'd worked with these girls for days back at base camp hence justifiably afraid when it seemed I'd have to endure them again. A pair of jet-fueled harpies that know too much, do too little, complain incessantly and are simply impossible to look at. Let somebody else enjoy the company of those buck and gap-toothed cranks. The work here can be ugly enough without the hagfish scavenging the remains of your patience. The girls had slithered into the Rover to secrete ill will all over the seats and I couldn't have been more obvious about wanting out. During the escape I nearly smashed my face on the rocks as the door on the rolling truck took a grab at my ankle. There is no teamwork with teammates entrenched offside in the ugly behavior zone.

I skipped the surface fossil scanning for nobler reasons. Differentiating tiny bones in a landscape cluttered with rocks of the same color is as much a gift as it is an acquirable skill. If my wishes come true, this business might afford me many years of walking in circles staring at the ground. It's the heart of the organization. For the time being, while still a fresh dog, it seemed wiser to garner some tricks which were not included in my genetic package. I've already become adept at setting up map grids, sight-leveling localities and adapting to an atmosphere which is 99.5% dust and carries oxygen in trace. It's the screening for me now, sifting through heaps of dirt for prehistoric bat fingernails and fossilized fish teeth.

Think I'm kidding?

I was only at it for short while when Dr. Waybill tagged me out of the sifting. He was leading an expedition *upstream*[2] to map outcroppings of volcanic ash in this dirt flow. It was 109° when we set out at midmorning. That's about par for this neighborhood, it was only going to get hotter and still there was an awful lot of grumbling about the heat. We're in Africa, for crying Pete's out loud sakes. So it's hot. I think back to where we were in Boston six months back and I want to whimper in any warm corner and deny the horrible cold we faced this past winter. It was like Santa had given us Wisconsin for Christmas. The freak wind chills shriveled my nuts so far up into my bladder I was internally impersonating a uterus with ovaries. There was a night when the pipes burst in the club's stairwell and I began menstruating amid a freezing flood because a –30° wind chill is just too fucking cold. Galloping through the water, before it froze at my feet, to the men's room to chew the gloves off my frostbitten fingers and stuff in a tampon. This heat has been a wonderful treat.

Not everybody takes hot climates the same way. We've got mad, whoring Lujurio who grew up in Argentina and joined the French Foreign Legion after a badly timed return to the Italian homeland. He mentioned something about an unsettled phone debt; but I've only got his trilingually expressed assertions and few of his reasons. He's familiar with freezing his ass off in nothing but French military-issue panties and he knows the swelter of South America's muggiest spots. He tools around the Karari in only a great white hunter hat and khaki shorts. Not even a minor hint of rosy sunburn has betrayed his skin. He'd said he deserted the Legion because there were too many morons in its ranks. It's tough to picture an organization where he was the sharpest stick but with those standards he should have gone AWOL from this field school a couple of weeks ago. We attract fools like cellulite to our class vegan.

Fool percentage is what's on the rise too, as we've lost one of the few decent senses of humor, Sheila, to heat exhaustion. The older student had been keeping the camp in stitches since we unloaded at Koobi Fora but she's had it rough ever since the

---

2 The Karari itself is a fossil slab of a once humongous river/lake system

76

gastrointestinal calamity on the road up to KF. She hasn't left the school entirely; not quite a screaming head case ready for airlift by the Flying Doctors. Not yet. But she's no longer sitting around the kerosene with us, singing deranged lounge tunes in the sand. Dehydration had turned her from comical to crazy and she was lorried back to base camp. They could better monitor her condition there and re-soak her innards to prevent her psyche from immolating. I miss her already.

The few women remaining here in the Karari are from the Odds & Ends aisle at best; each emphatically humorless and all afraid of the heat. Notably there is this obese, premenopausal dyke who slumps away from the sun into her tent most afternoons: a thick gummed, cod-toothed, bottle goggled, newt-eyed troll slouching her cephalothorax forward through the zippers to leer out at passersby. Just like mounds of spoiled tapioca pudding bulging from a split bag on the verge of a melting collapse into the sand you can't quite taxonomically pinpoint her. Human? Her clothing and language suggest so, but *Horta* or *Hut* or section of self-aware gristle all vie as possibilities. She gives God-fearin' folks the willies what with our primal distaste for amphibians, sci-fi chubbies and what not.

The rest are gripped by desert gripes, their utter distaste for the climate bursting thickly from the dense paste of UV-Block on their puckered maws. They lather themselves blue with sunscreens only to get fried like paper rubies anyway; a fitting color adjustment for the crabby pack of them. Simply exhausting the skin with chemicals cannot save you if the sun also hates everything you have to say. Failing to take notice of Lorenzo's example is their general mistake. The this vast cube of gravel and vaporless sky needs acceptance and embrace. Exposing the clean flesh is a ritual of respect and in return it anoints with a little splash of pink to your peel. A mark of initiation and then your skin is free to acquire warmer tones. This is an unshakable truth, no matter how rooted in horseshit it may be, high in my stockpiles of flimsy dogma – all accrued in the event I wish to start some dingbat cult. Naturally, these cosmically ordained tenets do not apply to Kalle McInnis. She treads across the rules and leaves better principles delicately calligraphed in the sand beneath her feet. Must be the wide-brimmed hat and cooling ringlets of hair which keep her limbs unblushed. Even the dust infusing her clothing can't mask the store of diffuse starlight in her skin or the small blue suns of her eyes making it all very hard to recall whatever point one is trying to make...

As far as my own measures against heat and skin cancer go, I just wear a baseball cap and a shirt and pants and hang out under trees when there's nothing to do. It's fucking hot out, for Christ's sake.

Our lorry, laden with Sheila, left the Karari this morning before sunrise and was back by eight p.m. An amazing event unfurled with its return. The big blue rolling ship docked with a bounty of fresh oranges, mangoes, eggs, and ice cream. Wow, fresh fruit and hold on just a goddamned second there what the hell was that? *Ice Cream?* Oh puzzles of the Cosmos! Befuddled be my ass! There *was* ice cream on that freaking truck! A screwy, naughty fantasy that just could not possibly be true. But it was true and I got my fair share of the loot, spading a sweet solid lump onto my tongue before the rest puddled in my bowl. Perplexing. Had to check my Lariam supply to make sure I hadn't taken any extra tablets today and was mistaking *ugali* corn paste for Ben & Jerry's. The vanilla rivulets dripping down the gathering of chins made everybody look deranged. There wasn't any freezer apparatus worth shit back at the Koobi main camp; the fridge's ice box produces one modest cube per week so they quit trying ages ago. I doubt there's ice anywhere for a few hundred kilometers. *What was the hell was the story?*

It's this: To get freezer desserts in super-rural hot zones somebody in your group has to go berserk. Then you can ring the Flying Doctor's of Africa to come pick up said lunatic and simultaneously place an order for fresh fruit and ice-cold tasties. They'll unload goodies upon landing at the airstrip up in Ileret and you just stick your cackling freak in the cargo hold where they won't infect anybody else. Then grab your spoons and propeller beanies – it's ice cream time!

Sometimes the Air MD's don't make it in time. Dessert will still come but not before the madness spreads among the

populace. Heidi (my favorite of all Nazi chick names) lost her anchor a few days ago, right before the camp split up to head to various dig sites. She'd been reduced to a puddle of babble; bawling, cowering, giggling up tears, hiding, whimpering, moaning spittled pleas to her pillow, and all that good stuff. She was blaming the Lariam. So many folks have just prattled on and on about the psycho side-effects of the drug it became inevitable that somebody was actually going to go nuts. The power of suggestion is extra powerful when the suggestion gets repeated and repeated and repeated. Anytime somebody got a headache or felt dizzy in the heat or had an itch or saw a bat somebody else was sure to suggest that it was actually Lariam boring holes in their brains. There were even faculty members who were guilty of keeping the drug's fear factor on high. Poor Heidi. It's possible her psyche was shabbily-equipped the extremes here and that it may or may not have been tweaked by the poisonous malaria pills. The murmured drug hysteria didn't help. I left for the Karari here, thinking it would be a crying shame if we had to lose her. Kind of a cutie, she'd been cheerful and pleasant to talk to before the crazy took root. With both breasts on level and warm teddy bear eyes, her departure meant the school had become appreciably uglier.

The paranoia then possessed her hutmate. Reports had her screeching about outrageous, unbearable headaches and smashing up her banda at night. Lariam again? Maybe, though Dengue fever was her own professional diagnosis. Can't say anything was surprising except that Nell hadn't been the first to crap out. She'd shown up at the Nairobi Museum *with her mother*. They were a joint package during the first week, shopping at the swankest knick knack stores and passing notes during lectures. After a week apart, the rough of the field without a nourishing, protective tit must have been an emotionally unacceptable prospect for Nell. She joined Helen in the belly of the doctor plane and they're in good hands now. The shamen of the twin-engine Pipers are professional and finely learned in the best cures for hysteria. When the girls get to Nairobi they'll probably get shot hyperglycemic with sugar water then have their damp, puffy faces slapped. *Smack! Smack! Smack!* Mighty Hippocratic hands will whack out the demons. Back in the states their mothers can snuggle them and lick the Aesculapian welts of their sorry faces.

Painting mean murals of the life here, but they're far from the whole picture. I'm actually in love with this place and a good few of the humans as well. I just need to flush all the needling crap from my soul. Don't know what I'd do without a belly full of hate to remind me that all this isn't just a fantasy. For all the beauty and stunning magic there necessarily has to be individuals who fuck up the vistas. It makes it all seem more real. The assholes and slackers are doing their important cosmic parts and they're fewer in number than might be indicated in these paeans of loathing for those lousy chicken necked dinks and their simpering ways. Torrents of contempt for their every minor groan or bitch squeaked out against this golden world. But when the day is done I feel like Adam. Without Eve. Or maybe with Eve but no apple trees and agave plants which distill themselves and all the Lariam I can snort.

In my sleeping bag I lose the hunger to slit jugulars and eat the writhing dumb. It becomes happy time. Frankie time. The moments to sleep and dream vertiginous wonderments. Hermaphrodites with cupric skin and succulent jugs cooing stammered odes of passion. Squares of caramel lolling in cool streams of blood. So...very...happy...

Fistful of Nickels

It was as good a morning as most are. Having no rigid course to these musings it feels like I need to get back to the things which brought me to Lake Turkana in the first place. Chances are healthy that I'll ultimately fail to become anything in any form of paleontological pursuit. But come midlife, some night while stuffing a pair of grease-stained, Size-50 coveralls into my locker at the mill, I may want to recall what I did in my twenties. There'll be this tattered journal, right under the one documenting my subsequent sucking off strangers for crack two years from now, to take me back through a time spent searching for stony ancestors in Kenya. So I set myself in front of one of these antiquated, marbley black and white notebooks and sketched out a tour of one of the workdays here. Starting in *Area 130* of the Karari, in the eroding sediment deposits of the *Upper Burgi Member.*

Looking for fossils was what everybody was up to. Elusive black, green, blue and white flecked[3] *former-animal-cum-rocks* strewn in fields of pebbles and stones. Imagine looking for dirty nickels at a city dump and you'll get an idea of how easy it is. No, that would be an incomplete analogy. There's no shortage of visible fossils here; they're all over the place and you can't walk without crushing some. It's finding our target ones, the rare and evanescent fragments of hominids, that's the improbable chore but one that needs doing according to the title of the field. Back to nickels in the dump: there's only four of the sort we want on the surface and they're the old buffalo variety. But all around are

---

[3] yes, ours look like sculpted, petrified goose turd

forty million quarters, dimes and silver dollars. There are a moderate amount of Jefferson nickels as well but those are just monkeys and of lesser interest. And handfuls of Canadian nickels that some joker threw in for shits and giggles. And trash – gum wrappers, cigarette butts, ostrich turds, etc. Ready? Go find those buffalo nickels.

A check-list of what we'd seen by eight-thirty this morning is as follows:

Ancient crocodile teeth (*neat!*)

Atlas vertebra, *Equid* (cool)

Croc teeth (neat.)

Hippo mandible with incisors (Wow, crazy huge!)

Croc teeth (uh-hunh)

Primate tooth (boo-yah!)

And some croc teeth (.)

Fish bones too. Mustn't forget the fish. *Pisces* galore. You'd think the crocodile teeth had monopolized the monotony but the tedium is really all about fish parts. Spines, ribs, head plates, vomers, vertebrae. *Fish, fishes, fishy, fish, fish.* It's obvious what sort of environments had been here - Aquatic theme parks and cat restaurants. Or possible rivers and/or a lake. There are enough land animal fossils, however - horses, antelope, elephants, pigs, etc. - to indicate it was a good place for anything to grab a drink and die. Terrestrial beasts may have been mired in shore muck, murdered while they stopped for a sip, dehydrated at a dry lake edge during a drought. Or passed on after downing bottles of pills and fifths of Jack to the sayonara hymn of lapping waves.

Fate is hell-bent on making me look like a crank and a moron. Every time I jot down some slander on the state of things the state of things turns itself upside down. Within twenty minutes of noting the languor that comes with a million fish spines people started finding baboon parts. They're not hominids, but they were big monkeys and not fish so even our prospecting instructor, Jomo, was looking elated.

What we labeled for museum baggies was as follows:

Left Mandible w/ P1, P2, M1, M2 teeth (*Papio* sp.?)
Right M3 w/ Mandible fragment (*Theropithecus* sp.?)

The Latin names and alphanumeric diddles up there might be confusing but it's the way we like to communicate as people of scholarly bent. It isn't kosher to say something like,

"If that baboon tries to take another jar of peanut butter I'm going to kick it in the nuts."

A smart-sounding dude would better phrase it as thus:

"I wouldn't go near that *Papio anubis* if I were you. It'll fuck you up bad."

It's not that I'm any sharper than a donut when it comes to knowing what the bones are as they're pulled off the gravel. The highly specific designations came from Jomo. He won't give up a straight answer when it comes to goats and their fucking horns, but he can spot a two million year old *Papio* tooth in a crowd of *Theropithecus* dentures. Those would be the respective genus names for baboons and their badass Leroy Brown cousins, the huge geladas. The P1, M2 stuff refers to teeth and where they sit in the dental arcade - *Premolar* 1, *Molar* 2. There's shorthand available for canine and incisor teeth too, but we didn't find any.

The baboon thrill wore off quickly as we swam back into the sea of rocky fish sticks. But we kept the bright hope that a *Homo habilis* waited for our eyes to catch it. Lujurio's patience, on the other hand...well, he never really had any to begin with. Every time a student picked up a piece of fossil and said, *"Ooo! Ooo!!!"* he hauled ass over to the kid, crushing many bones under foot. If Jomo gave it the old *"This...tch, tch...is monkey"* Enzo would vomit invectives, grab the bone and hurl it at God. He didn't desert the French Foreign Legion for Curious George's freaking ancestors and he would accept nothing less for his efforts here than an

Australopithecus. When no other authority is on hand he'll analyze the specimen himself, s*tarting with a lick*. Something about real fossils being sticky on the tongue, he'll tell you. Keeps him from getting fooled by all the fugazi fossils the Gypsies bury here.

About another hour later he was going apeshit berserk. We'd hit slopes that were jammed full of teeth. And not just those of crocs and seafood, lots of primate dentures were found. His disgust was terrifying as he snatched fossils from people's hand and cursed the mouths of all monkeys. Folks learned to keep their discoveries quiet and enjoy ancient jaws in peace. There was just something about shiny, snot-green monkey teeth that made the world taste like cold beer and uncut coke once again. Between mad dagos and magic molars from eons past, the morning really was a blast.

My personal discovery highlights had been *Papio* premolar, an elephant tusk, an elephant tibia and a half eaten rhino jaw. Fucking huzzah! It's hard enough seeing live rhinos around here anymore and I'd been pulling the rock-hard mouth pieces of their great-great–great-etc grandmomma's forefathers right out of the desert. But as cool as it sounds it probably won't get me laid back home or even here for that matter. We probably scored about a dozen primate tooth and jaw fragments all day. And the bastards back home still won't be jealous, am I right? Nobody will want to ride this bicycle even though it's sleek, slick and has tight coasting brakes. The work simply isn't a Grace Kelly fantasy which feels like life tied to a obscenely wealthy Tickle Fairy. It may still end in skidmarks and burning metal, but it just wasn't that fluffy to begin with.

It does come with fleeting moments of luxury, however. Yesterday I helped myself to a short bucket of water to cleanse my clogged skin. It was an opportunity to stand naked in feral lands. To let the testicles swing free in the zephyrs blowing through my sweat-muddy legs. There just ain't nothing like being naked in a pristine setting; something to the situation that's pretty smooth. There I was, marveling at how much like a comic book hero I'd started to appear - bright red from ankles to thighs. Maroon from the fingers to the shoulders. And a glaring titanium oxide white hailing satellites from my torso and feet. Not to mention the blinding pale of my ass. Bent over to scrub scab and scum from my shins, I was struck by the sight of my pecker dangling off its living room set in the breeze. Soap and sweat clinging to its wrinkled peel. While the wind flipped razor-sharp sand grains into my unprotected stern I understood how way-out ridiculous it was to be enjoying any of this. But screw reason. Love is getting buck bare assed in the East African wilderness. Adventure, people, begins with the basics.

I was waiting for a cheetah to run up and try tearing a hunk off my chalky haunches. Just hoping one would try and take a bite out of me. Without clothes to hinder my sinew, a charging cat would be without its head in a blinding instant, long before my dual carotid pulses gave its whiskers a tickle. Perhaps the cat's brain would still be alive enough to hear me belching around its fuzzy skull descending in my esophagus. What can possibly daunt a man of Africa when he is clean? Bring on the snakes, boys. I've got an immaculate ass and we're ready to throw down in the dirt.

After a visit to the Toilet Tree of course. It's of a nice Karma for Enzo and me since we claimed it on arrival. Our shovels alone till its soil and we are the sole providers of its fertilizer. Good fertilizer, that is. What sane tree gives a flying fuck about ground squirrel feces? Ours rewards us with under-heated shade and protection from the deadly asps which ruin sound bowel movements and it smiles to us from the distance in a continually greener grin. It's a ficus-looking thing though I haven't a clue what the hell it is specifically beyond a source of balm in a sea of boils. Defecation is powerful mind medicine; an Rx for stress, weakness and the embitterment of human spirit. Besides, being significantly short on conventional spots for pooping, we defecate wherever, and frequently whenever, our rectums find opportunity.

Obviously, considering where we are, that peace comes with many, many, many risks. The Karari is a place where the sight of some ground critters could scramble the mind of a goblin, riddle her heart with fear and make her run back through her own colonic production to slam face first into the stump of a broken tree branch. Mean beasts lurk at dirt level here. Forget the psychological terror of seeing rock-eating poison monsters, just imagine one of the little demons crawling up your bare leg en route to your genitals. That's why I always carry my dagger to the

Toilet Tree. Should its magic fail and some solifuge manages to clip into a nad, I can just slit my own throat.

Thinking it over, there is no place in Kenya where the toilets, dug in dirt or cast in porcelain, are truly safe from the nightmares, invisible or otherwise, that wish to murder us. I'd bet even Nairobi's uppity Norfolk Hotel gets the occasional spitting cobra slithering up the potty towards an unsuspecting Anglican fanny. There needs to be some ground rules for evacuating ones intestines in East Africa.

Or only one: *Just don't do it.* Hold it until you leave the continent. If your stay is going to be longer than two weeks take anti-diarrheals way beyond the recommended dosages and arrange for a Caesarean removal of the impacted mass when you get home. Constipation is nothing when one ride on the pot is worth five Nairobi hookers and a ruptured condom. It's a solid principle but if the syllogism can't sway you there are options...

Have a colostomy bag installed before travel. If unfeasible, consider staying home.

Intelligent Design

Ten of the bone pups are leaving for *Area 104* to seek and destroy hominid remains. There's been an ideological revolution within the camp brought on by Holy Crows and tongues of flame above our heads. We've seen a new light, hallelujah. We've recognized the errors in our thoughts, Good Jesus. In unity we've become fundamental, frothy-mouthed Evangelical goons and will no longer stand for any of this evolutionary horseshit, blessed be His Name on High. It's the Devil's business and as such we take issue with it, amen now. We're going to find those monkey bones where they hide in the dirt and bash them all to powder before any more heathen anthropologists find and use them to spread their heresy, praise be.

I will not be content to be just a Christian reactionary firebrand. I want to add a Republican flavor to our goon pack. Tomorrow we will commence hurling truck batteries into the lake and draining crankcase oil into acacia stands. I find the current pristine state of this land arrogant and there is no place for it under my watch. Time for the animals to go too – make us all rich on the sales of topi glue, zebra oil, crocodile jam and cheetah cakes.

Amen, Blessed Be My Name and Screw all you Nature Pansies.

Goats Can Go To Hell Too

You can never place an honest value on tough, stringy goat meat until you've had the singular experience of watching that goat die. Then the tendons and radial-treaded slices of fire-roasted beast garner a fuller array of nuances from brightly buttered sorcery to bitter aftertastes. This afternoon our white, kitchen-storage banda became a slaughter banda; a temporary goat shelter and now the place where they'd be killed. I just had to go up and see it all happen.

Goat slaughters are one of the occasional perks at Koobi Fora. It's protocol for the Kenyan members of the staff but they make a special ritual out of it for sadistic and meek students alike. Goats are bought wherever we run into them up here. There are herders roaming the region, gorging their sheep, goats and camels on the succulent grass stubble found beneath rocks. For bureaucratic reasons we buy one or two of their goats but do not eat them on the same day. Cohabiting with chattel just long enough, say one or two days, for the field school to become Little House on the Prairie. Each and every Halfpint Ingalls then desperately begs Pa not to kill the ol' gruffy billies on accountin' they love 'em so. But their fate was already penned and most of the kids will just refuse to acknowledge the slaughter, pretending the goats were never here in the first place. Some won't cave in to denial, pleading and shouting that the things be spared to fulfill whatever spiritual or intellectual promise goats have. More than a decade into running this program, Dr. H is used to it all and there will be no commuting of the sentence; not even if the vegan goes into hysterics or violence... The murder is on even if the timid wail and gnash, fingers knuckle-deep in their ears as the rotten death bleats resonate through every last quiet place in the camp.

The cold, omnivorous fiends among us savor the scene as the rest of the children force supper down in morose swallows. They may refuse to accept how dinner got to their plates but almost everybody eats. Except for the vegan twat and the Canadian Princess, even though their big, lazy behinds look like they were made of cheeseburgers. Oughta rope those chunky hineys into the abattoir while the knives are still sharp. Doubt anybody would speak up for them.

Allow me to explain the joy as I experienced it...

A teacher, a teaching assistant and I had gone to the Kenya staff's little kitchen banda out back, where victual victims are held when nobody's cooking. There was one sultry, white bitch goat. She came to the chicken wire preening for caresses and flaunting her thick goat udder. Engaging her slutty leer, I smacked my lips and named her Nickie.

In a corner was a smaller, roan animal quivering like a freshly whipped stepson. Poor Goldie, an overgrown squirrel constantly pissing over his own legs, was inconsequential unless the white goat stood near him. We had time to talk with the condemned, taunting cross-eyed Goldie with blue jokes about getting the *big haircut*. We were all having a laugh. Drinking sarsaparillas and crocked beer, singing *Rock of Ages* around the gallows, hawkin' loogies at Jesus and howling that Pilate let Barabbas come out to play.

Hot Dog! The mob jeers and blood frenzy unhinged my tongue as language ran vulgar and haywire from my throat. I snarled at the staff that I was going to do all the killings myself with no guarantee that I would stop at goats. Lunging at the window I screamed for a *panga* to chop off heads. Finger flesh and tongue meat tearing as I wrestled and chewed the wire, barking and hollering for a rusty pail of mint jelly.

"I am the Omega! The Sizzle of Night Eternal coming to hack the lipstick off your neck, you goddamned whores. But not, let me tell you, before we measure the life of your fuzzy boy-toy in puddles of syrup! I mean jelly! Now! Out in bubbles! It's not jelly? What the hell is it? The red crap...what the fuck is it?! Blood! He wants blood, blood, blood, bloody darn blood. Exsanguinations! Exsanguinations, nicks, sticks and tricklies! Exsanguinate now you slunt goblin and spatter the chiseled nickels out of your spangled bum!

Women came running from everywhere to subdue me, pin me down, tape my eyes shut and stroke my convulsing belly. Spirits having took my reason, the brave females brushed aside my demand that each of them fuck me powerfully to slake my mighty thirst for getting powerfully fucked. I needed to be pancaked in stacks of soft, tangy labias but they weren't giving in. They had control now, squeezing berries of the famine tree into my mouth and holding *Commifora* resin below my nostrils. There's a trick for everything at Koobi Fora. A fix for any situation that those bastard retards running the show allowed to happen in the first place. I was feeling more human with each inhale of the frankincense, nearly regaining my sanity when two *Dassanetch* tribesmen arrived. Time to dispatch the goats' souls to heaven, in a more decent manner.

I was calm again so they let me return to the killing floor. There was another delay while the men sought a proper stick for stirring fresh blood. Catching sight of the sweat percolating on my lip and afraid I'd go batshit again they grabbed instead the first functional twig and moved to begin this gala of carnage.

It's perplexing to see how little goats actually fight for their lives. They make some rhythmic bleating, perhaps as testament to their sense of being as fucked over as it gets but not much else. One guy seized both sets of Nickie's legs while another took control of her horns.[4] She didn't kick or make even a moderate twist in resistance; physical acquiescence to fate, an honest surrender and it was poignantly unsettling to see. All other thought was eradicated as I tried to fathom how the hell this could be. Why wouldn't it take a cloven hoof to somebody's shins? We were going to kill it, for chrissakes. Didn't it know that?

---

4 By gum, there's the answer to the goat horn conundrum!

Nothing about the situation was right anymore. As my brain kinked and conflopted over this tangle in common sense a knife was run up into the animal's neck. The cleft interrupted a final groan, turning it into a crimson spray sputtered from her windpipe.

The slaughtermen of Lake Turkana flipped the dying creature up by the hind side, strung her from a banda cornice and held the unlatched neck over an aluminum bowl. They collected a quart or so of fresh, hot blood. It was stirred and salted, to keep it from coagulating, then passed from man to man as a tepid, ritual quaff to an odd victory. Or maybe they just liked blood and one doesn't let food soak into the dust. I took a slug of her life fluid as well, surprising the guys more than a bit. Can't say I really liked it. Tasted fucking bloody and could have used more salt. As I was trying to wipe out some of that vital liquid which had splashed up a nostril, the goat was sliced down the midsection. One of the men cut out its bladder, drained it and blew it back up into a small ball. A forty-second soccer match was on before it deflated. Not much dignity in that – I hoped the goat's brain had died enough not to see it.

I wouldn't exactly say that I've come to thrill at the thought of killing animals. It is death after all and witnessing its occurrence feels lousy for the most part. Knowing what's about to happen as another life is led to its final moment right before your eyes, well, that is almost nauseating. But something occurred along that nerve-battering path to a goat's demise. It felt like a fork in the road with two paths leading to the same place from alternate sides and very different views of what might be seen. You could skip either path easily as it's something we do every day. Forget the ultra-fresh meat, drive to a butcher shop and buy a pot roast. All with full blinders over the rearview.

Or you could take the little curve that would put you not only in front of the last animal you'd ever see murdered but also the last one you'd ever consider eating. I'm sure most vegetarians got off the road long before this point. But for some who do come this far, the sight of supine creatures and cheap blades rasped over whetstones in an open-air abattoir signals that it's time for a lifestyle change. I just had to go the other way. And as the knife neared the first goat's neck it felt like a rock-eater was boring toward my center and when the blood spilled it had found its mark. I experienced a sharp spike of primal anger followed by billowing eruptions of unexpected calm; an effervescing spiritual analgesia which soothed through punching throbs. Then the normal pulses returned within my decreasing heart beat. An odd Voodoo comfort, smoothly meshed into the circle of life.

Dying animals are a captivating sight regardless of the emotional direction they send you in. Maybe this attraction to the receding life of a 'lesser' being is an extension of my need to comprehend human death. Comparatively, that is, without suffering an actual human loss. That makes some sense, macabre as it is. Who is free from the urge, whether tormenting like a radiant crystal spur or buried deep within the psyche's bedrock of terrors, to know as much about that terminal line between being alive and not? To see if something in those last moments of dying will reveal anything at all about what is beyond.

There is nothing there though; something I've only ever been able to state from a strictly logical stance. It doesn't make any sense whatsoever that there should be some existence beyond what we've got here. We've given ourselves way too much value in the hundred thousand something years that we've been thinking about it. Growing too intelligent to accept that we're really nothing more than a recent generation of biological hardware. All post-mortem universes are illusory – all there is are the machinations which operate for the sake of keeping the sum of everything moving through cycles of creations and destructions. For us that means nothing more than matter back to the earth and energy back to everywhere as we are fated to run-of-the-mill entropy rather than sacrosanct perpetuity. No favored treats of life everlasting or the eternities of consciousness that have been our collective ego-trip. Those are just the futile demands we've made on unknown, possibly non-existent, and most certainly unconcerned, creators. Bleak as it is, that's all I can accept as the final outcome to life. Of course it doesn't matter what I think. I can whisper or scream my convictions everywhere I go and they will still fall, as with anyone else's beliefs, into the hiss and fizzle of the universe's white noise.

There's why I've fallen into atheism. God, gods or nothing at all – if I can't see even an outside chance at an infinite duration for my alleged soul then there's no room for religious experience while it's still covered with my living meat. That's wasting better spent time on a futility. There are hockey games to watch and fucking for fun if I need to squander hours. Even sinking in the sand of a dry riverbed over this hooey sucks plenty of time away from experiential existence. I mean, I've discussed this with myself in the past so why waste heartbeats doing it again and again?

There is, however, very little else to do in the heat of the afternoon. Go for a walk perhaps? In that there is a chance to get ripped apart by a lion or a pack of hyenas or forty-one jackals, which I bet is the worst way to go. Might take a bite from a cobra. None of those are ways I want to assist in settling the arguments against the great hereafter. No matter what opinions sputter from my mind, I'd really rather not put them to the ultimate test for a good while. I'll even accept that I am wrong for the duration. But I will stick to this idea forever: going to heaven may be somebody else's paradigm of immortality. But not dying in the first place is mine.

Digress and Digress. Gotta get back to the goats, so here's the non-hyperbolic account of how goats die at the hands of my *Dassanetch* buddies: Goat lying on its side, legs held, horns pulled to stretch the neck and a low-quality, though freshly sharpened, knife slices open the throat with a sound of a trowel through wet cement. They slit the windpipe a couple of more times, though you'd think the first cut would have done the trick. The animal will keep breathing deeply for a few moments through the severed duct. But shock takes over quickly, the inhalations become shallow with its pupils dilating half a minute after the initial incision. Once some blood has been taken into the bowl the guys release the legs. They kick out feebly - *at last it gives back a little violence!* For a few moments they strike out until a final spasm leaves all four limbs rigidly outstretched. Around the head blood has spread like a silky, candy apple halo while an intrusion of grassy vomit slides into the pool in olive swirls. The goat's head relaxes with its passage past living and a few seconds later the legs collapse as the muscles receive no more electro-chemical signals from its dead brain.

The pupils will always stay with me – the eyes seemed to look right into me even as they bloomed full and black. I thought there was a microscopic spark in each, like the kind which remain as ghosts when old televisions are turned off. When the head eased into the slick of blood and the legs went limp those sparks vanished. Light no longer came from the eyes. The sun filtered into them. They were empty.

Dirt Eaters, Fish Flayers

I'm getting a second round at the Karari. That's not the way
things are supposed to work, however. Normally the class splits
in two at Koobi Fora, one group heads south for field work at
Jarigole and the other goes north to here. After a week all return
to base to rest, kill goats then swap field sites. With the exception
of one other sharp woman, my group went south to the Jarigole
hills without me. That's archaeology down there. *Neolithic*
archaeology, if you can grasp how that's even worse, not
paleoanthropology, which is what I came for. So with a pinch of
masterful groveling blended with a forceful plea for clemency,
Dr. H granted a stay of sentence. I'd get a little more time in the
Karari badlands. The homeland; our cradle. This part of the
Koobi Fora region has been among the most fertile dirts for
harvesting the ancestral bones of our kind. There very well may
be productive gravel down by Jarigole, but course rigors mean
student have to keep their heads bent in a 4,000 year old burial pit
down there. For now, an established nursery for mankind with its
rocky carpet and thorny romper toys was where I needed to be.
Waybill stayed back as well. From this sedimentary guru I have
learned more geology in a week than could be gleaned in a
semester course back home. At least I think I have because there
has been a little suspicion that once the subjects shift from local
sediments his disseminations become less reliable. My inquiries
into characteristics of the mantle, and other gut parts of the earth,
have left him with the oddest looks on his face. As though the
questions had pierced a vacuum in his head and he was waiting to
see if his ears got sucked inside. And whenever acting a little
surprised about some astonishing, sense-defying tidbit he'd given

about the local biology he has gotten downright testy. Still, I've been feeling geologically smarter after working with him.

While I was making a topographic sketch of Area 130-1 this morning, a girl from Washington U. hit pay dirt. Found a hominid molar. Not quite the mother lode, but it was the first trace of the old people discovered since we got here. *Australopithecus boisei* was the first guess at who'd lost that tooth. It had a crown pattern which was still fairly ape-like and *A. boisei* has a rap sheet in the Karari. But that particular species of Australopithecus also has a massive maw - try to picture the thing's cranium as a Darth Vader mask with a dorsal fin and Popeye's chin - and this tooth looked too small to come from the mother of all hominid nut-mashing machines. Perhaps a wee *boisei* lass? Or maybe a *habilis*? *Homo habilis* was worth a bet on size alone and size, you see, is so fucking little to make judgments with. So '*hominid tooth*' was the best, safest, and vaguest designation we could give it when it got dropped into a labeled baggie from the brand new locality, *Area 130-2*! Whaahoo! Finding teeth and naming vacant lots. Who wouldn't want to be me or any of these other dusty geeks?

The parades and luaus following the discovery wiped me out by evening, leaving me as a whipped hound concentrating my ass off on avoiding malaria. Trying to stay sharp for new mosquito attacks. Back at base camp the other night the wind had taken some time off, allowing the air to sticky up and the skeeters to organize a blood raid. The day gusts soften the blaze of the atmosphere and night winds are supposed keep the mosquitoes off our blood supply. They can't fly, or land, in a good wind. When we finally did get some air movement it was a light, loopy breeze *in* from the lake – it normally blows out, or in but aggressively – which was just enough to tumble every vicious, infected bug up to the bandas and no further. Netting is almost useless as skeeters can slip their needles through the tiny holes of the mesh. They could probably get them through sheet metal, for that matter, which is why you can't kill one once it's punctured you. You can squash the body but its titanium siphon will snap off at the hinge and remain in the capillary, bleeding you to death over the course of three years. Any sleeping flesh in contact with the net is an all-you-can-eat buffet for the insects. Only those skinny or still enough to avoid touching the mesh over their narrow bed were spared and no one was spared. Well, netless and foul-tasting Lujurio was spared and that kind of irony just ain't fair. That bastard really deserves to get bitten by something. We've all gotten perforated and left with tiny red and rock hard bumps and Lujurio chews off his fingernails because there's nothing to scratch. Could somebody hand me a snake, please?

The Karari has its own brand of flesh suckers, Koobi Fora's country cousins. Louder. Meaner. Carrying whatever strain of malaria parasite that's fashionable in these parts. I'm still a few days away from a new dose of Lariam as my stash of that wacky prophylactic is back at HQ. Sitting on a banda shelf waiting to jump in somebody's mouth and lend a hand. Of course my vigilance against them aerial smidgens of virulence has been exaggerated. I can't do crap against the mosquitoes.

Arthropods may have little to fear of me but I can certainly help bring holocausts to things in the vertebrate phylum. The day after the Festival of Goats I was allowed to join the guys in a fishing party. In the late afternoon eight of us moseyed on down to the shore with a fishing net. The expedition was easy as pie. With about fifty feet of mesh secured to two end poles we dragged the net straight out into the water, until the lead guys were waist deep, then began arcing it back towards shore in a big "C". Those of us inside the curve bent to hold the net against the lakebed to pull it back to shore as the men on the ends moved towards each other. I could feel things swishing by or banging into my legs, hoping the collisions remained minor – there had been an eight-foot crocodile trapped by the net during the previous class's session. The net turned out reptile-free on the beach and it was crowded with fish. There were a few nicely sized Nile perch and a pair of toothy tiger fish but the bulk of the trawl was a few dozen tilapia. It promised a hell of a fish fry ahead but we went out one more time to see if we could double the bounty.

Kalle came along to the kitchen banda where the men handed me a knife to help fillet our catch. She opted to just hang and watch. Now, I'm a fair hand a marine butchery back home but I was out of my league with my *Turkana* and *Dassanetch* friends. They were all cleaning four or five each to my every one. The speed of their knives was highlighted by the growing pile of filleted fish – they'd had their flanks sliced off so quickly most were still quite alive. The glistening, nearly skeletonized bodies of tilapia continued to twitch and bend as more were tossed in the heap. Quite the crazy sight and it brought on some minor pangs akin to what I'd felt the day before with the goats. Perhaps it was the lack of rushing blood, groans and the density of mammalian eyes or maybe I was more inured over killing but the defleshed fish just didn't pack the same spiritual punch.

Mudfish

For two hundred shillings, or whatever you've got on you, the answer is: "Rain"

The question: "What almost never occurs at the Karari?"

This, as you could guess, is bullshit. But I'd had that in my head ever since flipping through *Fodor's Guide to Kenya* back at the Wordsworth's store. Their immense authority on Every Last Place on Earth led them to print that the rainfall around Lake Turkana amounts to a *few centimeters* every five to ten years. They might consider upping the payola to their informants if they wish them to stop lying. Because it rains every year up here, often in the form of ark-floating deluges during October and November. I guess the donkeys at Fodor's never wondered how all the gnarly shrubs and wildlife in their desert photographs were sustained by a drizzle of water every decade. Journalists, remember. Travel journalists, albeit, but still without a solid concept of the truth or how to get to it. Need a fact? Make one up. Who the fuck goes to Lake Turkana anyway?

October did show up for a night this August, showcasing impressive feats of wetness. Gave a washout performance in early July too, according to staffers who'd gotten trapped in mud rivers at the time. After last night's slop show many students will be tossing sopping copies of Fodor's into the toilet pit. After they've fished them out of the ponds in their tents, that is. I had no losses to count. My tent was humidity saturated, if that's at all worth mentioning. Polar caps aside, weather is weather no matter where you're at on the planet. When the clouds roll in like bladder-troubled aunts and the air goes cadaver clammy it's time to get preventative. I strapped the flysheet on my cheap little

Sears tent which had been pitched atop a little mound, my yard grading away on all sides. When the sky bawled I reached through the zipper to hook the last hooks then lay back to listen to campers scramble like hens in a weasel pit infested with wet desert pneumonia. A dozen people repitching tents on higher ground in a deep, black downpour makes for a lot of noise. Rain and Suffering... Beats creaking jackals or goat quacking for lullaby effects.

There were plenty of damp, under-rested bellyachers who set off for the paleontology this morning. The field technique du jour called for preparing a complete, though busted up, fossil catfish for removal from Area 130-1. It required gouging a deep moat around the remains then splinting and spackling the top. This was a big fish - fat kid sized. Wouldn't want to hook one like it lest it chomp a leg off on deck. We bandaged the homely bones in toilet paper, burlap strips, sledge sticks and Plaster of Paris. Later we'd return to see it some more and see if it needed more splints and goop. The goal was to dig the fish out for cleansing and reassemblage at the museum, which will probably never happen. They've got old catfishes there already but we need the training. The rain came back angry at noon so we excused ourselves from the fossil mucksucker and split for lunch.

The weather went bipolar for the rest of the day. At one-thirty it was partially overcast and nippy, at around 82°. An hour later it was getting warm, jumping to 94°. Another hour passed and the clouds burst again as the air held the greatest chill yet. My watch's thermometer still insisted that it was in the 90's, but it had been stuffed in my pocket for a while so I wouldn't plaster it while casting the fish.

Back at Area 130-1 we made the final preparations for getting our mudfish out of its grave and off to a lab. Digging under and flipping the thing over brought it awful close to getting destroyed. It did get turned, though, and its belly got a spackle jacket as well. Then we abandoned it again once the sun was seen getting eaten alive by a continent-sized thunderhead. Where the clouds had lost control of themselves along the horizon it was plain to see the falling towers of rain. Like charcoal smudges wiped down a sooty canvas. It was heading our way and looking just a bit pissed. We hotfooted it, scrambling and rolling ankles to get back to the Rover.

Mad as hell or just looking to rinse off the badlands, those behemoth water pillows got me all soft and whatnot on the inside. Especially for the rainbows left in their wake. *Two* of those spectral arcs side by side in brilliant color made for a powerful scene. Wicked nice sky magic. For half an hour or more one rainbow was the complete package with *both* ends on the ground. Didn't know that ever happens or even could happen. We drove about a hundred meters from one terminus, a plump column of at least five distinct colors which altered the hue of the acacia trees and red dust it enveloped. There was no getting around musing on pots o'gold, only figuring that somewhere beneath that refracted band of light a Turkana leprechaun had buried a complete *Homo habilis* skeleton. Mighty vibes emanated from that sight – but what sane *Homo sapiens* would buy it? Certainly not Dr. Waybill who chuckled off my idea. It felt a little stupid to bring up the suggestion but it's not like whole hominid fossils were throwing themselves at us over in Area-130.

The flora and fauna hereabouts are amazing even in the usual, anhydrous climate. The survival of acacia, *commifora*, *salvadora* (the famine berry tree) and other plants is impressive. The lions, cheetahs, caracals, gazelles, antelopes, squirrels, zebras, and dozens of birds who call this arid badland home are also astounding in their ability to exploit and survive. None of it fails to be beautiful in the searing white sunshine. But when it rains, even for a day, the transformation of this neighborhood will flatten you right out on your ass. The vegetation is adapted to go into overdrive whenever there is some extra water. It gets greener and blossoms within a few hours after a rain, taking advantage of the pollinating aid of increased insect business, and even growing new leaves in less than a day. Along one of the gully paths to the catfish there were sprays of violet, Morning Glory-like flowers on freshened vines. The new, vibrant greens and a deeper rust colored earth shock the mind with an awareness of the true speed and resource of Nature.

Animals get entrepreneurial as well. The cats and other predatory machines had been out killing as evidenced by scattered crowds of gigantic, clownish vultures. Birds with more color than the freshly painted flora go on the hunt for the insects and the little animals that the wet trees bring out. All around gazelles play like inner city kids around an open fire hydrant. Unbelievably resplendent.

I am a nature pansy after all, there's no getting around it. Might as well suck in as much damp desert beauty as I can. This has been my last day in the Karari and I may never see it again. As per my deal with the director I'm shipping out for Jarigole in the morning.

Pith Helmet and a Hair Trigger

It was 4:30 a.m. when I peeled my head off the gin-soaked sweater I call a pillow. Early. In these parts even the sun doesn't have the guts to be seen at this hour. As for me, well see, I'm a P.A. man. The P.A. is for paleoanthropology to the squares. And it's my business to stand blinking in the dark before dawn, eyelids as crusty as a baker's boxer shorts. But it pays for the bread and the booze and it's just the way things get done.

My head was still throbbing from the night before. Might've been the rum. Or the scotch. Or the spider bites. But the smart money says it was the beating. I'd been up in the Karari for some time when the big man put the word out on me, time to haul my mug in. Down to the skids of Jarigole.

Jarigole...the name rang out like buckteeth on a headstone. At the moment I was feeling like a resident under that gravestone, getting banged up on the back of Bedford cargo lorry-slash-hearse. Apparently Doctor H, the Big Kahuna, thought I might not come down without a little sweet persuasion. He sent a few of his goons to perform a sock-hop on my cranium. They really got into their work, probably thinking that the best rides across the desert include a brain hemorrhage.

When we finally pulled in at Jarigole – four hours, a nose bleed and some dry heaves later - the good doctor was there to throw his arms wide in welcome. After getting tossed off the truck it took a minute for my eyes to uncross and my marbles to settle in a corner before I could see a lone Dr. H standing on the cinders before me.

"Hi, Frank!" he said with a childlike glee that masked the menace and power of this nefarious man.

"Morning…how goes it, H?" I grumbled back. "Thanks for the skull fractures…"

"Well…" he caroled, pulling an olive toned Gilligan hat off to scratch his graying hair, "I knew a formal invitation wouldn't get you away from your rocks. You've been on the North Side long enough and we've got enough loose cannons up there as is. It's time you learned the business as it goes down here. Koobi Fora is a big place, no point in any of my boys getting too comfortable in their own neighborhood."

"So that's how it works from now on, eh?" I smirked, nearly passing out from the effort. "I suppose there ain't any choices in the matter, right?"

"You're a sharp kid, Frankie. A bit too fond of your own ideas, but that's why you're here. And don't worry too much about the change of scenery, in time you'll come to appreciate our operations here. So look around, get some shut-eye and we'll bring you up to speed tomorrow."

With that a couple of henchwenches dragged me over to a tent on the banks of the *Il Nyongololong'atuk* laga. Now there's a name that sounds like an alibi you gobble at your wife with lipstick on your collar and a tongue drenched in bourbon. Just before she bats you in the puss with an ironing board. The goonettes thoughtfully pitched my canvas within the overhang of a giant, saggy thorn tree. A combination leopards' nest, spider hut and fire ant slum: they must've figured the neighbors would keep me indoors at night

Now, Doom is a lot like restraining orders from ex-chippies. Or school teachers that make you swallow bags of thumbtacks. Either way it makes you thirsty. I grabbed a mug of water from a burlap sweat-bag…nice and cool. Stared into it for a moment, wishing that it was a glass of tequila. I could curse up a thunderstorm right now. But nothing was gonna save me from Dr. H's wishes.

Neolithic Archaeology. That's what they called the racket in Jarigole. The swishy sound of it made me feel like a tulip. But it beats snorkeling in Lake Turkana with concrete flippers. Or worse: getting a failing mark on a pricey transcript. I figure I'll play the game for a while. Get on Dr. H's good side. It never hurts to know all the angles.

Next morning I went straight into it with of the Koobi Fora Cultural Reconstruction gang. A seedy bunch, I knew this rabble from the old days, when the cons were run in squalid tenements at the Koobi Fora spit. They still gave me some slicing glances. A biology stiff shoved into their archeological pickle jar really boiled their onions. They were wondering what the hell Dr. H was up to, kicking a guy with a rap sheet in science into their ethnographic hell-hole. But there was no time to worry about their bunched-up undies. Barely time to fill a burning gut with a little breakfast. A shot of pineapple juice, a swig of tea, and some *mandazis* – little wedges of fried, sugared dough that help lube the angina. I didn't have any cigarettes yet. Smokes came if the boss let you get 'em and this current nicotine seizure was the Doctor's way of letting me know he meant business. I just stared down at my *mandazi* and mulberry jam wishing it was a deep-fried wedge of tequila with lime jelly.

Nobody talks during the breakfast minute. Maybe it's some sort of crazy time of holy silence in this ritualistic society of dingbats. Maybe everyone here is too full to the eyeballs with bland morning angst to be social. Gee whiz, I was missing the peppery tobacco banter of the fossil thugs back at the Karari. But soon enough the riff raff grumbled up to a communal murmur and the time came for the serious work.

At 6:49 a.m. some crammed into a bestial, green monster Mercedes cargo truck belching mustard gas off bad pistons. I got in Dr. H's filthy, egg-white Land Rover.

At 6:50 a.m. Neolithic archaeology tasted an awful lot like getting back out of a filthy, egg-white Land Rover and pushing the damn thing to get the engine to turn over.

The morning was full of spectacles. Glorious stuff that came at us by the minute. At 7:13 the Land Rover spun to a dusty halt like an Okie tripping after a rolling nickel and having a heart attack. Dr. H needed to throw some rocks off the road. The Master in his Kingdom, he doesn't take sass from rubble on the highway.

At 7:15, H's right-hand behemoth, Ives, tore the hinges off the passenger door and jammed the speeding Rover to a stop with his left foot. It was his turn to clear basaltic ruffians off the freeway. He heaved the boulders overhead like they were light as a ton of Italian money. The raw, red earth shuddered and rifted beneath his feet as he flung the stones over the horizon into the Indian Ocean.

The landscape gets ominous as you near the Jarigole sweat-pits and strange things pop off the roadside. Large, skinny cats wearing cheetah-fur blazers. Zebras giving impalas the business. Or piles of ominous, white-washed stone blocks in the middle of nowhere, lying without a reason. As you stare at their enigmatic presence they begin to hum, *"Hey Ace, whaddya think? We're ominous white-washed stone blocks...in...a...pile..."*

The view on the runway to the Jarigole Stone Pillar Site gets grimmer. Basalt columns the hue of dried blood angle out of the ground, circling a pit like one of Satan's mouths gasping for air on a sulfur-blasted hunk of the planet. At 7:19 it was plenty clear the Prince of Darkness needed an orthodontist and a barrel of Blistex.

Us Rover jerks had already unpacked our chain-gang equipment, and some comfy canvas stools when the Mercedes Beast rolled into view. Kalle McInnis was twisting out of the back of the truck and shouting to the goon at the wheel. Couldn't make out what the hell she was hollering about because I was too wrapped up in the view. McInnis is a Class A dame. The sort of sultry broad that makes a paleontologist feel like his brain's been splashed with acetate and bedacryl. I stared hard, wishing she was a bracer of cool tequila in a curvy highball tumbler with a nice ass.

While the drool on my chin stubble dried and caked up in the blazing morning heat I realized Kalle's crowd was minus a couple of the Neolithic mobsters. Mastodon Lujurio and Squeaks Hixon weren't in the wayback of the Benz anymore. So that's what happens when you get on the wrong side of the boss. Tossed off the back of a speeding truck like chum from a shark trawler...

But it wasn't the case. The pair poked their domes up from a low gulch. They hadn't been flung from the vehicle, even if they'd deserved it. They'd jumped of their own volition after seeing some cheetahs chasing some gazelles, wanting to grab some glossies of the African weirdness. These were tricky people. I knew I'd have to stay alert or get eaten alive out here.

There was some quiet time as we gathered around Lucifer's Jaws – the crew was keen to find out what Dr. H had to show them. One veteran, Tommy J, sat like a slick bowling pin of squishy, beige granite. A lipid, cool-staring man of ethnography. A wedge of fat slush waiting for a command from the Don to fire him into medium-low speed action. The word around town was this kid had taken a nip in the jimmies from a scorpion last year. That kind of awkward agony can turn a man dangerous. I made a mental note never to have my back to Tommy and never to wear loose, open shorts.

A Toast to the Little Pricks

The Jariogle bunch were paraphrasing *Barfly* in the dinner pit tonight. I have trouble stomaching movie quoters, a condition which stems from the excessive script reiterations I performed myself years back; cloying John Hughes pap and all the fucking Monty Python. Realizing my habits were identical to any jackass ruining flicks for everyone else, I shifted gears and kept to brief lines plagiarized from art house cinema. Then the word *cinema* began to pretentiously burn my fucking bowels as it was clear I was cheating myself out of any originality. Now I make up my own gibberish, repeat it to death and nobody seems to give a crap. At least the lines will never plague them from any other direction but mine. This crowd's childlike glee for glorified alcoholism and the myth of Bukowski nevertheless had me pining for a violent, purple *Sauza* erection and a nasty whore to fuck me like she's got rabies. A quality slut who craves hours of fine madness getting sticky and beating the shit out of each other. This is where I find the Koobi Fora Field School to be deficient.

Work-release at Jarigole had ended in the afternoon and the closing remarks were made from the dry bed of the *Il Nyongololong'atuk*. Sounds like Eskimo, doesn't it? Or do I mean *Inuit*. Or is it *Inuktitut*? *Inupiaf*? Whatever the fuck I mean, if I learned anything in cultural classes it's that Snow Indians have names for stuff which sound like the title of this sandy trench we've been camped in.

I can't say I learned to love the Jarigole Pillar Site. Spending hours in a little strung-off square meter of a 4,000 year old grave, digging very slowly to discover many, very similar stuffs as the students one, two and three squares over. Little chips of pottery, *sherds*, with nothing on them. Sherds *with* marks on them. Thousands and thousands of little ostrich eggshell beads which strike as more grommety than beady. There was a little, pink soapstone bar decorated as an animal with its nose snapped off. It *was* interesting and promptly described as *phallic* by Dr. Ives.

Of course it was phallic. What isn't to archaeologists? Well, all the stuff that has breast aspects, naturally. As a matter of fact it's pretty much all jugs and pricks with archaeologists. So, spears, needles, carved antlers and rib bones are phalluses. Bowls, wide bottomed jugs, burial mounds, and tortoises are *mammarian*, I guess. They don't use actual breast references, opting instead for lighter blushable terms like *fertility totem*. The only time archaeologists will refuse to employ *phallic* or *fertility symbol* is when they come across actual carvings/painting/etchings of penises ("Naturalistic Male Figure") or little clay dolls with giant tits ("Venus Figurine"). Notice that archaeology tends to get more delicate when it comes to the female references? That's because most archaeologists have traditionally been male. Not that things are going to change too quickly as more women populate the field, mind you. On the whole here, this is a group of professionals who were always sitting down at school dances. They've a got lot of sex on the brain and little experience in directly expressing it.

Back to ostrich beads. Funny how neither they, nor anything ancient with a hole in it, is ever referred to as *rectal*. Funnier still, when you take stock of how many assholes are employed in archaeology.

By now you can see why I'm viewing this departure as liberation from The Hell of Dull Bastards Who Like to Spend Precious Bolts of Time Ripping Busted Ceramic Pieces Out of Neolithic Burial Cairns. Much the same as getting sprung from The Hell of Being Hung Face Down in Lye and Getting Skinned Alive Staring at Your Nuts. Okay, alright, yes I'm exaggerating in a stupid way again. Let's just say getting out of Jarigole is like a doctor calling off the prostate exam.

But there's sure to be things I'll miss about this district. Maybe it's the perfect breeze that comes down the laga when all else is still and hot. Or the cicadas droning out charming, ear-rupturing renditions of *The Outer Limits* theme music. At lunchtimes the only thing audible above the bugs' sonic assault was the vegan's shrill objections to the buffet. She's squealed about suspected egg or lactic intrusions into her meals. She's whined that she's unable to enjoy the cookies and French toast for those same reasons. She's grumbled distrustfully over fried dough, rice and boiled *ugali* over the potential taint from utensils which had touched the margarine (Kenya's *Blue Band* margarine is a spreadable fat combo which includes lard). The kitchen squad has done its best to set aside separate, animal-free meals for her which she'd wolf down without a trace of appreciation and never a word of thanks. The only person to visibly gain weight during the desert month, her voracious ingratitude led to one of the worst displays of thoughtlessness seen on this trip.

The crew gaffed one of her lunches, setting out a trough of canned tuna mixed with Bermuda onion and some oil. Having trouble understanding vegetarianism as a *choice* it was harder still to get their heads around the concept of veganism. Nobody but vegans really understands what the fuck a vegan is all about – it seems more a disorder than a lifestyle. So they made a simple mistake, forgetting that meatless also meant fishless, and Rachel went out of her tits. Storming over to the cooks she screamed at them, demanding to know why they thought she could eat tuna. Dr. H ran over quickly to pull her off the cooks, gently explain the tuna issue and ask if they could throw together some vegetable thing. Perhaps something apart from *the big platter of tomatoes and cucumbers on the lunch table*. And they did it. Their ability to graciously overlook transgression ought to be legendary. Rachel might have been the first vegan vermin they've encountered. But fat, white idiots have gone by like a parade over the years.

The thing that'll probably get me the most wistful is this: lying in the river gravel with Kalle McInnis, under a midnight sky that's about to tear under the weight of all the stars. Driving my sexual hunger to a Latin frenzy while talking about all the screwing we haven't done since coming to Kenya.

Kalle talks freely about her love of mattress company. The sheer enthusiasm of her banter had me thinking she could go into the throes of ecstasy with a single moistened finger in her ear. And once she had my nerves burning in rivers of sparks she'd fishtail into musings on abstinence, saying she'd need to be chained to a tree during the full moon phase. Now there was an idea – chain her to a tree! Hell, chain her to anything, especially my tent poles. I couldn't be sure what I was supposed to infer from her discourses. It could have been that I wasn't supposed to infer anything. I was just the guy lucky enough to audience her fantasies both dirty and chaste. Fortunate enough to go to bed a few nights in a row with cramps in my patiently clenched jaws. Falling asleep hopelessly with teeth ground to stumps of raw nerve-pulp and enamel gravel. I'd lain down with agonizing erections, but at least sleep brought the violent dreams needed to ease them.

Vlad the Mothsucker

The atmosphere has been strikingly subdued since the sun went down and the dinner plates finished their trips through the wash basins. This is the final night for us at Koobi For a base camp. Tomorrow we're headed south again, to begin a week of ecology surveys before bringing it all back home to Nairobi. I was expecting more hubbub – kids scrambling around to pack or take some last photos or recount the crazy points of the session or to revel in the fact that they're finally getting the hell out of here. Most everyone has already packed and even the distant background noise of lorry loading had ended before dinner. There's an air of wistfulness among all; even the few who'd made no bones about their distaste for the region now seem down about leaving this special place.

I know I'm a bit depressed about saying good-bye to this place and I've been taking in the bat show at the main banda one more time. Koobi Fora's hometown bat, *Nycteris hispida*, or hairy slit-faced bat, provides peripheral entertainment for us from around 7:00 p.m. until whenever the last person pulls the chain on the fluorescent tube overhead. The light brings bugs and the bats come for supper. They seem to really enjoy moths. The main table is notable for its litter of moth dust and wing splinters.

Amazing what people get used to. For some, a bat doing aerial stunts around their heads at home would send them screaming indoors in a molten panic. But bats are part of the package here, so learning to live with them is the rule. By the second night at the main table we were all just sitting with dopey grins as wacky sky rats careened and caromed at our faces. Their senses are as uncanny as anything you've heard. Or maybe they are cannier.

Either way, it amounts to rarely ever getting hit by a bat since they'll pull ninety-degree turns a blink before colliding into your teeth. If the pickings turn out a little slim, during strong breezes or after the bats have eaten most of the bugs, they'll flap around in mad figure eights over the tables until extra helpings buzz in. If a big insect gets snagged they'll whizz it back to the archaeology or geology lab to enjoy a noisy munch. A big, bright green praying mantis, which had also come to eat bugs, got nabbed one night. Didn't see it get consumed but we heard it getting chewed up loud and clear within the dark of the archie-lab. Gonna miss the bats and hoping my banda bat will be home by dawn so we can formally say *"So long!"* to each other.

There is a bonfire starting to ignite down at the beach, and I hear a bottle of rum or vodka made its way down to it. Time for me to follow it and bid adieu to the crocodiles...

Potty Reprise

Though it doesn't seem like school work the course gets tied together as though we'd spent six weeks in an auditorium. Took the last exam today and it cemented the idea that I've at least got the aptitude for this field. So absolutely fucking bright when it comes to this business, I play like an ace and beautiful ladies will soon be rolling over and sinking their teeth in the wall just to be under my knowledge of human science. But now my mind needs rest. No tales of inter-disciplinary intrigue or politics and especially no ruminations on women or cheap fuck treatises. Softer thoughts are called for, the perfect time to return to meditations on Third World Toilet Precautions...

Carpet the Mezzanine! A rule beyond debate: Always lay some paper on the rim of any john you intend to set your bum on. Forget feeling foolish. Men should ignore the notion that only women and fuss-budgets do this back in the States. Every place on this planet - except the US and maybe some homes of the Canadian *Ultra Riche* - has nothing but infected, infectious, contaminated, contagious, virulent, and poorly matched toilet seats. I had a nice potty at a flat I stayed in while in Paris. But it was in a broom closet and Parisians seem happiest peeing in the street. Here, even if you'd just watched a janitor or char-woman or Special Forces agent scrub the ring down you still must beware. The nastiest germs, particularly the Nairobi strains, laugh at bleaches and acids, completely ecstatic to get a polish on their lethal membranes. So pad the damn seat and save thyself, even if you have to walk out of the head with toilet paper hanging from your shorts. Nothing looks as foolish as a person with dysentery shitting searing liquid through his khakis every two minutes. Dignity means doodlysquat with holes in your colon and ulcers on your flesh.

Geyser Insurance. Pack the bowl with toilet tissue before excrementing into it. The reasoning is similar to the defense against seat disease, only more terrifying. With a lot of loose water underneath, the happiness of your southern portal is gravely threatened. The liquid must be sponged up or paper-thickened lest a dense stool plummets in to send a tower of horror fluid splashing all over your bum. Diphtheria bidets are awful things. Never let them happen. A bottomless intestine ain't correct, socially or physiologically, earnestly wiping out the desire to go on living while you're on vacation. And who knows? Maybe the sopping wet state of your buttocks will have already wiped out your *ability* to live.

I may or mayn't have developed an art of defecating wisely. I will, regardless of point or taste, outline the basics until I'm comfortable enough to construct a philosophy for the movement. These sagacious tidbits are handy in regions where the term *toilet* is idiomatic, untranslatable or thoroughly meaningless. Onward!

Laying Cable in the Great Wide Open. Dig a hole. Dig a really deep hole. Honestly, you gotta have a hole. You'd think that's a self-evident notion, but it isn't. Many folk just ease their bowels on the level earth and it's simply a bad idea. Firstly, it is nice to bury the business once it's done; better for the panorama and most people go home to louse up their own countryside anyway. Then there are the hyenas which seem to like any crap they come across. They'll dig up anything you bury but why make it easy for them?

Off the mark again. The burial is about staying healthy. You have to get the dung in a grave quickly before it can do any harm. Those funny, dreamy and soothing postludes to evacuations are just the window the bugs from inside you need to make a final play for your life. There's probably some science to it, but for now just accept that bacteria that's benign *inside* you becomes instantaneously rude and deadly upon reaching the outside. Ever see *Gremlins*? It's just like that. Cute, furry bacteria in the guts and vicious, toothy things in the open air. Keeping your distance from a live turd is the priority. A foot or two of dirt over it is going the extra mile to protect oneself.

Posture. Pretty important as well. Like the depth of the hole, how you perch your tushie above a fresh-dug abyss plays a role in keeping microbes off you. Too low, hence too close to your ankles, spells trouble. The tropics do weird, unforeseeable things to a bowel, its volume and content composition. You might end up with legs plastered like camouflaged Doric columns. Or have your ass swimming in a swamp of things which once looked and smelled better.

Too high has a less intuitive risk. If the poop is rigid, you'll have an event not unlike dropping a canoe heavy with Kung Fu-Grip GI Joe's from a high roof into a pit of Darth Vader action figures. Here's the Newtonian physics – the boat, with an odd shape and an odd landing spot, will have very little bounce of its own. The hole and planet underneath it won't be knocked out of the way either. No, the collision of boat and pit requires an equal and opposite reaction which will be visually fulfilled by GI Joes and Lord Vaders flying up like popcorn. Leading to this terrifying image: protozoa, bacteria, viruses, and slightly larger crud varmints soaring high in a small, dirty cloud created by fecal impact. Tiny things with the micro version of rubber hands to clutch the fine hairs of your loins en route to rotting your flesh from the bum up.

Eeeeewww, n'est pas? Then consider this – the feces is not firm, but rather a choleric fluid blast. *Vesuvius effluvius*, as the Caesars would say. The scatter range of such projectiliquids probably means you're walking back to camp with the hot stews of your innards stuck to your socks and shins. The shame of the shit streaked is often worse than his death.

Dumb Animals

On the first day into the Koobi Fora exodus I'd spent the last twelve hours in our big blue people lorry. A rolling, mechanized monster trolley, which has no compassion for human asses, spines, or bowels. The trip was savage, long, and hot for anybody any in any of the vehicles. A protracted snuggle in the Devil's hoof cleavage, from the keys penetrating the ignitions to the cracked teeth and the cigarettes after. We were all viciously brutalized by this Sunday drive in the country.

I'd sat in the last bare space of splintering bench near the rattling tailgate and just a little less near the flesh-eating gravel tearing backwards beneath us. It was an ideal mount to meditate on mortality. I hadn't truly taken the danger to heart until sometime after falling prey to a fit of napping. Sleep proved almost fatal, my wake-up call being an enormous bang into a pothole causing a violent truck-lurching that left my ass airborne and halfway *behind* the lorry. With eyes open to widened slits in the torrential dust I managed to flail a hand around the roll bar and, with kids clutching at my shirt and arms, grappled back into the truck. I have no idea how long it took for my heart to start beating again. Snoozing on the bus is now on the growing list of stupid things I've done since getting to Kenya.

That list would also include that pitch-black night in South Horr with Janet a month back. But headline coverage ought to go to this incredibly brilliant example of humans whose common sense had been pathetically maimed: *Morons molesting hippos at midnight.*

Now how on earth would something like that happen? Messing with a hippopotamus? There ought to be a reason for such lunacy. And there is. Sure isn't a good reason, though. There was a humongous hippo fuck-up this year and I was at the heart of it.

Gathering down on the beach for the last night, a handful of us were sipping a little alcohol and reflecting on our past six weeks at KFFS. Beautiful night. A few tattered, lonely clouds, nudging the breeze, which in turn kneaded the low rolling, slate waves. The crocs were lazy, at least the big ones were – the little ones always get active when you try to grab them by the tail. Even the jackals and hyenas had tempered their usual racket. And Louis was with us.

Louis was a fascinating dude, *Iree Ganjaselassie*, or whatever the hell you want to call a Kenyan Rastafarian who only becomes visible to the living at after-dinner campfires. Roasted goat and tinkling rum bottles cause him to materialize from the dark. He's an NMK-Koobi Fora guy and doesn't actually work for us. He's more of a tour guide for the National Museums and its little exhibit a few kliks back on the spit. Since he'd banged a student in the Richard Leakey Banda the other night he does warrant a slightly deeper study. Ethno-specifically he's Wakamba, though anyone's first guess would be Jamaican, what with the tricolor yarn bag he uses to trap his dreds. And the weed. Or at least the *fumet de ganja* which is the fragrant clarion of his arrival. But fucking a student, a nice girl from a pretty white suburb no less, in the Big Man's private hut? That demands praise doesn't it? For *her* I mean. As she also mentioned nipping a little Johnnie Walker from ol' Dickie's dry bar I can only grovel in deep admiration for her.

Louis, sucking on a joint the size of a baby arm, joined us at the beach with our memories, our rum, and our folding chairs. My chair was less for sitting and more a ludicrous piece of weaponry. I figured I could, if the occasion came along, bash a lion in the face with it just before it ripped the trachea out of my screaming neck. Besides it just seemed wrong to be propped in canvas when I ought to feel the Lake Turkana sands directly under my ass one last time. There was a bonfire. Well there was some flaming wood which would have been incredible had it been bigger, the fuel supply being fairly spare. Tree overcrowding is not a noted aspect of northern Kenya, particularity in the scrub deserts of the

Turkana basin. Finding fire-worthy driftwood meant increasing foot labor which Lou and I took on.

One trip brought us a quarter mile west along the spit before we had decent armfuls of dry driftwood. I bet most of it had floated in from Ethiopia, though the labels had been washed off by happy lake splash. That's when we saw it, a huge hippopotamus about fifty meters off. The moon just beyond it, it grazed solemnly in a powdery luminescence. A mammoth silhouette on a grass hummock a few meters up from the shore. Stunned by its magnificence, mesmerized by the thick nocturnal wonder of the scene.

Then Louis turned to me and said, "Hey! Lit's go scare da sheet outtadet 'ippo!"

"*Okay! Heck Yeah! Let's do that!*" I sang, "*Right on!*" and followed him as we jogged, hopped, hooted and howled like monkeys on bourbon, trying to get a little closer to chuck our logs at it. *Fuck yes!* I was going to shout and huck sticks at that wonderful creature. I, a nondescript pork pie smudge from Woonsocket, was going to be part of driving that beautiful behemoth back to its muck-bottomed sump, assisted by my man Lou, a Kenyan and thus an expert on how to put fear into 6000-pound amphibious mammals. A goddamned authority, by golly! He had to be or why the hell else would I go trotting towards one of the planet's most dangerous grass eating monsters to toss driftwood at it? Since the hippo hadn't scampered out of harm's way I could assume that, at the very least, it didn't mind.

It had been grazing with its rump to the lake as we lobbed our missiles at it. Then it turned. All the way around to face us. With the moonlight shining behind it, it was impossible to really gauge its expression. But it wasn't giggling. Maybe it was starting to mind a little…

It made a kind of snort, then a roaring yawn, a bellow and additional other pissed-off sounding noises. Then it moved one of its front feet in our direction. Then all its feet started moving. In the microsecond it took to glean the gravity of what was about to go down there was barely time to develop my new image of Louis: just a jackass stoner from the Kamba highlands who didn't know dick about hippos. Microseconds, however, were ample to fill with the reflection that I was nothing more than a terminal asshole about to get processed into a puddle of guts, sand and grass by a humongous beast that we'd irritated for no good cause. *Gonna die, gonna die, gonna die, gonna die* was all my brain gave my face to sputter as I sprinted, faster than I ever thought I could go, across the razor grass of the Koobi Fora Spit, my soon to be last resting place. Not even a folding chair was going to save me. At least I would go down running away. How *français*...

But something in my head was still working on a way out. A survival mechanism which heard the thundering hippo behind us and still thought we could make it.

"*Water!*" blared the internal PA system, "Get your ass in the fucking *water*!!!"

Many might think that was stupid idea. I, however, felt it was pure, unadulterated genius. At least as smart as anything anybody could come up with a few seconds away from a horrible hippo stomping. Sure the beast was gaining and sure it's as at home in the water as on land. But there was no way three tons of animal was going to maintain speed if it barreled down after me into the lake. The water would put a brake on it and I'd be saved; it could go off and squish up Louis instead. *I was going to live.* Just so long as the beast didn't stop at the water's edge to prevent me from getting back out – but there was no time to worry about it. Into the low surf of Lake Turkana I went, my own gallop slowing to the resistance of the water. I took the span of a gasp to look behind me and then a double take to confirm a miraculous sight: the hippopotamus quit charging about thirty meters back. Thank god they get sick of running quickly. It had made its point anyway and I was absolutely fucking positive that I got the message. It was over, and I started to slow down looking east towards the dull red scab of a smoldering campfire...

Then... *BOOM! WHOOSH! AAAAOOGHAH!* Geysers started exploding in the water to my left and maelstroms sucked the air from the sky. *What the fuck?* Were there small beach break volcanoes ready to kill me too? Actually, amid the roiling lake and deafening blasts were terrifying roars reminiscent of sounds I'd recently noticed coming out of an aggravated hippopotamus. But this was more than a solo. The streaked moonlight revealed at least four fat hippo heads pushing up through the surface of the lake, jaws far too fucking open, spouting liquid wrath and hellish gusts of steam that barely hazed out the murderous tusks in those pale red mouths. It was Godzilla storming out of Tokyo Bay with some cousins. I was thigh deep in the front yard of a hippo nest while the leader of the gang was back on the grass cruelly laughing its ass off. *Fucked again. Dang.* With that realization my mind imploded and I tore out of the lake on primal instinct, bent on running all the way back to Boston and screaming like a retard with his hands on a hot plate.

Back at the fire there'd be a story to tell, but only after some heavy, wheezing inhalations to get oxygen back in my body. My leg muscles were burning in a bath of lactic acid and I needed to replenish the spent rum in my system. The fire was in its final crackles too, but we couldn't save it. The fuel we'd collected belonged to the hippos now. Louis had beaten me back to safety. Cocksucker. He was sweating, panting and giggling as he rolled in the sand. That fucking Bob Marley hat was still in place, not a single dred was loose. Cocksucker. I needed more air. To get up and rip that damn bag off his head and break his dopey skull open on the rocks. No, that wasn't fair. My near demise was my own damn fault. Lou had only suggested the asinine idea; he didn't have to hard sell it in the least. Sometimes I get too hopped up on the '...*do as the Romans*' vibe, to the point of forgetting that the strict *caveat* in this Rome is: *Leave The Hippos the Fuck Alone.* Nevertheless, I can't think of Louie as anything other than a big old cocksucker.

It might have been over and it really looked that way this time. The only way to be absolutely sure was to get back to the hippo-proof refuge of my stone banda. As far as I know they can't spring over stone walls. Hopefully none of the animals have tiptoed up to my hut to ambush on the way home. If I'm lucky they've also got phobias for solifuges and potty-mouthed Italians. I needed to go to sleep and dream about baskets of hamsters.

Beautiful, magnificent, wonderful and amazing creatures those hippopotamuses. The name *Hippopotamus* derives from the Greek terms *hippo*s (horse) and *potamus*, (river). *Riverhorse!* Isn't that just precious? They're reputed to kill more people than any other animal in Africa.[5]

---

[5] [5]More than any of the big mammals, though some say that Cape Buffaloes hold the record. Mosquitoes, Tsetse flies, crocs, snakes, and even snails, are good at killing too. But, and this is just for factual accuracy, in Africa no animal kills Africans in higher numbers than other Africans.

Jug-Head Humanist

We've been rumbling down the eastern shore of Lake Turkana, battling the rocks, ruts and dust cyclones of the Chalbi Desert. It's been tiring, but it's been a fine time to commit places to memory. So many strange names and all the newness blurred my intake of the landscape en route to Koobi Fora. But now each place sings itself out in catchy tunes. The evaporative hum of the *Karsa* and *Hurran Hurra* waterholes under the watch of *Gabbra* nomads with their goats, guns and magnesium glares. The *Bura Galadi* hills and the *Lowasera Gorge* leading to *El Molo Bay* and the dwindling contingent of *Elmolo* fisher folk living on a rocky spit, uttering out the final phrases of an extinguishing language. Their tongue has lost ground to Samburu and more of their fish are winding up on the sport lines of foreigners staying at *Loyengalani's* hot springs at the southern reaches of the lake.

Twice now we've rumbled past the ridge above these disappearing people. It was mentioned that they now numbered less than fifty heads and we hadn't even stopped to take a good look. It doesn't seem right to give only the quickest distant glance at a people verging on vanishing. It could be argued, that relative to all the human history prior to this moment, the *Elmolo* really can't receive anything more than a quick look. Their bloodline will trickle into the damp gravels of their lakeside home or into the Samburu pool where it will eventually dissipate into the blood of greater Africa, one day arriving as a trace in all of us. Ethnographers may have already written down their tongue, cataloged their oral histories and placed it in a book for ready reference by the handful of humans who still care to know of the lives of the *Elmolo*. But that tome will be delved by fewer and fewer spelunkers of the arcane until its final shelving as a dead mass in a museum library.

Perhaps we need to see it as simply the expiration of a village and language only. However sad that notion might be we shouldn't see it as the demise of *special* human beings of a physical consistency or quality unlike the rest of us. A world bereft of a town of grandparents and their peculiar way of talking isn't a net loss in terms of human potential; we'll only be short another means of expressing that idea.

On this leg we had daylight views of big *Mt. Kulal*, the shield volcano responsible for much of this landscape over the eons. I thought about the crazy thickness of the *Tulu Bor* tuff. So much ash fell from the sky three millions years ago, burying so much of what was the universe to the lanky apes who had just begun standing straight under the slight swell to their heads. The *Elmolo* are not the first humans to gaze over the emerald ripples of Lake Turkana and see the vista of oblivion.

Veering off the somberly philosophic road we made a stop in what must've been the business district of South Horr village. It was enshrouded by condensing woodland, but had a shack where you could buy cigarettes, soap, and petrol out of dirty milk bottles. There was another shanty where passersby stopped to speak with an old gent leaning over a split door. *Information booth? Telecommunications center?* I liked the place. Having motored through here at dusk last month I never had the chance to scope it out. It's a little stunning in the morning. Coming from the north the low, rocky hills and scrub of the South Horr desert swell ahead into high green slopes and coalescing woodland. Along the western escarpment there was a bank of dense cloud cresting the high, steep hills. As we pulled in the gossamer pudding was at rest. But it was soon flowing downhill like tongues spun from platinum floss. Nice. Just plain nice.

It was a great day for haggling. Not a hell of a lot of tourism so far north in Kenya so it's amazing to see how the Samburu locals suddenly fill this dirt rest stop to sell stuff. Good stuff, too. The Samburu are northern cousins of the Maasai - think tall, red kilted people; women with scores of bead chokers in descending circumference and men with red, well-ornamented Bo Derek hair. Or bald dudes looking like well-tanned Scots without pipes. Nomadic herders in the past to settled pastoralists now they've also got solid a reputation as metalsmiths. Maasai spears are also Samburu spears; lengthy iron blades hafted on short wooden handles sitting upon long iron pikes. Good for killing what's after your cattle, whether big cats or *Rendille* warriors, from a secure distance. And they will sell them to you, using the proceeds to buy AK-47's – much more effective for guarding cattle and killing *Turkana* and *Gabbra* folk.

The girl from Long Island bought the niftiest odd commodity – a war club. Eighteen inches of straight stick the diameter of a rake handle, banded with blue, black, red, and yellow electrical tape and capped by a heavy sprocket. The crown gear from a Land Rover to be exact and a tasty take. Jealousy set in and I offered to buy it from her at a profit. So did others, reinforcing its novelty value as well as her resolve to hang on to it. I did get a spear though; a steal at fourteen bucks. I'm guessing that it was a bargain as the *moran* who let it go didn't seem pleased to be parting with it for a mere 750 shillings. He'd started at 3000, but surrendered at the urging of a squirrelly dude who showed up halfway into the bargaining. Maybe he was the local sales agent. Speaking crystal English and sporting a plaid blazer over his skirt, he'd arrived to negotiate and get a taste in the deal. I'd soon gotten the feeling that this greaser would hock his mother's ovaries if the price was right. Or if there was just a price...

While shaking the *moran's* long hand to seal the transaction, Bwana Shifty suggested I give the spear's former owner another hundred shillings...*while he held onto the rest.* He wasn't an agent after all: he was a freaking pimp! I tried to give the man his spear back, suddenly feeling terrible, which shocked the plaid bastard into stutters and protest. But the warrior smiled and refused to accept it. The tacky-jacketed middleman then explained the *moran* had honored the sale, regardless of his paltry recompense, and would not go back on his word. I gave the warrior the previously suggested extra hundred plus a hundred more out of sheer guilt. Then I headed for the lorries. No more joy in owning this genuine article, only a boatload of shame over the thought of dry-fucking a guy while his brother pushed a knee in his back.

The rest of the day stayed on that emotional low, kept there by the insidious, crunching sacroiliac cruelty of the lorries. There were no beer runs at Baragoi and the hope of paved road in Rumuruti was of little comfort to our battered bones and arterial hemorrhages. But we did make it to Maralal early and took care of business in order of importance: bought cigarettes, got the tents up at the Yare Safari campgrounds, and then we got smashed. Knock-down, hi-pollutin' shitty drunk. Also had a long, overdue talk with Kalle McInnis. The way I see it, we're soon to entangle our privates like adrenalized mice in a musky sock, or to just become closer friends for the next ten days. Then we will leave East Africa and never speak again.

My journal clearly shows that I had attempted to document something at some point during the evening. I'm unclear on what I thought I could accomplish on paper after settling into so much alcohol. The script dabbled in *Cuneiform*, Etruscan *Linear B*, pretty little ant trails and not a single word in any language I actually know. I recall the pen spending so much time hauled into my throat as I tried suckling nicotine from it it's surprising I hadn't barfed all over the book. At least ten Tusker half-liters splashed in my belly before I ceased protesting the flow of that pernicious ale. Those were the ones I could recall having paid for or which had been donated to me. There were other incidents when one or another Kenyan guy would pull a full beer from a phalanx of empties and insist that I take charge of drinking it. Everybody was cutting loose. There were also thimbles of Camino Real Tequila, giving me one more thing to jot down on the list of Kenya caveats – *do not drink the tequila*. Tastes ever so faintly of agave and reeks oh so strongly of paint thinner. I wouldn't be the least bit surprised if they strained turpentine through a sisal plant before putting it into a used bottle.

But the nips added just the right boost to the beer's formaldehyde to get me out dancing. Chukumbi, the Zairean Lord of the Dance, gave me a quick how-to in the Zulu Hustle and Belgian Backslide. Then I got a few Kamba steps from Kitila and Ben Sila. And then any rhythm I'd managed to muster unraveled and left me with my own Frankenstyle footwork - stomping like an autistic gorilla and kicking over tables.

Somewhere in the dense smog of carousery I wound up in close quarters with Kalle. Sex talk again, always a popular topic for her, flavored this time by the subcategory of *Unusual Gratification Forms* and followed, naturally, by her lamentation over the present lack of any forms. And me sitting inches away with a platinum boner sponging up blood my contaminated brain couldn't spare. Is it necessary to explain the discomfort of sitting next to, getting howling drunk with, and listening to a beautiful woman rant about how crazy horned up she's become? It's just swell. Like having cramps in your eyelids.

She had yet to resolve the "is it alright to screw somebody in the few short weeks of scholarly endeavor?" issue. *Groovy sana,* we've got all the time in the world to sort that out. And I'm the pair of ears that gets to hear about it a whole lot. Whee! She weighs this shit out between her head, heart and vagina while I get mentally bound, whipped, and quartered. Largely because I don't jerk off. Never tried rubbing the urges or frustrations out manually and my screwball preference for the electrocuting brilliance of wet dreams no longer matters. While Kalle was getting misty solely on the *idea* of having a warm cock all I wanted to do was punch mine till it was nothing more than a fine, rusty powder. *Frrrggggh!* Just as long as she's airing it out, yes? She'll feel better for talking, no? Keen! This shit has just got to stop. If there had been more shots of that Mexican oven cleaner in me I might've suffocated her with a pillow, snipped out her genitals with pinking shears and taken them someplace private to scream at them.

I shouldn't put it that way. It belies the fact that I've become so ridiculously enamored by Kalle that I can't even bring myself to make a clumsy, drunken pass. Wouldn't have recognized a set of shears in that state anyway and tackling this woman and hoping passion trumps all her misgivings isn't the thing I want. Don't get this wrong - I want to screw her silly. Right after she brings herself to my tent and slides up to my face to say she's falling in love with me.

When she had become sufficiently unburdened she skipped off to bed. There was not a chance in this universe that I was going to hit the sack lonely so I went back to the Yare bar and bought a White Cap, the classiest dame Kenya Brewery keeps in the stalls.

I took that sassy brown honey back to the crib, popped her lid and sucked the brown out of her glass. She did her trick for me. Not only was my libido obliterated, that terminal beer rendered me completely senseless. The last thing I recall was feeling like a rubbery cicada nuzzling into the soil for a long rest; a good seventeen years before these grievous mating urges would need further attention.

At 10:38 a.m. Maralal Central Time I was face up on my sleeping bag staring at the ugliest animal I've ever seen. A god awful huge, mutated wasp. It was as grotesquely deformed as I felt grotesquely poisoned. Two thirds of it was waspish enough – head, thorax and wings were like the stuff of God's most badass bug. But its abdomen was something entirely different, extending like a tumorous knockwurst or parasitic maggot, the color of a spoiled yam. Maybe it was a queen hornet looking to discharge a glob of eggs into my chest. That nasty gut was of a similar fashion to the egg bag of the mother bug in *Aliens*. Aw fuck, it was going to pump eggs in my thorax so I'd burst into a swarm of gruesome little girls at the supper table. Dammit, that just wasn't the way I wanted to go out.

Then it came to me as I risked the agony of a chuckle and repeated the words *tumorous knockwurst*. The dirty little thing was a *sausage fly*, the winged male *siafu*, or safari ant. I'd run across this entomological oddball while reading a bug guide on the road to Koobi Fora. The *raunchwurst* dangling where a regular bug bum ought to be was a big old bag of sperm. That went a long way to explaining the ant party at my tent's doorstep. The girls were on the hunt for the guy. When they get him they'll chew off his wings, carry him home and then I'm lost on the process after that. Should have kept reading.

The sight wasn't making my morning a happy one and its soundtrack built on my nausea, drilled pits in my glands and spilled sewerage on the nice white slacks of my discontent. It clawed its little dagger feet over the net with a noise of a Pontiac being dragged over a guardrail a couple miles down the road. My hangover was coughing out nightmares so they could crawl over the mesh dome of my tent and take in the air. No doubt the acrid vapors leaving my skin and inflating this nylon morgue were vastly sweeter than whatever the fuck was braising in the casserole of my flesh. When there had been enough of this monstrosity I started to flick at its underbelly with my finger hoping for it to leave but expecting an explosive shower of angry ant semen. Each strike thudded on the surprisingly hard rind of the beast and it simply ignored the assault, intent on staying out of reach of the ladies out front. There was no evicting the vile squatter, so I crawled outside to have a cardiac arrest. Or at least to vomit.

I didn't throw up, incidentally, though I'd sorely needed to. The Maralal sun, burning off the morning cloud blankets, dumped buckets of hatchets and tonic water through my eyes. I fought back on the notion of barfing, positive that my cranium wouldn't stand the pressure of retching. Besides, all the caustic liquid in my gut ate holes through it, bypassed the rest of the lower GI system, and flushed into a sump of turpentine and radish pulp sitting heavy on my anus. I got to the toilets before the hot mess cooked my sphincter off, discharging all but the hookworms, leaving my innards ready for a refill of internal bleeding. A filthy story, but a distraction from uglier issues waiting outside the latrine.

Last night's near, *too close to call* and *never meant to happen* tryst with the exquisite Mme. McInnis had repercussions that went beyond her and me, resulting in restlessness among others. Sheila, specifically. This friend of mine, as far as you can judge the development of friendship in a six week crash course abroad...

Hold on, false start. A rephrasing is in order: It's less that she's a friend of mine than that she sees me as her friend. Wonder if I can explain that in a brief way that'll pave the way to the troubles today. No, I can't. My head's too scrambled. Good fucking Jesus do I feel sick.

We grew friendly while giving her a little attention a few weeks back. That last day of the road trip to Koobi Fora, she'd gotten intestinally fucked over by nanodemons which had previously lain quiet in her tubing. By the time we put in for the night in the sandy bed of the Il Nyongololong'atuk the bugs struck and she spent the dark hours geyser-puking and shitting right through her clothing. I'd slumbered that night at the thought of wild beasts howling in the wood, but apparently it had been the stricken Shelia wailing in distress. Later, as kids passed by in embarrassed silence I broke down her tent, and packed it. After giving it a badly needed wash down, as it was still wet with the anger of a Satanized bowel. This thirty-seven year-old fat lady quickly became very helpless, feeling like a whipped, incapacitated and very lonely child begging through her sobs to go home. There wasn't much of a chance of that happening right away. One night of rambunctious guts isn't enough to proclaim malaria and call a plane to pick you up.

In the big scheme it's become harder to get overly concerned as to when people live or die or get sick or feel blue. There are far and away too many individuals on the down side of life to get compassionate for anyone who hasn't already got history with me. But this is a different circumstance; a short-term artificial family was forming with lots of geographic isolation to deal with. Barely a week into this thing all were still just getting acquainted. That's why a vicious night of cramps and vomit and rectal magma could be the worst living hell Sheila may ever experience. Being sick among strangers – in the jackal and arachnid infested desert out in the middle of fucking nowhere – is a special brand of loneliness. Who does she turn to? Whom does she share a past of reciprocal warmth with? Absolutely nobody and that's devastating. That's when the stench of shit in your clothes stings a lot less than having to turn to a stranger and plead for help.

Fortunately, the director of this program is Dr. H, a walking well of kindness that could flood the Rift Valley. Luckily she hadn't first found slackjaw Waybill in her deep anguish. But by the time I'd been enlisted to help, the geologist had arrived. He was standing tranced-out near her fecaled tarps, craning his neck forward either to get a sharper gawk at the stains or help his gay-scooter mustache shade the saliva pooling in his lower lip. But her luck would run thin after that. There'd be hours to ride ahead and a couple dozen kids who hadn't come thinking they'd need to consider the feelings of ladies who'd soiled themselves in dysenteric nightmares. Unfamiliar peers who hadn't suffered so terribly themselves, so Sheila rightly had thin hopes for empathy. Crushed with stark embarrassment she could expect nothing more than cheap pity and backseat snickerings on bus rides around the Koobi Fora Spit. Alone in misery, how could she lift her gaze to meet the eyes of other students? She couldn't, that's how, so she focused her watery stares on her shoelaces for quite a while.

Ailing people aren't necessarily a drain on my personal resources. It's no complication to look after them for a while. Stuck in a prefab family for whatever it's worth and the survival of the clan requires spoiled siblings and cheap uncles to protect and tend each other in need. To the ends of expedient productivity, a group either repairs weak links or all goals are compromised. Besides, sick people snuffling alone and aloud are terrible for morale.

Strip away all superfluous motives and my concern for Sheila was nothing short of selfish. The deep tuition investment and profound interest in evolution had me expecting big returns from this field school. In turn, I expected a lot from the fellow gunnabees, lookieloos and seasoned bone monkeys. Doing my part to keep the experience working and not fucking it up for anyone else. On the same day Sheila went bitterly liquid I'd also helped H fix the radiator on his Land Rover. From greasy fecal stains on a tent to getting scraped, greased and gravel rasped under a truck, all the crud I'd gotten my elbows into that morning went for the same greater good.

From then on, Sheila became attached to me and in a very needy manner. Her situation stayed shaky, fingers precariously pinching her sack of marbles in an expanding decline. The severity of the intestinal episode lobotomized her sense of self-preservation as she grew oblivious to thoughts of keeping healthy out there. Desert living is a tough gig even for well-equipped field schools and kids with four-hundred-buck REI tents. Her psyche couldn't accept what the environment was doing to her physiology. Or she was just an idiot.

Maybe she *needed* the care. The *attention*, the artificially sweetened substitute for *love*, which debilitation had brought her way. Whatever the root, she started skipping food, shunned water and when her bowels dried up she was ridden with a fat case of heat exhaustion. Pale yellow, splotched with magenta and unable to sweat, she went wacky delirious. Clinically apeshit. We rehydrated her, but nobody had the correct wrench to screw her head back on. I kept up the visiting nurse routine, checking her bed in the mornings to see if she died in the night, making rounds to where she lazed away days under the open-air roof of the labs, fanning her flushed round head and waiting for her pores to get back to the business of perspiring. I was a good auntie, fetching things she needed and massaging her misery with a bottomless pail of jokes. Though thoughtfully tended by others, her mind insisted on slipping a little more. We kept at the supportive jive and I threw more jokes at her – those dredged from the abyssal part of the bucket were increasingly tasteless, insensitive, and appalling. Fucking hilarious, that is. Then I turned on hard sarcasm to get a rise out of her. If the patient wouldn't get happy, then why not piss her off? At least it would break her monotony of depression. Humor was failing so what the fuck? Nuns would laugh at some of my most depraved incest jokes - it's all in the delivery - but this bird quit chuckling before the gags got funny.

Sheila's participation in the Karari and Jarigole excavations never happened. Though she gave it a try the waterless Karari had midday temperatures knocking at 120, often burning right past it. The afterthought of bathing meant a half bucket of warm water every other day – if you were obsessed about cleanliness – and in the end she lasted about a day and a half before getting driven back to the convalescence of the Koobi Fora spit. The *Il Nyongololong'atuk* base camp at Jarigole was slightly less hostile than the Karari, as the proximity to Allia Bay cut the heat by a degree and offered daily bath trips to the lake. Somebody in Sheila's state could always catch a lift to sit in the cooling waters or wait for some crocodile euthanasia. But bad memories lay at Allia Bay for the old girl. Koobi Fora proper offered the best amenities for the infirm and there she'd remain. She did her field requisites with Burrows and the pile of dirt and arrowheads he administered on the spit. That lecherous, insane professor probably didn't help her much. His style of humor, corner window pervert with a touch of Dixie queer-hater, made mine look Quaker. When we'd regrouped at Koobi Fora in the final few days, Sheila greeted me with streaming yammers about Burrows's vices, mud storms, obscene diseases and animals that lived in certain parts of the Ozarks. I had to shield my eyes, as the screws were now flying out of her head.

The buddy thing became an itchy, allergenic albatross during that last week. She'd clutch my arm hourly to make me re-promise that I'd be there if her sanity went. *If?* Our porcine neurotic was snapping like mice under a truck tire. Sure, I'd be there - pouring water on her head to prevent combustion or strapping her up to pack in a truck. She needed to hear that things would all be ducks and bunnies soon; that there'd be hands to hold through the worst. We hoped the worst had already passed for this batty pumpkin.

This portrait of Sheila is probably more two-dimensional than she deserves. Look past the plagues Kenya had foisted on her and she's an alright gal. She is pretty sharp on humor. Or had been. Even without the heat exhaustion or flushing guts she was comically batshit to begin with and thus brought something important to the party: laughter and morale. Whether stroking our inner-Samaritans to assist her or laughing to the piss point as she unleashed her wit, we were mostly a smiling herd on the spit. She was driven by a desire to be liked by everyone. But aching to be universally accepted would work against getting back to a rosier state. Her physical and emotional health was far and away the most precarious but it certainly wasn't the sole trial on any given day. We had more issues than snakes on the spit, and Sheila relentlessly reached out from her shaded slouch to insinuate herself into the solution of each mini-crisis.

Yet issue-resolution was not her strong suit. She was more of an empathy-vacuum, sucking up tribulation until she was a co-sufferer with the original complainant. Picture something to the tune of *"Zoë said something really unkind to Rachel."* This would strike Sheila as strange because it's so unlike Zoë to be mean to anybody. Unless, of course, deep down she really is a viper which Sheila finds hurtful as she hadn't realized that *she'd* done anything to deserve Zoë's antagonism of Rachel. The world as it is would fog up for Sheila (Rachel is an unlovable twat; something even Jesus would point out) and the jokey gourd of the morning became a sobbing lard-ass you'd quickly lose sympathy for. It was frustrating to watch our efforts drain away like burnt orange urine pissed out in the Karari. Her do-gooderisms were self-damaging and invariably chafed the crap out of the original squabblers. Their issue would be settled via common annoyance at the deep cushioned invalid.

Ack. The better intentions go nowhere. I'm trying form a better picture of Sheila but I'm smearing it with ugliness. Something inside tries to re-imagine what's fair and objective, but my heart chokes it back, reminding all internal, conscience-related parties that we're always striving for that anyway. The subject matter can't always be perfumed and airbrushed into a dreamy haze. We don't go nose to knob with a daisy-covered shit heap and pretend to only smell the flowers. That butterball basket case couldn't cut life through a humid New Jersey spring, let alone survive doing field work near the equator.

So, we're pals for whatever the fuck that's worth. I've got a fistful of headaches and they originated at last night's party. Sheila was there with all her new friends and got wasted right along with us. She bought beers, danced and sat at low coffee tables shrieking with laughter as the group went through a drunken catharsis. Each of us owned up to special foibles and fuck-ups in liquored-up delight. She chummed up to Kalle who'd rant to anybody about the libidinous seethe in her tropical zones. And the divine McInnis whispered to Sheila that she may even "...*just ask Frank to screw her, as a favor from a good friend.*" Had I even known such an idea was being tabled, my current thoughts would have brighter tenor to them.

The intimation was innocent on Kalle's part. Nobody had any idea that Sheila had taken a romantic shine to me. The woman who does consume me with thoughts of long stemmed roses and matrimonial semen gave her a secret which was like poisoned ribbon candy in her beer.

As Kalle and I slipped off a couple of times to chat tongues wagged and Sheila's gut burned. Tethered by floss to a tiny anchor of emotional cohesion, the Tusker's and what she thought Kalle must be doing with me snipped her flimsy safety line. Off she sailed into a night of histrionics and hyperventilation. While lying face down this morning, having *not* been recently fornicated upon, I heard the big girl going through some paces. It was still dark, or I was suffering optical damage, as the wheeze of things brushing across tent fabric roused me. She was trudging among the teepees huffing, sighing and intermittently bawling like a fresh Syrian widow. After a bit of this weirdness zipping noises whizzed through the air and her wailing became muted. Turns out she barreled into one of my bigger classmate's wigwam to weep the morning away on the Sugar Bear's shoulder.

The *why* of all of that was yet an unknown in my crippled brain. Sheila braying mournfully at dawn, or at any hour, was nothing new. It was somebody else's turn to talk her down. I just turned myself over to discover that I had a crawling bratwurst on my ceiling to deal with.

She didn't want to give up the why when I ran into her that morning, all crawdad red and smearing tears across her face with a puffy backhand. That was good; in my state I didn't give a fuck if there was peace on Earth or inside of anybody. I also had inklings that what was eating her was something I'd never wish to know. Nevertheless, she was compelled to tell me anyway that afternoon. There was no escape from another one of her barreling inner-purgings. She wanted to say something, had been saying it to everyone else she'd cornered, and my running away was improbable. Any time I've tried to move quickly, the ground would shoot up vertically to greet me with wallop on the chin. Mean hangover. Cruel. There was hot peroxide still streaming on brain rinds and I felt like I was standing in the middle of a pool cover. Slowly sinking and unable to struggle out as it cocooned me into a blue vinyl submarine banana. And there was Sheila at the edge of the pool poking at me with the handle of a skim net and telling me why she's sad. She's got a crush on me and I was stuck in some lame wet metaphor with no way to cut my throat.

It was more than simply her romantic inclinations towards me; she'd started to believe that I felt the same about her, as I had been so nice to her, and when she saw the drunken chumminess and multiple exits with Kalle she realized that it just wasn't the case. This in turn made her "*feel so stupid*" and compounded the pain. I honestly understood what was going on inside her. Who hasn't been attracted to someone else under similar contexts? Somebody pays a little extra attention to you and, *whammo*, you're snagged. My first year of college was filled with women who really liked me, *but not in that way*. It's not exactly a mistake, but it's one we all make once in a while. At eighteen I was a comical, intriguing, overweight stoner who just shouldn't have been shaving his own mohawks. Sometimes our cannibis-slitted eyes dim the view on our own particular shortcomings. I was interesting back then but no calendar boy. On the other hand, you'd think she would've noticed that I'd spent five weeks trailing Kalle with all the lust of a chimp after a pie wagon.

We did smooth it out enough for her to be less uncomfortable around me. But it was plain that she wasn't going to be fully right with the whole business anytime soon. She made steps to chat up Kalle and even got some jokes in with both of us. It all came out forced, however, and every time her nervous giggles cease that heavy face drops back to the expression of a beaten puppy with a sour pickle in the kibble. Getting home can't come soon enough now. Back home, getting away from a social encumbrance is as simple as not answering the phone. Working to keep one hypersensitive freak grinning with some semblance of sanity through three squares a day has ruined my taste for people on the whole. I want malaria now more than ever. What sweet delirium that would be, yes? No one to hassle me except the guy who sloshes my bed pan away and the girl that sticks me with needles. I'll bet they'll be nice quiet folk.

Sweet Ass Freddie Odede

The paved road at Rumuruti slipped under our wheels today. Halfway from boozy Maralal to the dry gulch at Lake Nakuru. The ride became fat and smooth, promising far less dust-clotted snot to shovel out of my nose. But the luxury travel was short lived as our convoy thundered into an inertial sit a klik or so from downtown Rumuruti. There was a cracked plate around the stub axle of the Bedford lorry. Unfortunate shit of that sort leads to wheel wobble, something undesirable in a truck hauling people over the Rift Valley. The differential was also leaking oil *into* the brake drum. Again, something we don't want. Thousand-foot escarpments, students, truck, greasy brakes...no good.

There was an upside to losing time in that backwater camelopolis and it wasn't just the occasional stands of cedar and olive trees. Nor was it the peculiar population of tree stumps around the area. It wasn't even the pervasive aroma of dwindling cedar and olive trees being turned into charcoal. The bright spot was the loss of a day on the "Ecology Safari" down in Nakuru and Naivasha. My heart, tired and for once in tune with the rest of this gang, would be a hell of a lot merrier without too many days staring at a billion more antelope.

Don't get me wrong, I love Kenya's natural side and there is a good point to the ecological education. We've spent a lot of time kicking through dead earth looking for pieces of our ancestors, but finding them is just a step in understanding our evolution. Getting a picture of where and how they lived helps tackle the questions of what got them there and, maybe, why we got here. A quick look won't reveal that the Karari wasn't always a skin-cracking, hot gravel wasteland. But the ridiculous number of fossilized bones says otherwise. It was a more hospitable spread a couple million years back. What we need to get our heads around is just what sort of hospitable spread has a modern analog. Since the Karari (in geologic layers where hominids have been found) is lousy with hippo, big buck, small buck, gazelle, croc, hog, cow and monkey bones we need to look for places where we can see something like living hippos, waterbucks, reedbucks, impala, crocs, pigs, buffalo and vervets. *Lacustrine* forests like Naivasha, Nakuru and other wet, woody places in Kenya. A thorough comprehension of those environments means a better grasp of what ecological situations probably nursed us in our evolutionary cradles and which factors could have driven our development. So the ecology safari has an inarguable point to it. But now that we've *slept* in so much of the East African landscape and its animals, and have grown tired, whiny, cranky, hung-over and thoroughly *Sheilacked*, it's a point threatening to be over-made.

While kicking around in the brush, my friend, Frederick Odede, trotted over to hand me a mitt-full of *ochwoga*. That's the *Dholuo* word for the little red berries he'd been pulling off shrubs and gobbling up at the pit stop. Fred's had me eating off hedges everywhere we've been. That's taken some faith on my part since he's the type of mischievous bastard who'd trick you into swallowing a naturally violent laxative just for giggles - if he didn't like you in the first place. But we've gotten along swimmingly since meeting and now I love this lunatic more than many people in my own family. I'd eat a strip of thorny bark if he told me it would be delicious.

Now I just referred to Freddy as *my friend*. That warrants some reflection since *friend* as it pertained to Sheila caused a flooding vomit of discourse. Fred fits what most of us would define as a friend - doesn't ask for much and gives easily. He's been a wellspring of info on everything Kenya and a pretty good liaison to the various people and cultures we've run into along the way. And that wasn't always easy; though infinitely charming, he passionately loves to dick around with people. Being *Luo* doesn't help either. As the country's second or third largest tribe and noted as an intellectual people, many other Kenyans detest them. Goes to show just how racism can also be colorblind. On top of all the cross-cultural ambassadoring, he's freakin' hilarious and a hoot to get drunk with. And he's almost always ready as a drinking buddy since he's almost always drunk. Yesterday he took Vic and me through Maralal. While making sure we didn't get taken on the souvenir hunt he did an excellent job of crawling up the craws of the trinket hawkers. Already on edge from gobs of *miraa* stuffed in their cheeks, they stammered and spat like indignant gerbils, awfully pissed about the *Luo* who kept "putting his nose" in their deals. Once or twice we felt that violence was a heartbeat from eruption, making us wonder if saving a few shillings on spears and bracelets was really worth a gang fight.

Getting out without any scrapes was definitely worth a drink in Freddy's book. Getting out of bed without pillow marks is a boozing occasion in same book. It's a big book. So off he dragged us to some woman's home to have a taste of the *local beer* - Freddy's term for anything alcoholic from other places. At this lady's joint, *beer* didn't even come close to describing what we drank. If you added suds and took away eighty percent of the alcohol you might end up with something beerish. The shit was moonshine. The pernicious result of distilling sugar and molasses as far as they can go. Like rum with Hell's Angels' tattoos; full of damage but surprisingly smooth in its approach. The lady added a couple drops of water to my glass, as though it wasn't cloudy enough, and I had a drink that dangled dreams of a pleasantly fucked-up evening ahead. My stomach was so ripped up from the previous night that I restrained myself to a single greasy tumbler, providing me with ample fanny-tingle and swimmer's ear. With extra float in our eyes, Vic and I sank in and watched the Odede Show. Obviously he'd sampled the woman's supply earlier since his buzz kicked in like it was launched off a trampoline. For a bit he alternated from urging the beer lady to kiss Vic then advising her thusly,

"I am *fucking* you today!" It was the first time I'd heard an African use that word.

"Victor, did you hear that?!"

Vic didn't respond. The two of us were extra-relaxed. Internally massaged by the local beer, it left us more interested in letting Freddie roll than joining in the discussion.

"Victor! Did you hear me?" Freddie erupted again.

"Did you hear that, *Crocuta*? I am fucking her today!"

We had a howl, but the proprietress was under-amused and visibly irritated by his turgid eloquence. The juice filled our throats with giggles and my head with vile mischief. It crossed my thoughts to restrain the woman, should she fail to oblige on her own, if Freddy really wished to be fucking her. It abruptly occurred to me that this *changaa* was worse than tequila in its deviant incites. My demon was starting to salivate but I no longer felt like feeding the gluttonous fucker. Paranoia squeezed my head like a big humid buttocks, compounding an incipient claustrophobia. That was it for me. I got the guys up and out, half lifting a gleefully cackling Freddy as he downed a fresh tumbler and took one last swipe at our hostess' ass.

Outside the air was fresher, regardless of the humidity and hints of elephant turd. It all began to look sane again. For a moment I closed my eyes and sucked air in deeply. Bad move. I'd inhaled too hard because when my lids flipped open we were surrounded again by hustlers with those unblinking yellow eyes strangled by lacelets of umbilical neon and their gritty teeth with shit green gums. That's all from the *miraa*, which they stuff into their cheeks in small bales. This narcotic got some press coverage over the last year or so during the Somali War. Over in Somalia they call this weed *qat* and it was notorious for keeping Somali guerillas, or warlords, or *technicals*, or whatever the fuck we called them, at a high pitch of electrified meanness. Near as I can tell, *miraa* is like caffeinated sugar dusted with cocaine. Makes people viciously chatty and free to never sleep again. Some of the kids had five times as much vegetation crammed in their faces as the most chaw-addicted Major League first baseman.

66

[1]Freddy liked to call Vic *"Crocuta crocuta"*, the Latin for spotted hyena. He'd been using it ever since coming across it in our East African Mammal guide. It was also popular among other students and staff. It had a catchy hook to it; as nobody had even seen a *Crocuta* there wasn't much to warrant hearing it so often. Freddy Odede also called Vic *"Okote Member"*, referencing a strat layer in the Koobi Fora geologic formation. Really hard to say what these two had going on in terms of a relationship…

We were trailed back to the Yare by John, Francis, Nick and Isaac who still had knick-knackery to pawn; mostly cheap miniature spears and beaten copper bangles. I traded Francis some clean gym shirts for some shiny crap since we were *"brothers by name and must make business with each other!"* Isaac had a swank

Samburu lion spear he wanted me to buy and I really wanted to buy it from him. The school was crawling its way back to Nairobi, where getting anything authentic was going to cost me a hell of a lot more. And I had yet to score anything really unique. The spear in South Horr, although legit, looked a bit like any spear from the city's knock-off shops. It was a spear to throw at moderately sized animals, or people, but it was pellet gun next to Isaac's magnum. My loose funds were running low. I haggled casually, not letting on how badly I wanted that weapon to live in my apartment.

Half a mile from the Yare we stopped in a field so Isaac could demonstrate how to throw the rather heavy spear. He took a few jogging steps with the shaft on his shoulder then launched it with a motion that had as much upward thrust as forward, making it more of a lob rather than a hurl. The two metal sections wavered in the air as it flew about thirty meters and landed with a deep 45° stick in the grass. Neat!

Then he passed the spear to me and told me to give it a try. Oh boy, was I going to huck that spear for a record! I'd done some javelin throwing in high school and arrogantly believed that I could send that mother twice as far as my instructor. I took some powerful strides, almost breaking into a full run as I began twisting my torso to the right and back, lowering my arm and the spear behind me – that fucker was gonna fly heavenward and burn out on reentry. Isaac was shouting as I catapulted the lance…

"No! Don't! Oh my God…"

There was no time to worry about what was eating him as I watched the spear soar up in a magnificent parabola. Then it sped back to earth where it jammed with the piked tail end leaning forward, cracking the wooden shaft so the tail section could topple off and drag the head shaft down with a bridge of splinters.

Whoops.

I heard my mother, father, hobby store owners, K-Mart clerks, motorcycle salesmen, packie managers and a host of others chorusing: *You break it, you buy it!* Crap. This was the first time in twenty-six years that I actually did break the merchandise. Always have to do things my own way, even if I'd just been shown what to do. *My, my, what a jerk.* Oh, what a flair for slipping my head right up my ass on the drop of a dime. Isaac was hurt, let down, and deflated all over looking like I'd smacked him with a bag of dicks. Vic was chuckling in disbelief. It disappointed Fred, who wagged his head in reproach.

"You cannot throw a spear like that, man."

The haggling was over. That cocky hurl cost me my bargaining rights. The best I could venture then was to screw a whole lot of remorse into my voice and suggest that if he got me a new wooden shaft I'd buy the spear at his last price of 650*Ksh*. That brightened him up and he ran back to Maralal immediately.

It took us ten minutes or so to get back and it only took another twenty for Isaac to pull up on a creaking 3-Speed Schwinn with a completely refurbished spear. The walk from Maralal to where I broke the spear took close to an hour. But there he was with the new shaft carved from a fresh, white length of acacia, which fit even better than the first. That was some impressive ass-hauling.

"Stronger," he assured me, "Though, I think you know how to throw now…"

I gave him the dough and he asked if I'd throw in my hat. The black ball cap that I'd loved selflessly even though it fit funny. But he could've had my shoes for the asking, considering what I'd put him through to make the sale. He'd used up saintly amounts of patience, impressive geniality in his sales tact, and an awful lot of perspiration to close the deal. I got a stunning piece of African weaponry for twelve bucks and a used hat but could not take pride in my dickering skills.

Thinking some beer would shim my head to level, I set my sights on the tavern. But an ugly bovine lowing had begun beyond the Yare fence where Isaac left me - the sound of a clinically depressed cow with a stomach ache. It emanated from the direction of our tent city and within the camp enclosure the noise just got worse. It was like a gargantuan barn door roaring out moans as it was dragged open on antique hinges. But it was just a camel. I think I'd heard camel vocals in *Lawrence of Arabia* but the dromedary dialog never stuck to where I could put a face to the groan. But I'm sure Peter O'Toole's costars never performed any baritone caterwauling like this beast was making.

At issue was the saddle getting strapped on the animal, a situation that seemed to grieve the living shit out of it. One sees so many films of quiet camels hauling people on their humps that you'd have to assume they don't mind the work. But this guy was far from happy and only got madder as its Samburu handlers helped a fat white German get onto the tack. The groaning bullied other sounds out of the air but the jiggling maws of the rider's pasty pals made it plain they thought it was jolly fucking hilarious. The locals tried to find it funny too though they seemed baffled by their animal's displeasure. They finally got the clammy lump of Munich ham on top then pulled at a rope bridle and hit the creature with switches to make it stand and take a walk. Which it did, angrily and haltingly, as what was really vexing it came into view: the rear cord of the saddle was wrapped, strapped and pulled tight across its genitals. That kind of abuse is what gets broncos to go berserk for the rodeo. Yet all this animal did was complain up a storm. The jerk astride him couldn't see but guffawed heartily as his dumbfuck chums explained that a rope was nearly cutting his ride's pecker in half. Unbelievable - *a jackass on a camel.* How the fuck do people come to such disregard for the pain of other beings? All that mattered to these idiots was a lame tale attached to a mediocre snapshot from that dipshit's safari.

Now I needed to get into that bar. To get some beer inside me to cut the stress knotting up my neck. To cool the anger that was simmering up aneurysms in my head. And to write. But writing can be such a filthy fucking mirror. Seeing "*twelve bucks*" penciled out filled me with pangs of guilt. Fuck, I got away cheaply again. Of all the guys I've met in Maralal – no, in Kenya - Isaac was among the nicest. A sweet soul. After all the extra shit he pulled just to get me to buy the spear, after all his patience and refreshing, pleasant demeanor the least I could have done was to invite him to the bar for a beer. What was I doing there alone? *Where was my camel?*

With little else to say in my self-soured state, I just did some pencil work as per the request of Freddie. He wanted to know what Eskimos lived in so I doodled him up an igloo. He also wished to know how many shillings it cost me to come to Kenya, so I broke it down. Calculations of trip costs translated into Kenya shillings: 279,550. A little mess of numbers representing tuition, airfare and gear. It was a little shocking to Fred when I showed him later. I'm a bit stupefied too knowing that after two months and northwards of six grand I'll be flat broke when I get home.

Getting Murdered by Snakes

Going Potty Outside, reprise. Bunches of places in the world have huge populations of venom loaded snakes. Where'er thar be snakes of poison stock, ye be hard by to find a yon crapper, cozy and safe, nigh, aye. 'Tis because poisonous snakes...*What the fuck did I just write?* Christ, two-day hangovers and Lariam are bad combo. Anyhow, venomous snakes are intelligent, sagacious, swaggery and downright smarmy reptiles. Real ruinous jerks from time to time too. Sorcerers of camouflage, they're indistinct from their surroundings, looking exactly like dirt, or twigs or the hole you scooped for a toilet. They will not reside in well populated towns or cities because humans look ridiculous, smell funky and are notoriously loud. Our astonishingly inane conversations confederated with clattering utensils directly influenced all urban (and a high fraction of suburban) vipers to take their own lives. Suicide is sacrosanct among snakes and their Supreme Being routinely sends such sinners back to the mortal coil as sterile turtle eggs or mongeese with Down syndrome. Naturally, this peeves the shit out of their country cousins. So they hate like hell to see us arrive on their real estate and take great pains to drive us back to our street lamps and department stores.

The best terror tactic in the snake book, whenever it finds a bipedal moron curling feculence in their yard, is to bite it square in the anus. Once the individual has been envenomated, the rest of the group, if there is one, will be stricken with mass constipation, screeching and shrieking back home like bastards from the whip. And what would you do if you were to receive an adder bite on your bare hiney? Why, pull out your survival knife or loop your belt over a tree limb and kill yourself!

What else could you be expected to do? Where in the heck-all hey-now would you twist a tourniquet? Maybe, and it's a very outside maybe, there's a friend who might suck the poison out? That would be a mighty fine friend without a doubt. Somebody to put their lips at your taint to slurp venom-laced blood right after you've defecated? That just sounds deviant. Not to mention useless, even dangerous to the sucker, so there isn't much room for this variety of fun. It's as hopeless a situation as you could ever dream of. You're a weak link in the food chain now. Your brain failed to warn you that you have no natural need to be any place where it isn't safe to have a bowel movement. Own up to it. Pull up your trousers, smile wryly for wasting the potential of your parents' sperm and egg and cut your throat. Our god no longer holds suicide to be a sin. He has seen what we've become, how we live and how we fuck it all up. He's come to expect it and wouldn't mind having us clear out sooner for earthly dominion to be assumed by the octopuses and cuttlefish.

Nyahururu

This had been the most surreal of evenings I've had in Kenya. I've come as close to an animal related death as I need to, been terrified by phantasmic clawed spiders and I've wandered over the edge of my former cosmos into the unbridled night of the mean desert. But putting in for the night at Thompson Falls has barely registered as an actual event. It was more a fatigued dream, reeled out a day or two into a methamphetamine crash when the brain conjures banalities with no spare energy to get very ugly or frightening.

As shit falls off truck chasses or out of the engines we never know where we'll end up bunking at the end of the day. There's the goal - *We're headed for Nakuru this evening.* And then there's the contingency - *Plan B (We do not make it to Nakuru this evening),* which is what ultimately brought us to the Thomson's Falls Lodge in Nyahururu. Still had to sleep in tents, but it beat pitching them in ditches on a feral roadside without a bar. Or showers. I couldn't have hallucinated that because I don't think I'd freeze myself like that on purpose in dreamlife. Dr. H worked out something with the proprietor, allowing everyone a rinse in an actual bathroom with an actual indoor floor and *fresh* water. With the exception of the coffee cup baths in the Karari, we'd been bathing in saline lake water, which also fed the base camp showers, for about a month. It was nice to have some unsalted water to asphyxiate the seaweed colony in my hair.

I hadn't had a good look at my hair in over a month. Hadn't had much face time in mirrors altogether, as I'd never packed one. In the swankest motel on the Equator I got myself fully undressed before turning to the looking glass over the bathroom sink. My limbs jolted askew, almost downing me on the wet tiles, ambushed by the sight of a shaggy, goobly-eyed maniac in the latrine with me. Reddened rills snaked through the dusty, dark wool falling over his chest and back. Having left home at a healthy two-hundred five pounds, this skinny infiltrator and his scraggly red beard were in for an ass-whuppin' if they took one step closer. But what a good deep tan he had – all my Irish skinned life I'd longed to get good color like that. *Holy fucking melanocytes!* That homely bastard was me and I was tan! All it took was a few deep base burns from the African sun and I browned up as nice as anybody. Wow. I stared at me for a bit and wondered how long that Alpine whitehead had been poking through the whiskers on my chin.

Twentieth in line doesn't get you much hot water and that's a little rough since Nyahururu has a cool climate. But clean is clean, and getting to the bar later meant my beer came from deeper in the fridge. Cold beer is cold beer, whether you've walked twelve blocks in Yuma or woke up at the South Pole, it does the trick. There's no other way to drink it.

Whether road weary, lit up with lagers, in shock from the self-encounter or thickened by a case of the sniffles, the rest of the evening gyrated around my dampened senses. Thick pillows stuffed the atmosphere while my irises polarized and halved the light of the dusk. I got chummy with an apple-green chameleon plucked from a tree and who turned charcoal to go with my faded black sweater and damp, dark hair. I called him Paul. I thought all my friends would love Paul too, but it turns out that a little lizard on my shoulder made my new Kenyan pals recoil with profoundly horrified expressions. Some believe that chameleons are quite dangerous – venomous and vicious. Line up to assess that one you ethno-historian jerkoffs! How did this little reptile, ferocious as Frosty the Snowman, come to strike terror in the local souls? Was it the teensy horns on a wee triceratops head? Its habit of moving its cowled eyes in different directions at once? Does it tear people's ears off as they sleep? I made efforts to have Sila pet Paul, to no avail. It was getting dark and I worried that Paul might catch my cold so I gave him back his tree. Its limbs were drenched with the exploding dew. Everything was getting wet and cold.

Dank and frigid enough for me to nuzzle deep and tight into my bag without taking off my pants, sweater or ugly, blue foul-weather coat. Socks remained on too and that's how my family would come to know that I'd died in a cold, cold night. I can't sleep with stocking-bound toes unless the chill makes my fat metatarsal sausages hurt. A far cry from undies-only sleep in the unmoistened air of Koobi Fora, the contents of my tent clumped to me like sugar on a bead of spit. I felt like a snail in cheap sheets and endured a prolonged, hazy consciousness itemizing all that I found distasteful about camping. I've never had an issue telling good buddies to take flying fucks over invitations to join them on sleepovers in outdoor New England. Karma was riding my ass again; after days spent on hot, dry African roads, I still have to go to bed in New Hampshire.

Exhaustion was squeaking past discontent for the win when the tent flaps began whispering to me. I pulled them in to tell them to shut the hell up and wound up nose to nose with Kalle. The murmuring nylon must have gotten to her too, but she asked to come in anyway. She'd been lying awake and didn't want to be alone any longer. She wished for a body to lie against and an arm to pull her close. She just wanted to be close to me. In my fatigued state I brought her in and only managed to understand that this was *something*. And something probably needed to be done about it. I could not, however think of anything. Dutifully, I draped an arm over her and softly squeezed her into my multiple layers. The scenario was a tight arena begging for action, but my thoughts pawed at missing doorknobs, unable to gain entry and make it to the stage. Libido beat itself against portals in distant halls while romantic proffers, tangled in bathrobes and stilts, lay at the exit locked out from within. The Sandman shouted torpor from the pulpit and I was at the collapse of consciousness again when Kalle abruptly got up.

"I'm going to go now," the canorous shadow of her voice slipped from the tent as the flaps shushed out my goodbye. Despite the desperate, far off harangues from romance and carnality that I get the hell up and go to her tent, the lights went out on it all and plunged me backside into slumber.

Such a sound sleep. I woke late, allowing the cacophony of plastic tea cups and daybreak banter to fully crescendo before finally pulling out of my low-temp humidity chamber. Kalle was finishing a mandazi as she smiled a tired "Morning…"

I held her last night. Regardless of my enervation I knew that it was Kalle, not the tent door, who whispered for me. It was her; she had lain full against me while the fresh water smell wafted from her curls into my dreams. But nothing about the atmosphere steaming across from our morning drinks lent much support to this idea. She'd driven me in yet another circle to another morning as usual. We were headed to Nakuru now and another night in a tent where I could see if this crazy dream kept on looping.

Nature Boy

Business tonight was scribbling pictures of chameleons and stick figures of fossil 1470 into my beaten book. And some shivering. Shivering because it's cold again. I'm wrapped up uncomfortably in my sleeping bag - *Buy the fairy blue one! It's rated as toasty down through 40°!* - with a sheet inserted around me in a bunching, constricting fashion...*for warmth*. Don't that beat all? I'm in Africa, close enough to the equatorial line to hang laundry on it and I am fucking chilly. Camping had been a pleasure up until last night, but that's because it had been mostly desert camping. For sleeping outside you can't beat the feeling of crawling into an arid tent with your camping sundries moving independently of each other. You can shift anything you've got in there, sleep sack, notebooks, dirty socks and without a molecule of moisture to stick it all up the litter responds with a dry, soothing whisper. The only liquid is what lies trapped in the orifices or beneath your bulk on the bedding. You can sweat freely in the heat and it will leave the exposed parts of your body in vapor to be annihilated in the sere atmosphere and scattered through the fabric screens at either end of the teepee. Whatever you ooze from pores in contact with the open sleeping bag will get sumped deep into its thirsting fibers, parched from a day without a perspiring body inside. It's only a few hours before the sandy earth outside radiates away its store of heat and the cooling desert gales swirl through the tarps so sleep can be finished with the bag folded over your torso. Nice, nice. Not like this raw clammy crap again tonight. This bites. Worse than living in a Cape Cod basement. Fit for salamanders or summering lungfish or Bangladeshis, but not for me.

This is what I'd dreaded when I'd heard the field school would be living in tents for extended periods. This is precisely the repugnant experience that had turned me off from camping as a kid. There was my first outing as a four year-old in woods near Ft. Bragg in North Carolina. What began as a magical journey into my dad's Army life – picked up at home by a military transport truck, taken with other boys for a Father & Son's weekend at an 82nd Airborne Division training camp with toy guns and real Howitzer canons – became sullied with the chores of digging circular trenches, pitching huge musty tents within them so we could sleep in a viscid, mildewed shelter.

Later, as a third grader in Yuma the old man took me and my kid brother for a night under the sky where the Colorado River ran close to home. Desert camping, my first taste of it and it was sweet. The annual Inner Tube Race was on and we cheered the sight of fat folk slipping through the current while drinking beer on inflated tire guts. Kenny and I thrashed about in the river and dug up riparian clams until he got swept into the stream. I had to rescue him by pushing his flailing body into the weeds by the bank. That ruined it for him but left me with the new game of hiking upstream, jumping into the current, then paddling furiously for the reeds as it brought me back to the campsite. There were hot dogs for dinner, a trillion stars smeared like paste across the sky and going to bed in the warm, dry night.

Camping could have worked its way back into my blood after that night. But then Dad cooked us breakfast - oozy scrambled eggs and sausages under-fried on tin foil over a charcoal hibachi. Something went wrong, and it may have been the old man's culinary ability. Or the Arizona clams we'd eaten were catching up with me just as the half-cooked breakfast links were going in. Dad's cooking had a fairly damning track record. Of the three creative dishes I can recall him making us in the years before that outing - Ptomaine Pheasant, Cheesecake Porridge, and mac & cheese baked with tuna – it was only that last box and can combo that we were able to keep down. Either way, clam poison or botulism, a hot afternoon of barfing left me with no stomach for camping, desert or otherwise, for years to come. I was done with breakfast sausages as well.

One more stab at this outdoor living horseshit would come later on a visit to my father in Arkansas. Outdoor sleep seems stuck in the hearts of Vietnam vets or in his generation in general. What the fuck is wrong with roller coasters for family fun? In the end, the caving and bat watching turned out cool. Canoeing and trying to catch a water moccasin with an oar while my stepbrother bawled in terror had been exquisite. But a syrupy tent, a sleep sack cloying as a duck's vagina, a swollen hand oozing from a brown recluse spider bite and fuck all that back-to-nature noise! There was no way I'd ever camp again until I was old enough to be drunk enough for it to make sense. After high school, hippie convert pals would offer spots on their woodsie outings,

"We're going to Maine to camp, wanna come? We got acid..."

"You wanna go to Purgatory Chasm? We got tents...and acid!"

I'd say that going along would be swell, long as they understood that after the acid wore off and we headed for bed I'd be kicking everyone in the balls, girls too, to make sure we *all* had a lousy time. Now I'm back in the cold. Nakuru's mucky mists and my squishy sleeping gear are almost a kick to my own nuts - if there were anything left to boot beyond the glistening, tightly collapsed testicles hiding beneath my wet fatigues like violet raisins tangled in a toupee. This is Africa? Where'd the hot go?

Of course, it can make fine sense to be cold in an equatorial place. Lay out all the pertinent geographical data about Kenya and there you have it, the reason the school directed us to bring warmer clothing: Here at Lake Nakuru we're about 5761 feet above sea level. That's a mile and a half towards the stratosphere and good cause to feel refrigerated at night. The high side of the eastern Rift Valley catches all the climatic slop sliding in from the perimonsoonal mayhem of the Indian Ocean. Nakuru's sun can still cook you into a chicken-fried tarheel, but that's only when it's shining. In late August, at least this year's late August, the clouds dominate for much of the day, breaking only at lunch. Under their jurisdiction, wind, mist and rigid nipples are the rule.

A moistened, fitful course of sleep was only one of the nocturnal irritations. As I lay griping about meteorology in the tenuous safety of the tent our camp was being raided by olive baboons. *Papio anubises*. Three-foot forest thugs. Smart, sinister, high stepping dandies with their polished fangs and naugahyde bum patches - *ischial callosities*, the Latin smart-talk for 'chapless backs'. They were in the trees as we all turned in, waiting for the village to go quiet so they could sneak in and steal anything left unsecured. Hard to judge by sound exactly what sort of vandalism they were up too. But every so often there came a noise like rain falling on a tent. One thick stream of rain at a time. Some of the dirty fucks were swinging up in the fever trees and pissing all over us. They were making one mother of a racket and it sounded like more monkeys were circling in from the forest. Higher pitched *wheeeets* and *eeeechts* so my guess was that the vervets that had been scrounging our digs for peanut butter earlier were on the way back and stuck in the queue. They were waiting for the baboons to finish going to the bathroom all over the place so they could comb the camp for any finer grained leftovers. Good for them. Industriousness is a wonderful quality for a monkey.

Since I've been lobbing around the Linnaean names and bland trivia I might as well give fair time to the vervets. As the name suggests, they're also known as green monkeys. *Cercopithecus aethiops*, with subspecies all over Africa and in laboratories the world over. The green monkey has often been a suspect as the primate who gave the world a virus which kills people who pump opiates into their arteries, worship Liza Minnelli or just like to fornicate a whole bunch. The original HIV patients, or their kinfolk at least, were swinging all around with the high hopes of finding spoons that the baboons didn't already snatch. I don't really have anything more accurate to offer on AIDS or vervets. Can't even recall what the original virus was called. *Simian Immunodeficiency Virus*? *Monkey Pox*? Did it spread to humans via wild monkey love here in Africa or, as conspiracy dinks love to think, was it inoculated in vervets lucky enough to get government housing? All of a sudden I couldn't care about it. I was getting real drowsy even in the din. Vervets are sweet little twits anyhow, loads nicer than baboons. Not that baboons are emphatically nasty. Unprovoked, that is, and it's probably better to run into one while holding a fat rock.

I stepped out to pee and to rouse myself enough to finish my field journal coherently, having just logged an entry which ran

"...going to my fist don't like the to take to he punching for face..."
Drowsy belligerence towards monkeys. The baboons were
moving to a nearby camp and sped it up when I got outside. The
vervets were indeed right behind them, followed by giant forest
hogs, rooting up deeply buried garbage and feasting high. Deep
snorts countered the trebling cacophony above like subwoofers.
Hogs are easier to slumber along with than *a capella* monkey
screeching.

The big, huge animal racket started in earnest an hour later,
rousing me from a funny nightmare. The hogs were pitting grunts
against the Virginia girl's snoring as they rooted in rubbish pits
for pig treats. The baboons went out of control, wailing like
banshees with stubbed toes as the vervets screamed like home-
schooled crack babies. And something suddenly sounded like
elephants, so much so that I forgot about sleep and grew worried
as hell that pachyderms were coming to town to squish tents like
snails.

But there'd been no elephants, or even baboons doing elephant
impersonations. In the morning the crew said the strange bellows
had come from two lions swaggering through camp. That had
sent the baboons batshit, though it's suspected a leopard may
have grabbed one of them as well. Who knew? As far back as
watching Marlin Perkins on *Wild Kingdom* in the seventies I'd been
led to believe that lions growled menacingly like '69 Chevelles, or
just roared. I know now that they also sound like blasting
trombones with murder in their slides. Good thing I'd gotten out
early to take a leak. Any later and the cats might've seen my tent
as a red and gray hippo birthing a fresh pink entrée.

Learn Yerself Dumb

We began the Eco-Safari in a fogged-in Lake Nakuru morning. Spinning towards the mists of the shore, we came across the desiccated remains of a female waterbuck, *Kobus defassa*. Wasn't it a *K. ellipsiprymnus*? *No...ok...you're sure about that?* The voice just said it was definitely *defassa*. A big pack of bones held in their original arrangement by the animal's dried up leather outfit. The mouth had been drawn shut by dehydrated facial skin making it hard to see the teeth. The dental work of an animal, especially where adult creatures are concerned, is what offers a fair idea of how old the beast was at death. A glance at the choppers won't provide an exact age like *"This ellipsiprymnus, Defassa, whatever the fuck it is, was eight and a half when she died!"* But tooth wear, excluding animals that eat lots of rocks or only pudding, will point to a relative age. As in, *"This buck was a young adult"* or *"This girl took the shuttle bus to bingo."* It's very important in paleontology because knowing relative ages at death allows us a picture of what was happening to a group of ancient animals at a particular point in time. A fossil assemblage consisting of mostly old animals could suggest a healthy, thriving population where everybody got to retire before croaking. An even mix of old and very young animals insinuates that a group was subject to standard predation. A high, concentrated count at all ages speaks of catastrophe – flood, famine, extreme predation, disease, cult suicide, et al. Finding the bones of a single creature of any age doesn't do much for population info, but today it was beside the point. We're being educated in the *Tao of Paleoanthropology* here; there was a deceased waterbuck lying on the crusty salt shore of Lake Nakuru. *How old was it?*

The question was put to us by the instructors. Everyone had a good look at the carcass. Some tried peering into its rawhide pucker then stepped back to murmur their guesses. I got down and stuck my survival knife into the wrapping of the waterbuck's jaws. I really shoulda seen it coming...

"Frank! Stop! Don't do that – it's gross!"

"Eeeewwww"

"Don't do that, y'gonna have worms all over the place."

The last protest came from archaeopervertologist, Burrows. I backed away, disappointed as living fuck, because we're supposed to defer to the scientists. He'd been here before. He knew what was what. Praise Jesus that he stopped me from releasing the worms. The waterbuck was dust-choked like a vacuum cleaner bag and salt was powdered through the crisp fur of its hide. With such an utter absence of moisture in the body it, *oh golly yes,* had to be pure paradise for maggots and mealworms. A jizzlobbing jackass, but he had the support of many in our group. Freddy was chuckling; at least he was always on my team. I'd been growing suspicious of an increasing number of morons within our ranks. It had turned out far worse – many of them were becoming archaeologists as well.

Nobody had even bothered to ask how a tasty feast like that had managed to go uneaten. A perfectly good waterbuck drying into jerky without so much as a nibble on it hints at trouble in Nakuru. This is Africa, nothing should go to waste. Where were the predators? How about the vultures? Something was out of balance and whole antelopes decomposing in peace warranted some inquiries. Burrows wasn't posing any, so I did.

"How come it hasn't been eaten?"

"What?" Knocked out of a deviant daydream, Burrows scowled to find me asking questions again. The crazy butcher with sheep and goat head issues was at it again...

"It dried up but nothing took a bite out of it. Does that make sense?"

"Dunno. The hyenas probably didn't find it yet...it's foggy."

"What about cats? There wasn't any fog yesterday…" Burrows face twisted in like a bunghole, challenging his glasses to stay on his beak.

"They're all probably at the other side of the reserve. Geeez, what's the matter – you afraid of lions or sumpin'?"

Again I led myself astray trying to delve into the themes of our studies. On the Eco-Safari stretch of the school shouldn't we be focused on the ecological state of things? How can archaeologists expect to reassemble the puzzles of fossil ecologies if they don't really examine what's happening in the ones around them. It struck me that we've always been restricted to learning nothing more than what's planned or conceived of by teachers. Didn't matter that we'd spent weeks trying to absorb the wear patterns on a range of animal teeth, getting a lock on the waterbuck's age turned out to be on nobody's mind but mine and I wasn't permitted to find it out. The dearth of predators and overall health of Nakuru's ecosystem also appeared to be a lonely concern. Why ask questions? Why show an interest in anything? Every time I try on nicer thoughts about Archaeology, one of its bastards drops a turd on my shoe. *Vive! Vive les sciences préhistorique!*

The afternoon game drive was refreshingly identical to yesterday's. It meant seeing the same animals doing the same stuff – standing up, lying down, staring back at us. Similar monotone lectures as well, *"…each year millions of greater and lesser flamingos come to Nakuru every year from all over the world including Tampa to gather together by the millions the lesser can be distinguished from the greater by size and color darker pink or whitish they get their color from the tiny shrimp they eat here in the lake which has high salinity which is good for shrimp…"*

I gotta ride with somebody other than Waybill next time out. He can really suck the wonder out of a moment. Not by revealing the secrets in nature's magic, mind you, his voice simply suppresses awe of any kind. Probably safe to bet that when I get home I'll recall that first sight of infinite flamingos as a duller event in life. Other points of interest were huge herds of zebras. *There are really two types of zebra actually around here Burchell's and Grevy's distinguishable as both have black and white markings and are relatives of horses who migrated from North America after horses evolved there long long ago before zebras met Burchell…* I made that up just to be an ass. Drone it out in a monotone to see how easy it is to nod off as a hundred zebras thunder by your truck.

The warthogs were rutting today, so we all got a pornographic pig peep. As a man who's been there, I was full of empathy for one particular hog. Started to get into his girl's pants only to have her squirm away and bolt, leaving him no choice but to chase her across the lawn with a wagging boner. That'll teach him to hit on sober chicks. But, to get the animal stuff out of the way, here's how the rest of Nakuru's beasts get on:

Common Waterbuck, *Kobus ellipsiprymnus* - Do absolutely little but hang near lakes, as they are *obligate drinkers*, in herds with a 50/50 gender blend. They look at things and later they die. Hold it a minute, I think I mean Defassa Waterbucks, *Kobus de-oh-fuck-it*, the difference is brown vs. browner. We found another corpse at the park's waterfall. *Makalia Falls* isn't exactly huge, high or very awe-inspiring but it is awful pretty as the water cascades over a fifty meter wall of rock into a cavey, covey, greeny laced pool. It's almost famous since Tanya Roberts gave her tits a good rinse under there in that shitty movie *Sheena*. Maybe it was *Beast Master*. Coulda been both. Thank god she can't act. Real talent could lead her to serious roles and 'no-nudity' clauses in her contract. But back to the waterfall itself, which isn't the crystal shower of liquid seen splashing all over Tanya's magnificent rack. As it begins its descent, the water has the yellowed, dirty look of the shallow stream feeding it. My tits would need to be very, very dirty to make a shower at Makalia worth the wetness. But back to our other dead waterbuck. It looked as though, prior to its demise, the antelope lived above the falls. With an unnatural twist to its neck that couldn't have come from dying *in situ*, it could have tumbled off the cliff before or after it croaked. In the beating sunlight it stunk like a Spanish gym and attracted more flies than a Biloxi hooker. Some joker suggested I go cut it open. Not a fucking chance. The corpse was so bloated, its hide so taut over the ballooning, festered innards that if a fly landed on it too hard there'd be an explosion of fizzing guts and rotten ooze.

Waterbucks must taste awful. We've come across two that hadn't been scavenged by anything other than bugs and bacteria. Something is amiss with Nakuru's predators. Disease? Culling?

Poaching? *Hmmm...*I wonder how they cleaned the water to make it look so glisteningly perfect on Tanya Roberts' breasts?

Bohor's Reedbuck, *Redunca redunca* – Same habits as waterbuck's, only shier about it because they're smaller and socially awkward.

Impalas, *Aepyceros melampus* – One male impala gets all the women. That's a very twisted rule unless you're that one twisty-horned guy with the sex appeal. Then it's a golden life with a harem of thirty-plus lithe, leggy antelope ladies that you get to poke anytime the mood hits. The females are forbidden to even look at other males, quite an Islamic set-up. In the meantime, the other boys form their own bachelor herd. A goon platoon of gazelle dorks which loiters near the sex party looking disappointed and ribbing each other about who's the worst at not being able to score with the chicks.

Southern Bushbuck, *Tragelaphus scriptus* – Southern? Isn't this *East* Africa? I'm slowly learning not to ask... Kind of like impalas on steroids, these thick antelopes appear one or two at a time. They munch on leaves, because they're *browsers* and generally behave as though they should have taken a left turn at Albuquerque. Or Johannesburg. Is there such a thing as an *Eastern* bushbuck? Anybody?

Burchell's Zebra, *Equus burchelli* - Nothing like goddamned Europeans, particularly the freaking British. Naming critters after themselves as if God did such a swell job making them they'd better grab some of the credit. Yes, I know American scientists are no less culpable in this business. But fuck Europe anyway and all of its ugly, fucking Europeans. Got it? I have no idea why but it's just where I'm at emotionally right now. Anyhow, zebras: just like water bucks, only not drinking as much and they never die.

Grevy's Zebra, *Equus grevyi* – Don't ask me. Maybe Grevy could tell the difference between his zebras and Burchell's. But I can't and even with field books and doctorate degrees neither can anybody else.

Thomson's Gazelles, *Gazella thomsoni* - Tommies! Ain't that continentally frigging cute? Trotty little antelope shits that race in insane circles to make zebra herds go berserk.

Grant's Gazelles, *Gazella granti* - Not "granties" though. Grant, Tommies, Grevy, Aaaaaugh...Fuck! I'm going to hike through fucking Europe with brass knuckles and a bucket of urine. Somebody needs to take it in the teeth for this animal-with-people-names crap. Goddamn! Whoa! I don't have a clue as to why it's pissing me off so. I may even be entirely incorrect and all these English names could have been given by and in honor of Americans. Or Canadians or Aussies or little rotten pig-diddlers from Belize. I don't know, don't care and *fuck! fuck! fuck! fuck!* I do so loathe the British. But more about them and why they grate me another time.

Grant's gazelles do uncanny impersonations of Tommies, albeit in a dumb, bigger-brother ape sort of way. They lack the thick, black racing stripe of Thompson's gazelle's. And doomed to Thomson's shadow, Grant lacks his own waterfall.

Elephants, *Loxodonta africana* – Yes, we have no elephants here in Nakuru. Big ears, big everything. What else is there to tell?

Warthogs, *Phacochoerus aethipoicus* - At Nakuru, these pigs are the ruling class. There are more here than there are rats in Boston's North End. Usually they just grunt about between the legs of their giant henchmen, the Cape Buffaloes. At other times they run in trenches and ram their heads into the earth. And, on sunny Tuesday mornings (A lie: like I know what fucking day of the week it is out here) they pork for public viewing.

Leopards, *Pantera pardus* – No English goon has laid claim to the leopards. *Pantera* means lion and *pardus* means spotted. There you have it: a leopard is its own, unlicensed animal; just the way it would be with all beasts if strict Latin was still the rule for naming things. I wonder what language the Romans used for scientific nomenclature? Celt? I can picture some toga clad archaeologist excavating a Mycenaean site and coming across a decorated clam shell…

"Wow! Herodotus, come over here…I've found something interesting!"

"What is it, Asinus? Oh, that. We had hundreds of those at the digs on Crete. It's just another *cunt* from Atlantis."

We've run across much more evidence of leopards than we have actual leopards. The baboon retreat of last night could have had partial leopard roots and bones dangle from trees all over the place. On a little urine-related morning stroll after tea and mandazis I spotted the head, spine and rib cage of a reedbuck slung over a branch in a fever tree - about thirty feet up! The big kitty must have just finished eating it. What little remained of the buck's meat was still moist, glistening crimson in the breakfast sun. Wicked tasty sight. Ah, leopards! Genteel panthers! Quite on the beam, so to speak. Man's best friend in Nakuru as they eat baboons and frighten lady archaeologists. That statement reminds me that I've recently begun to toss out some real chauvinistic, misogynistic even, thoughts. Well, *hakuna matata*. I'd like to feel guilty over it but I'm pretty sure it'll get worse, perhaps devolving into a bad bigotry gripped in a seething rant about retards, dwarves and excessively freckled children.

Germans, *Deutschelandus dumbphucki* - Visual and audial pollution. Crane necked, jugheaded primates which dress atrociously and speak bowling-ball sharp gutterances such as, "*Ja, Sigmund, vere you seeing that funny bird flying near the tree vich is so very far from ein giraffe and the leaves it appears reluctant to be eating?*"

Whenever the Germans leave, game wardens have to go pick up the snakes stretched dead near bottles of whiskey and sleeping pills. Getting stuck behind some Germans while hiking trails, we find ourselves picking up smoldering cigarette butts and handing them back to the littering Deutsche *fuckvadzen*.

Italians, *Latinus stuggatzi* – Tough to find many around. Planes known to be carrying them to East Africa get shot down by Ethiopia. The ones that make it here, or were left behind after Mussolini retreated, have stuck around and opened trattorias. Of all the fucked up things I've come across since arriving, this one tickles me greatly: You can get some really fine pizzas here in Kenya.

Jesus. All this talk of animals, women and pizza has left me with a giant hankering for a basketful of blow-jobs. Or a good bottle of tequila. On second thought it doesn't have to be all that good. Just real tequila rather than the jaundiced liniment carried in Kenyan bars. But I can't see either gift arriving anytime soon. Tonight will be another spent in fitful slumber, unconsciously grinding my dork against nylon-covered earth while gnawing the collar of my sweater. A hamster burning off stress.

The locals suddenly burst into music this evening. A tribal drum and chant number. It was fairly loud but there's no way to gauge how close it was with the eerie way sounds travel in the lake basin. It's as though the salty expanse of water is a woofer, the cliffs resonators and the nighttime trees are thousand-watt amps. It might have been in a camp clearing next to ours or could've been a kilometer away at the Nakuru Lodge. Volume aside, it was so soothing that I'd wished to hear it go on all night. But it wasn't a marathon concert intended for us. Europeans, and American tourists admittedly, eat this shit up when on safaris at game park hotels. It gives them what they need to complete their tales of man-eaters and quaint natives. The Euros, far more polite than Americans, keep mum about their racism but often exude twice as much bigotry. This is how they expect Africa to be as a whole – abundant big game, ivory on the cheap, Africans barefoot and painted with mud. When they pop in on Africa for a visit it's what the austere shits wish from their niggers. The holiday fees must include native performances which have no meaning to the performers unless it's the traditional "shilling dance." If they were dancing for rain or fertility or even sheer joy there can be no doubt that it all goes to shit once two or three overweight Bavarians jump in the middle of performance,

"Helmut! Ulrika! Look at me! I am like ze natifs! Ich bin ein gleeful bunny in ze junkle!"

European racism is a tough thing to sell to many of my people. Early at the Chiromo Hotel it was a point I'd tried to make. Out of Lujurio's earshot, mind you, as that recalcitrant brute was a case in point. Some of the US kids who'd been to Europe immediately went on the defensive, avowing having never heard a single racial slur while abroad. Of course you *hear* very little unequivocally in the way of hate over there. Open attitudes and flapping mouths led to a lot of trouble sixty years ago – from Portugal all the way east to Arizona. The disdain for other peoples migrated beneath the surface leaving the regular, coarse American in awe of Europe's refined enlightenment. This is where crank cynics like myself come to point out how Enzo gives a light huff whenever an African student speaks. Or rolls his eyes whenever a black lecturer teaches. But during that little evening debate at the Chiromo, I didn't have Enzo alone to support my argument. A few minutes into explaining my thoughts there came a ruckus from the parking lot adjacent to the beer garden. A German guest giving a rash of shit to one of the Kenyan clerks. Didn't like the way his bags were being packed into a van. *Couldn't it have been honestly about the clerk's mishandling of the luggage?* From our seats the van had plenty of available cargo space and nothing about the bags looked in disarray. Unless the guy had just dropped a duffel full of test tubes or bone china then there wasn't an easy way to explain how he'd merited such a rotten harangue. The fat dude with the ugly mouth, possessed of that Hessian love of order in the universe, could've loaded the bags himself; something he'd do without a thought back home. But here there are Africans and Africans are meant to stow luggage for Europeans. Something they'll invariably fuck up, giving opportunity for guys like this doughy, white piece of crap to express his displeasure *"in the only way those people understand..."*

And just like that the music couldn't lull me to dreamland any longer. I was chafed from ass to midbrain with visions of stumbling white imbeciles mucking around within the dance. Unable to clap hands to the rhythm, making up their own chants and shrieking to each other like mongoloids on a merry-go-round. I prayed for violence to be brought swiftly down on them. I yearned for King Kong to stomp through the forest, to chomp their yellow E.U. heads off and rape them right in half. There was no hope. Kong was an island guy and I'm landlocked. I fell back to teeth gnashing and pig grunts, hoping to find the noise to incite giant forest hogs into a frenzied rut on the jamboree pigs.

Archaeology is the Glue of Brotherhood

This is my last night as a camping, tent-bound student of paleoanthropology. At the Fisherman's Camp at Lake Naivasha, nearby to Hell's Gate National Park, I haven't come to love anybody any better than previously. I haven't begun to love any of them less either. My judgments of character, whether seen as sound or not, are consistent and largely reliable. It can take a lot of effort for someone to prove that my early assessments of their personality were wrong. Take Burrows. Back in previous screeds I've viewed him as warped and possibly handicapped with perverse proclivities. Now those qualities are not a barrier to friendship, not in my book, you see. Many see me as one of society's deviants, at least as far as my world perspective goes. How I present said perspective probably needs polish and my circle of confidants, while generally good in their hearts, includes some of the most psychologically knotted folks I've ever known and sexual depravity is neither here nor there to me. Men must drain their testicles from time to time, women need to quell inner quivers or whatever the hell it is they get, and they ought to be able to achieve those goals however they see fit. Within a narrow band of reason, naturally, because one has to abhor venereal atrocity: acts on children; 'connecting' with others at knifepoint or one-sided violence of any sort while a genital is exposed. Barring stuff of that *verboten* sort, people ought to feel free to court animals or re-ingest their own physiological byproducts and the like. Point is: sexual inclinations don't weigh heavy when choosing between keeping somebody's company or getting him as far the fuck away from me as possible. The absolutely fascinating thing about Burrows doesn't even emanate from within his degenerate, cactus-like being. It's what the rest of the miniature world thinks of him. He's like the teacher in charge of Special Ed in a windowless classroom free, to behave however he feels. His colleagues give him some students, shut the door, hope they learn something and pray that nobody gets molested. But I'd adored the cranky fucknut. How often in life will I ever again have the chance to waste hours in the African sun checking out wildlife, smoking cheap Rooster cigarettes and swapping comedy with another human who likes jokes just for the sake of telling them?

We we're washing dishes the other day, see? It was after our first lunch at Naivasha. I was rinsing the plates, utensils, loose beetles, etc. in a *karai*. Out of nowhere Burrows grabs the *karai* and throws the soapy water all over Casmus. Knowing Burrows is a joker and that Casmus, the foreman of the Koobi Fora crew, has an infathomable sense of humor I already had a half smile ready for the punchline. Casmus was smiling too, doubtless excited for the one hell of a funny reason for the assault. But the funny wasn't coming. The funny was never there.

"I told you I didn't want those *karais* used for washing!" Burrows croaked venomously. "I told you to keep them with my things!"

Casmus' smile flattened, then rounded down into a look of shock.

"Why did you do it like that? I told them! Man, why did you do that to me?!"

"You're the crew chief!" Burrows hissed, "I told *you* so it's your goddamned responsibility. It's no joke!!!"

There it was. The final line to fill Burrows out from a intriguing, grizzled and funny bastard into one magnificent, luminous asshole. Instead of pulling Casmus aside for an explanation as to why he would ruin stainless steel basins with *dishwater* - they were designed for the gentle buffery of rocks and sand, you see - he deliberately sought to embarrass the man in front of every last member of our gang. Nice human. Sweet as swamp water. H jumped up for an explanation and was visibly disturbed at the one he got. He walked off for a few moments like a man trying desperately not to let his head erupt in a blast of magma and naughty language.

The rest of the crew was also upset. A hostile murmur ascended in place of the muted disappointment they usually have toward white dipshit behavior. Casmus sat far from us to simmer down and weigh out whether he'd really done anything to warrant retribution by dirty dishwater. I felt white-hot hate pushing into my simmering heart, threatening to thrust me far past restraint and into the fray. Standing, muscles coiling and starting to go furiously blind as though Burrows had just pissed in my mouth. How the fuck could that bastard justify humiliating another man, a very good man, over the trifle of putting water in the dirt pans? Was he coughing up the inane reactivity of the brat child interred in his psyche? I could give a flying fuck over the psychology of his behavior. He's a bronzed prick who needs to be pummeled, not analyzed. Nobody gives a shit for the *Id* of a tick. It's picked off and squished because that's what you do with parasites. I was sorting out the logistics of pulling Burrows' head off without getting my shirt dirty when H began a more sober way of fixing the problem. He went over to the offended man.

"Casmus," he intoned calmly while heated fluid glazed his eyes. "Go take Burrows' *karais* off the lorry and please put them in the white Land Rover…"

Ah, finally the punchline. And what a fucking terrible one. "…*off* the *lorry*…" The lorry, and the rest of Burrows' gear, was a good thirty meters from the kitchen area. Awful hard to wash utensils in his *karais* while they were buried under a ton of cargo.

Boy howdy, didn't that brainless beige mass of inedible meat just fuck up! Maybe we'd get to gut him and squeeze tart urine from his raisin heart into the final blinks of his sunken eyes. But Dr. H was simply planning to ship the twit back to Nairobi. Hopefully he'd buy a street boy with the severance pay. One with tetanus and AIDS whose jaws would lock, tear Burrows' pecker off and leave him with the immune system of veal fat. I was just frothing nastiness, making up horrible scenarios in my head as anybody would when they know they've no control over the balance of wrongs and amends. Frustrated and tilting at windmills, righting the situation was not up to me. So I sat with Casmus, talked trash about Burrows, then moved him on to sunny themes. Like which student had the prettiest eyes or packed the most junk in the trunk.

Dr. H is a man of infinite patience, almost to a fault. He thinks scenes all the way through and plans all the angles before committing to a course of action. The sentence for Burrows would be banishment *after* he'd been forced to sit with the crew and gorge himself on the ptomaine crow he'd cooked for himself. We set out for another game drive and left him to further atonements with the staff or to skulk in the hippo trench. I chuckled over the image of finding one of his rings dangling from a bone in whatever stew we'd be having for supper that evening. Windmills again. Burrows quite possibly could lose his position and, though that was neither a grim or gory process, it certainly was a heavy fine to pay.

Burrows' history was over. But I had seven more days in Kenya to add density to mine before saying goodbye to a place that's staring to feel like somewhere I could really belong, A place of bickering, love, lust, morons, sages, mosquitoes, heat, swamp ass and unrelenting beauty. It could be home more than any place I've been. Come mid-September I'll be just an American again; a chef or a bartender or a retail drone or whatever the fuck it is that will include nothing like the things I've done here. Living my usual ways as these memories dry up like crystallized sweat on my skin.

How soon will Kalle fade from the picture? It has to happen eventually. My thoughts may let her linger a little further on into the future, however, as dictated by the jarring romantic interludes and punctuated sexual tensions of these final nights.

Among life's maddening situations lies the Hell of Adoring a Woman Hornier than Yourself, Certainly More Beautiful Than You Deserve and About to Depart Your Life. I need less hells and fewer cutesy fucking metaphors. Moments stuck in this dumb state of getting a divine what-for can be abortive eternities where you can A) Battle yourself over better intentions and let her fly off in friendship or B) Get her in a chokehold till you've had your way and ask if she was okay with it as she runs back to her room.

Frustration is a circus of fleas wintering on your skin.

It's time to shelve the jokes about sexual violence. I can't hide behind a callous misanthropy and not feel the press of the softer side to this ordeal. Two months off from the home-style opportunities for companionship and the manic need to just fuck the hell out of somebody has finally yielded. Now there's only the desire to hold a tender heart close. A nice warm, weighted body to fit against mine. Lulling me to peace with sexual *intelligence*, good words and easy breaths. There's a gap running from beneath my chin down past my shins where Kalle fits with Incan precision. What to think?

I sincerely dig this woman all over the place. This is a college program and eighty percent of everyone I've met is under twenty-one. Most have witnessed life from under windproof umbrellas; books, campus and college radio have been their universe so there's an understandable naïveté about this planet. Yet they'll be quick to point out how nobody gets it. How guys like me don't understand the world. For elder scholars, cranky and crow footed at a mere twenty-six years of age, the social gaps are implausibly huge. It's a divide that's hard to bridge for those who haven't been pitifully broke, engaged to bipolar Irish women or prone to substance abuse and overnight stays in police 'offices'. The possibilities for congruent perspectives are slanted frustratingly away from me. Kalle, though, is a feminine, doppelganger of myself. Back to college late in the game at twenty-five years of age with a wild, sordid past behind her. Occasionally she's an ornery, stubborn ass with hips that passed by Jesus' bench on the assembly line. Why the hell shouldn't we get along the way we have? Hours stacked in each other's company have welded the chains dragged on by our hearts.

Yesterday we hit town for all sorts of *Only in Nairobi* affairs with Vic, Odede and Jen. Like eating lunch at the Hard Rock Café *in* Nairobi, this is the only place it can get done. I'd considered a spiny lobster because they were so huge and pretty in the tank. But I settled for a fiscally responsible cheeseburger; a treat that was as juicy and exciting as sticky crushed popcorn. Third World or not, The Hard Rock is a premium priced Western chain and they shouldn't be fucking anybody on the burgers.

But Freddie was aboard the tour ship. We helped liquor him up and he was the caretaker of morale in the waning days of these friendships. For dessert he took us to *Pegi's Palace*. Fred Odede is a special sort of stray cat. Doesn't matter where we've been in the country or in the feculent sprawl of the capital -Eastleigh, Westlands, Downtown – he sniffs out the moonshine like a shark after chum. He doesn't frequent standard bars, preferring to haunt illegal nickel *changaa* shacks such as Pegi's. We arrived at a dirt apse quite nearly impossible to detect beneath its towering glass, concrete and steel neighbors. Even within the only thing making it appear more than a fenced-in service and garbage alley was the shack. A varitoned blue collection of warped boards and stained corrugated roof. The Palace. Where Pegi and her boys serve *changaa* from pre-owned plastic jugs at five nickels a fifth.

Not that *changaa* is necessarily the right word. The stuff Pegi pours wasn't like the vicious distillates usually known as *changaa*. The stuff at the Palace drew better parallels with the Carnivore's *Dawas* or cheap wine coolers. Freddie described this *mnywo* (that's the word – just remembered it) as what you get when *"...you put pineapples and fruit and put it with the juice and some sugar. Then put it outside and you have this local beer!"*

The local beer went down easy. It was indeed fruity, but not in the sickly candied way of juice booze marketed to teenagers back home. Tasted natural, like a tropical cider. And if you didn't let your imagination get wrapped up in the sub-sanitary condition of the bottles there was nothing more adverse than an effervescent undertone of ethyl. I think the plan had been to stay for a few minutes so Freddie could fuel up and then we'd split.

But there was no rapid departure as the dirt bubble atmosphere and destitute hospitality of that plank cave took over our schedule. Hard to leave sticky seats as half-lit university professors and erudite lushes stood firm on seeing that our bottles were always near full. The drunks there were educated, not a single dummy slouched on the walls of that speakeasy. They wanted to hear about the States from firsthand witnesses, they wished to give us the African take on Rwanda and Burundi and elucidate the inner structure of Daniel arap Moi's administration. They inquired as to whether or not America felt it could *"...beat India economically"* and regaled us with figurative whoops and sssssss's when we divulged the current dollar/K-shilling exchange rate. We were in a think tank with dry rot in the walls and drunks catching society red handed in its disregard for the individual and his ideas. Yet they were all just a little too soused to do much about it. Pour a concrete floor, spritz it with morning vomit, scatter the Boston Herald's eighty page sports section and half sheet of job ads, stray a few know-it-alls staggering in a gin mist and Pegi's could be a bar back home in Southie. Policy experts all around us and all had probably passed out during the last five national votes. But we played well to our hosts, and they'd laughed when we laughed and we were often doubled over in glee though I couldn't get a thumb on what the hell had become so funny. In the cab back to the Chiromo it became clear the rib-cracking giggles weren't going to slacken soon. There couldn't have been regular street grade alcohol in the *mnyvo*. Perhaps a *'maybe-it's-clean'* jerrican of pineapple juice fermenting in the humid Nairobi sun produced something else in the beverage. Not necessarily a hallucinogenic by-product, but I did feel wickedly stoned. Dumbed up good with no way to stop cacking like a raccoon. My temporalimandibuloon clown face muscle locked backwards with polished apple cheeks crushing the crap out of my eyeballs. Life had at last driven me to the perfect booze and I'd probably never get another lick of it again.

Kalle and I passed most of the evening at the Chiromo, finishing some projects in my room. A little further into the night we broke for some room service: food and beer brought back to my stucco romance cave. We sipped Tuskers at an easy pace. Pointedly fatigued, with beer molecules pinging off the relaxation triggers in our bloodstreams, we called it a night on the paleo business. It was time to stretch out and just shoot the shit. The talking went on for a long time, as neither of us wished to stop listening to the whatnots burping up in each other's thoughts. We'd accepted something had developed between us, an incontrovertible connection the kind of which can take years to build. We were now looking to work backwards and flesh out a history. Our pasts were covered from the slightly better than ordinary to the unequivocally fucked up and back again to banal trifles, the missionary positions of life which would bore the tears out of anyone except us. We absorbed drab details as though our memories were scheduled to get erased in the a.m. We spun epics about drugs, hummed ditties about aunts and dry turkey dinners, railed about loathsome bastards, chanted litanies about books, chattered about mailmen, murmured about back pain piled over gland trouble, crooned above love and kept the eddy of words swirling back to hymns from the missalettes of adultery.

I made a pass somewhere in all that, quite brazen considering my first beer stood half full and completely warm. Exhaustion had hamstringed self-doubt and I needed to kiss her. We'd half-jokingly discussed this moment for so long there was no way I'd ever say goodbye to Kalle McInnis without knowing if her lips fit to mine.

It was weak, that first moment the kiss came together. I faltered and she wavered, one lip reaching as the other fell away; her left hand digging through my hair to grasp my neck while her right sought the door jamb for leverage to pull away. The vacillant tournament went on; Kalle reiterating a need to leave then staying, locking in soulful determination then floundering with slackened mouths. Passion struggled to find footing as climax seemed like a trip wire into the gummy mire of denouement. Ahead might be a tub of remorse. Attaching ourselves only to be severed and flown apart was as masochistic as drinking ipecac for the joy of dry heaves. This was the massive phosphorescent coffee table that I'd never stop bashing my shins against in the dark. The closer I've gotten the madder I am over the terminal prognosis. If we spent the night together the sense of finality would be an ugly motherfucker to live with. I'd want more desperately and yet probably never travel to Canada to taste it all over. Then again, there'd be no remorse for never having made love, slept and woken up with Kalle.

Kissing and biting her throat. Running my fingers down her spine and catching her lower lip in a gentle spring trap of teeth. A standing leg compressed in a triple vice of a hand on her ass and the squeeze of her thighs. Misgivings were finally blown from the room, making it possible to lift her without breaking the rhythm of her mouth and tongue and lay us on the bed.

It was too late to expect another chance but still too early in the dissolution of qualms to fall deeper than this erotic, tangled, bruising embrace. Had more happened, the emotional struggle might have drained away anything that could have been special about it. So we had some kissing. And we had a climactic cuddle. At least I did...

As much as I wished to plunge deep and bring her gasping to ecstasy or just screw her silly with her panties on my head, we were too tired to get there and too happy just to nestle into each other. She never left, almost did though - arranging herself, saying goodbye and grabbing the handle of the door. But she could only manage to crack open her exit. Giving in to something she really desired after all, she quietly locked the door, sighed with a smile and came back to lie beside me. We talked for at least another hour. We could have discussed anything or everything, so we did.

On the Seventh Day He Grew Fidgety and Irritable

I've always hated the hell out of Sundays. Admittedly, it's ridiculous to feel visceral contempt for a regularly occurring day. But the first twenty four hours of the *hebdomas* have nevertheless put me off ease throughout my entire life. They make me peel Latin scabs out of an atrophied vocabulary as the dry aura from this miserable fucking Day of the Lord chokes down my own sense for words.

Sundays fail to keep me occupied. Work or even holidays never seem to capture and divert my attention from the dismal introspections I avoid 85.75% of my days. On Sunday my mind gets uppity and refuses to ignore itself. There's no choice but to look inward, judge the past and over-read the maps of possible futures. I could take drugs on a Sunday or get drunk, but only to smear the jeering images in my head. Instead of getting rid of the taunting inner faces, I only get miserable headaches. Cigarettes taste awful; friends lose their appeal and strangers reek of spoiled *kimchi*. My self is driven to assess itself in the wooly itch of Sunday's light. Relentless and tenaciously determined to comprehend its ugly being, my mind has to slug it out hard to complete the job.

Another Sunday today. I can verify that because this is Nairobi again and everybody has returned to referencing their doings in terms of defined chronologies. *The Museum's Paleontology Lab is closed on Tuesdays; Allison is flying out on Tuesday and needs a ride; I think Savita makes a fresh batch of biriyani at the café on Tuesdays; Of course you can't park here, bwana – it's Jumanne,* and so on with other days coming into the fray with their own peculiar hashmarks. Up in the scrub of Koobi Fora, time wasn't really bound by the same strictures. I had a watch sure enough, but it was critical only at five a.m., when it beeped to remind me I'd better hurry to breakfast before the fat kids ate all the *mandazis*. Or late at night to keep me from staring forever into the thick Milky Way. Occasionally, during afternoon siestas, I'd run the 1/100th second function and watch the little LCD digits race by for giggles and the sullen joy in killing time. Beyond those there wasn't much need for chronographs – *sun up* meant off to the sites; *sun burning hole in apex of head* signified time for lunch. Since routines were the same each day, the difference between Monday and Saturday amounted to five morning digs, five lunches, five afternoon digs, five dinners, and five night snoozes. It was perfectly easy to forget where I was in the date book. But nebulous calendrics could only stand for a six day stretch. For once every seven days, without counting them you see, I'd be overcome by the dread presence of my enemy dawn. I sensed it with the regularity of a cabbage-fed clairvoyant. It usually came on after my first mug of tea in the morning, like my skin was being raked with burlap and desiccated marshmallow fists began bearing down on my eyelids. Suddenly disenchanted with everything, a freshly fried *mandazi* staling in my mouth, I'd sniff the null atmosphere and mutter,

"Fuck. A Sunday. Here we go again…"

Straight off I'd be broodingly pissed at the Vikings. What the hell were they thinking? Dedicating fractions of the week to a crew of deities nobody would soon give a fuck about? If the West had been content to leave the days with nothing to their names but numbers I may have been spared ever having to spend the horrors of a Sunday with a twenty-four hour, unobstructed view of the *succuba* within me. Without names each month would have up to five Sundays with at least one thing unique about them and the bad taste that comes with their utterance would have a dash of variation in flavor.

And now Sunday comes to abrade Kalle's figure in my heart. I've got her pen, rooked while rummaging in her panty drawer, and it's going to write about her until it bleeds dry or I learn to let the fuck go. She'd slept here for part of the night again. Having been over to my mosquito crib with Vic & Janet until three a.m., she split only to knock on the door minutes later. She'd begun the climb into bed back in her room and then changed her mind, returning to my threshold in her coat and underwear. Jesus, what a sight. It wasn't the first time seeing her legs in their entirety, but the rarity of the view kept it spellbinding. Her thighs were an added assault on my psyche. I was chest deep in this love swamp as is, I didn't need a set of elongated, smooth resplendences tempting me to dive. Son of a bitch if they weren't magnificently toned, sliding under her diaphanous panties where humidity loosened the cotton into soft pleats. How could that pair of stems be bare in my room? Legs untouched by sun through an equatorial summer, having been hidden by denim, long shorts and sheets of sunblock. Those naked pulverizations of my emotional sanity stood cold near my bed, the congregate shadow of a billion goosebumps only slightly darkening her skin in the light cutting through the room from the latrine. One leg could have been whispering *"please, please touch us"* as the other whimpered *"it will crush us if you do."* All I needed was to see a slight crescent of hiney slip from the cut of her brief and I was never going to stop crying.

Kalle needed to talk but she doesn't always get right on to the most pressing issue in her head, opting to just swing the satellite dilemmas surrounding it. One thing was a concern about me, wondering if I'd been angry or upset over the evening. Did I think she'd been blowing me off and spending too much time with Janet? I'll admit fleeting moments where there'd been minor but insidious resentment for time spent any way without me. Instances of a heart squawking pitiful, neglected whines until my brain roared at it to shut the hell up. Envious minutes were inevitable. The night with her locked in my arms brazed a nexus, due to corrode and disintegrate in a day.

To make her feel worse I'd been slipping into a calcified introversion, leaving a party at the bar from time to time without a word. I'd needed to think, to smoke in reverie and to breathe in all I felt about my time here. It instigated a bit of worry among the others as well. Why would I be in the midst of a drinking party saying next to nothing when it was normal for me to be talking too much? I'd gone mute with the taut brow and half-squint, acquired from the Syrian side of the family, which appears in interludes of aphonic contempt or deep internal deliberations. It tends to spook people. My feelings for Kalle aside, I felt these last few days were for listening, not being heard. To absorb anything Kenyan or the words of anybody who'd been with me here. Filling in previous gaps before Kalle punches a spacious new lacuna into my soul the day after tomorrow.

My beautiful, enigmatic affliction was again seated on the bed and she was apologizing to me. It calmed the nag noise within though it wasn't necessary of her to do so. We had grown tight, but she too had things and people to hold onto a while longer. And there were moments when I was off tying up some loose end, that she'd wished I'd been near her instead. A romantic germinal certain to get pulped under doom's mower we were still only parts of this finality. The paleoanthropology, career paths, contacts and international friendships were merely to be interrupted by leaving here. Those might find new ties at a future lace, but our end - an implosion of love under crazy fucking stresses and eleventh hour pressures - was at hand. In the wee hours of the morning we were trying to stretch this frustrating connection. I said I wanted to be with her in the coming day and night. But the words, part assertion and half begged, were unconvincing to my own ears. Constant companionship wouldn't be feasible. There was a dinner invitation in Eastleigh from a woman she'd met on a *matatu*. No matter what supper entailed it had to be an experience she couldn't pass up. And I was hoping to dine alone; to savor a final medium-rare Chiromo burger and keep my guts harmonious with the discord in my heart.

She hoped I wasn't feeling obligated to being with her. As I looked at her face, spectrally softened by the weak light slipping in from the bathroom, I dissolved in love and ache. *What the hell was going on here?* Her interest in my feelings had abruptly intensified. After the starlight of Jarigole, after Maralal, after last night she thought I might feel *pressured* to behave tenderly towards her? This is why Van Gogh sliced his ear off and gave it to a hooker: to state, *I love you, all women really, but this thing can't listen to any more emotional acrobatics from your mouths.* Wasn't I a swell guy? Hadn't I been the possibility for a friendly fuck on the frontier? Was it the heat? Was it the cold? Wasn't I the best conversationalist east of Banff and south of the goddamned Omo? Or was I merely a sliver above the rest when she needed a close mind to reveal her thoughts? She needs arms around her, needs space, needs my heart, my love and to assure me it's not necessary for me to reciprocate. And if I'd insisted she keep the crazy vacillatory flood locked behind her teeth, then I might never hear the lush alto of her voice again. The best road to be on was a route which kept a cool relation with me no matter what, even if fate revealed an insistence that we bang the daylights out of each other. If she were in her right mind she could leave right then and have an easy go back to the Americas. But...*but, but, but,* goddammit, can't we have a better conjunction? This girl that set a bonfire in my emotions, this being I hope I don't fall in love with, this woman that I am falling over, came to apologize and explain her actions endlessly. Staying chaste through an interminable babbling dialectic? I ultimately told her to shut up and to get into bed with me.

Chalk one up for shut-eye. She'd lain on her side taking up most of the blanket and I was behind her with my right arm over her body and my left hand caressing her head to help her to sleep. Her only intimate request was for me to slide my right leg over her left, interlocking along the bend of her right leg and hip. Good enough for me.

Though she'd later admit the platonic spooning tortured her, sexual animation had been limited to the wax and wane of an erection. And I hope she'd been acutely aware of it. My head was all messed up, obviously, as I congested with an odd desire to hold her respect by keeping a promise just to hold her. My sinister addiction to screwing slipped away for a night like a slime I'd finally found the soap for. I can't remember the last time any woman got under my covers without finding something of me stuck somewhere inside of her. I never saw it coming, but the only things I knew about myself at that point were that the erection ceased and that the warmest thing I'd ever touched was lying next to me. I lost that thing around five in the morning. She ran back to her room before dawn to avoid a public display of her undies.

The following evening was something to wait for. Though the last few weeks with Kalle had taught me to expect nothing, it was going to be the last night we'd be able to stay with each other and hearing her sleeping breaths close to mine in bed would be all I needed for a lifetime of sweet memory. The next morning I'd leave for Benjamin Sila's farm in Machakos. Kamba country, green, red and hilly, they say. I'll be there five or six days and she'll be back home, available to make someone else a happier man.

Karma's Prophylactic

The final exam results came in and officially made me the top ranking student in this outfit. Looks like the suffocating crush on the Wordsworth girl in Cambridge paid off. It also paid to be mildly evolution-obsessed in a school where half the students were just looking for something cool to do with their summers. Regardless, my nuts swollen with satisfaction, it's now easier to see continuing with this degree-seeking horseshit. *Dear Diary, will I ever be a gossamer-winged princess or only a libidinous, paleoanthropological jerk?*

Score one for stubborn kismet. Or for lousy luck or throwing in the towel or the milksop resignation to fly home with distended, unused testosterone and lasting regret. I mosied myself over to Kalle's room at ten. The light was off and that alone almost had me sulking back to my mosquitoes. But summoning up the mustard to knock, I quietly drew on a cigarette and waited for an answer. Her roommate, Ellen, finally stuck a chin whisker out. Seeing her putty mug was an unwelcome swallow of bubbling snail grease. Terrible girl, born under the stars of Anus in retrograde and not the face I'd hoped to see, see? I muttered some bullshit about saying goodbye before my early departure to Machakos in the morning.

She offered a puckered "Thank you. Now, goodnight."

The girl was a hair across the ass wherever you turned in the program and we'd gotten along as cuddly as spiders. Did she really think I came by to give her a warm toodle-oo? Kalle was asleep and I could have walked away on the whole heart wrenching business and stopped beating the crap out of myself over her. But I can't stop where she's concerned and pushed on just a little further, squeezing past the frumpy bouncer's saddle bags and on to the edge of Kalle's bed. There I whispered out my clumsy farewell. I should have scooped her up and taken her home with me. But the will to drag it out any longer had finally tattered away, probably snagged on some broken corner of Ellen's wide, bumpy ass. I kissed her temple and said good-bye.

I have no idea if Kalle ever came by my room earlier in the evening or if she'd ventured to seek me out in the Chiromo bar, as I never got in there myself. After a quick meal in the motel mess, I split to pack for Machakos and murder a few more mosquitoes, making a note to pack dragonflies if I ever come back this way. Roundabouts nine, I went to see Dr. H to pick his brain before screwing up the gumption to request a return as a teaching assistant. He complimented my performance and enthusiasm. On the way to his room I saw Kalle's lights were on, assurance that there'd be no trouble catching her after a sit-down with the head guy. But H and I talked for an hour, spraying hot asphalt over the gravel of my future and leaving the impression that he felt I was as good as any to fill a spot next summer. When I took leave, bidding him Godspeed to his lithic angels and whatzits, it would turn out that I'd left the last possible moments with McInnis in the dust as well. A fat slab of my brain had been betting on this being the case. Self preservation or masochism, it didn't really matter since either root drive denied me a final chance to sweep the sweet film of her mouth with my own. Any tarnish I may have put over her heart was being scoured away as she dreamt of home.

I bought three liters, six big bottles, of Tusker White Cap at the bar and cut through the kitchen to say bye to the cooks on the way back to the room. I wanted to write an epic love letter and set myself up for some morning nausea. The beer came along to help. Probably not the best of ideas as I have the road trip to Kamba country in the a.m. Going to Benjamin Sila's farm for the week and to get there I have to catch a ride in City Center. The nearby central part of this city, where we've tooled around so much, turns out to have no relation to City Center. So some discovery work and a bus ride is in line for the morning; not a lot of space for hangovers or heartache.

Then Maggie dragged her bags by my mosquitoleum. The grating out on the concrete was just the distraction I needed to throw down the pen, hop on a chair and peak through the high vent with its bug screen which *was fluttering* in the crumbly, courtyard-facing aperture. All of a sudden my heart was spitting tears through my eyes – the vent! The little barred window frozen in a yawn against the hedgerow of bamboo and lush, weedy treelets! My very last night here and the tiny windows had just now arrested my awareness. The fucking mosquitoes may or mayn't have been breeding under my bed but they've sure as shit been flying through the gnawed mesh of the screens. I could've halted the nasty nips days ago. The universe had been dropping stinging hints from high above in the cadaverous stucco of my room yet, I'd failed to look up. Well then, might as well misdirect my frustration and crap on Maggie then.

There are folks who thrive on tragedy or at least on thoughts of bad news. Sheila had a touch of that, but it's pathological in Maggie. She'd stunned us with a lengthy roster of *good friends* who'd experienced dozens of world-class disasters in their lives. Everyone she knows has cancer, HIV, diabetes, paralysis, Southside psoriasis, ear pox, reluctant digestion, gunshot wounds, cirrhosis, sarcoma, oblique halitosis, elephantiasis, ménage a papilloma, misplaced limbs, schizophrenia, Down Syndrome, Tourette's, Parkinson's Disarray, Tay-Sachs Dilemma, Lou Gehrig's DH, Alzsomething, MS, MD, scurvy, foot odor, kleptomania and Cucamongaphobia. As rancid icing on their lousy, mealy donuts most have since died of a sexually related drug murder. Or will before she gets back home. This should sound exactly as crazy as it is but her regales of woe left us with little room for exaggeration, pealing off the unimaginable plagues of loved ones on a daily basis. No matter what you've experienced in the universe of tragedies, if you venture to mention any of it, she's gonna unload a handful of examples of similar horrors gone worse by a factor of seven. Once Mag starts vomiting woe, your own remorse for a friend's real and miserable demise from affliction will seem plain silly. It's not even necessary to address her directly on the topic of loss. If the ear clusters on that chud detected anyone speaking sorrow a dozen meters off from her meal worm hunt, she'd lumber to the source to make their anguish insignificant as compared to yet another best friend;

the one who lost both legs and yet manages to coach soccer scores of disadvantaged children who suffer muscular dystrophy. Most of them, that is, because some are only severely autistic.

The punchline is that I didn't even make that last one up. Ugly is one thing. But lots of homelies crossed my path this summer without warranting a lengthy piss drenching. It was the unnecessary, outlandish fables one after that next that kept this bufonoid heap plaguing the overlooks of everyday thought. Double amputee teaching soccer to the autistic and tykes with MD...a whole lot of them? On its own it stretches plausibility but with one wacky load of shit after the next I had trouble producing my own dumb daydreams as my brain opted to rerun her neurotic scenarios. Was it my old man who went down on crashing airliners twice and walked off a third that would kill all on board hours later? Was it hers? If I stop to muse that my dad's Camel habit will eventually wrack him with emphysema, that minor apocalypse morphs into me as a future mass of symbiotic Sapphic lumps watching films of my lungless pop dragging a breathing machine up Mount Ararat with forty deaf altiphobics in tow.

Getting the picture yet? A Horror sent from the Zone of Horrors to horrify the living fuck out of decent citizens with messages of fucking horror. She's a year's worth of Reader's Digest melodramas where each story had its last paragraph amputated, the ones with candy scents of pithy hope. The saying is that anyone is lucky to count their number of good friends on one hand. Maggie is one fortunate, blessed sea cucumber. Scores of close and dear friends. Too bad none ever had a peaceful moment in their miserable lives and a shame that loving her means they're gonna die.

Suddenly I feel little bites of guilt inside. Granted her mind seems knotted tightly to one mother of a twisted universe but the woman is a disarmingly pleasant and polite lady. Can't think of an instance where she even looked as though she wished ill on any of us. Perhaps all her disturbing tales were actually true and I should have left Maggie's story out of all of this. I could have simply left her alone or turned my slander elsewhere. Towards the vegan perhaps? She offered far less to love than poor

Maggie. Then again, she hadn't walked past the rotten mood of my room tonight...

With half a carafe of beer left, I no longer felt like writing or slighting and headed to bed. I wasn't drinking to get drunk anyway. I was sucking down Tuskers to get sick, to replace Kalle with a stomachache. It wasn't working, but at least Maggie plodded past to give me an hour's break from the beautifully difficult woman whose lithe body will kick holy hell throughout my dreams.

Nunguni? No, *Nunguni.*

I finally made it out of Nairobi and southwest into the Kalong Hills. The Makueni District, specifically. Or Nunguni if you really want to bull's eye me on the map. Zero in on the spare bed Ben Sila set for my bus-broken bones and you've cornered me for the kill. Far as I've ever been from old friends, it's down to the business of making new ones. One would have to say that Ben's about as fine a friend as you can meet; generous and forgiving more than anyone I've known recently. When I'd arrived at the Nunguni stop and fell out of the *matatu* (literally that is, as my narcoleptic knees gave way to commune my face with the dirt) I was six hours late. Yet he was there with a welcoming smile. He must've just assumed I'd get lost in the hellhole of Nairobi's City Center transport hub and be forced to wait for the next over-packed, rolling tin dust-oven going to Nunguni. Despite the solid hour walk from his home to the bus drop-off, there was no wagging finger, no disappointment on his face. He was happy to see me and pleased that my journey was minimally uncomfortable, incurring only a sprained bladder, temporary paraplegia and nothing worse.

I spent the day sucking up the scenery; among the most beautiful I've seen in Kenya. I enjoyed the waning hours with Ben's family and getting a tour of his *shamba.* Mrs. Sila pointed out the animal pens, outhouse and rain catchments around their home atop a hill then took me down the slopes of java trees to the stream, aardvark holes and fruit trees. They've got mangoes and pawpaws and avocados and loufas and two little kids who had me playing chase throughout the arbors – as best I could with newly calcified knee cartilage, a powerfully recharged head cold and a mind still swimming through Kalle's rip currents. Plied over matatu fatigue it was a fantastic way to exhaust a guest to bed. Ben's big hill is actually a lower rise within a greater vale so night poured in rapidly before seven. I had a lovely, sleepy dinner and then my host packed me and the rhinoviruses off to bed.

Anxious, wistful and itchy I fought sleep in the cozy, dirt-floored room I shared with a rooster and a hen. I had some letterhead, swiped from the museum, and used it to resume gushing the tripe I'd begun writing to Kalle the night before. The epistle was good medicine for my symptoms but we'll have to wait to see how it copes with the root sickness. There's a good likelihood that I'll never send it to her. I needed the purge more than she needs a drawn out ode on the whole affair. And it knocked me out to sleep as soundly as a starfish dreaming of nothing but snoring chickens.

Things are more relaxed on this farm than in the field. From his work at Koobi Fora I'd figured Ben as compulsively industrious. Yet by nine a.m. the only stirrings I heard beyond my door were the dogs and other livestock which also sleep in the three-room house. The rooster had been busy. That loud, feathered fucker woke me up a few hours back, blasting out strangled hoots every half hour since dawn. But at least it roused me early to resume the pressing chore of blowing my nose.

Once Ben had recovered my busted body yesterday afternoon we had some tea and mandazis at a bus stop café. It sat among rows of closet-sized shops in a busy, half-crazed spot on the atlas where truck routes and footpaths tangles amidst shacks. All under the shallow gaze of rising hills as dusty, red earth and green life cascaded away to deep valleys. My arrival also coincided with the commencement of the exciting town games. Barely a sip into the tea, a downhill mob erupted in whistles, brays and gleeful whoops. The terrain was too steep and rutted for a soccer match, but something exciting was sure as hell going on. So we ditched our splintery stools for a better view of the hubbub outside.

A woman, we were filled in, had stolen the school fees from a little girl and now she was paying the consequences. In spades. The way they leapt on her, it looked sure as hell the crowd was going to shred her into fillets. But it wasn't that severe, they only tore off her clothes to chase her out of town in her birthday suit.

Scrambling uphill to escape, she took bare-assed diggers in the dirt and frequent slaps on her hiney. Mob justice, nothing objectionable about it in this case and darn funny if you ask me. To everybody else too - when it was over men and women headed off in all directions, holding each other up as they laughed and wiped the teary rills of funny from their cheeks.

Events today have been less spectacular, though it matters little as the still life of these here hills is staggering in its own right. Walking entailed constant stumbles and frequent paralysis as I lost myself in the panoramas. Gorgeous. Things have been much as they'd gone down since Ben brought me from town to his house: mostly people stopping us or popping in to greet the visitor from the US. I've met uncles, sisters, cousins, nephews, nieces, more cousins, patriarchs, matriarchs, babies, chickens and local businessmen. The poultry accost you chronically along the hilly paths, giving strangers a threatening once over before moving on. It doesn't take long for an unusual *mzungu* (troglodyte-type rather than well-trimmed average white guy version) to have his presence known throughout the neighborhood. For now, I appear to be *it*, the gotta-see thing of the week. Nobody wasted any time welcoming me to the area, putting me at a measure of discomfort as I've felt a bit foolish and undeserving of these receptions. I worry about acting in an offensive manner, figuring it has to happen at any moment. Happens everywhere, after all, especially at home where I'm quite in tune with the local customs.

They slew a chicken for dinner, all special and stuff, just for me. Sila's wife picked up the bird just as he announced we'd be having it for supper and wrung its neck so swiftly it never had a chance to disagree. It brought a pang of guilt as the bird had approved my arrival yesterday and we'd even shared a room. But killing the chicken meant something more than a hankering for drumsticks; it was a jubilant affirmation of friendship. Now that's something. I wonder if perfect love means having someone so enamoring that you'd be willing to snap the heads off birds to celebrate life's little moments. Maybe if I'd killed those goats myself at Koobi Fora I would've gotten laid this summer.

The chicken was fricasseed, in a lovely soupy way, and we ate it in Ben's front room with his uncle. His wife, little boy and girl didn't eat with us. Maybe the missus dumped the rug rats at a sister's and went drinking with the girls? No, things are divvied up socially into sex and age groups here. Men with men and everybody else eats in the pantry. Delicious dinner though, the chicken was densely chicken flavored even if it was a chore to tear the durable meat off the bone. I caught on to Ben's technique – stick a piece in your mouth, bone and all, chew until you got what you came for and spit out the hard parts when you're done. I cursed Colonel Sanders for giving me weak and lazy jaws.

I don't know what Ben has in store for me next. There's a possible trip to the coffee factory – Ben's *shamba* is part of a java growing collective. A pal from the coffee board was here at breakfast but Ben wouldn't commit a time for visiting, worried that news of a guest would cause the curiosity of the workers to prevent me from getting a real picture of normal business. The tour is up in the air so we can make a proper surprise intrusion. For now, he filled me in on Kamba coffee history and some current highlights.

Some men in the region were recently convicted of *illegally* selling coffee. They were channeling black market jamoke to some Germans who weren't registered with the Board. *Convicted!* As in tried, judged and sentenced unpleasantly. Sila believes the guys will get a few years in the clink for that. Imagine having to hear the gavel slammed down just for selling *your own beans* to the wrong coffee drinkers? Understandably, such transgressions undermine the regulations and markets Ben and everyone else here has to deal with. But considering that some of the priciest bags of joe at home come from right here and that the folks producing beans aren't the ones getting wealthy, even off the wholesale end, you have to sympathize with the 'crooks' who were trying to make a few extra shillings for selfish luxuries. Like pipes to bring water to their coffee trees. Perhaps it was the makings of a revolution. Probably would have failed eventually anyway as the rules protect the collective more than they hinder individual prosperity. Without local price regulatory boards, even as ethically hobbled as they currently are, the powerful coffee-buying concerns of the world would ultimately get most farmers back to their original barely-able-to-eat incomes. I'll have to keep that in mind next time I feel like stuffing myself with sandwiches and fudge bricks at Starbucks.

Near bedtime and Christ Golly was my ass spalling and threatening to crumble off. The hike from Nunguni center to Ben's, steep and grueling, had a similar day-after effect of having squatted five hundred pounds bare assed in a gravel storm. Laid a hurtin' in my glutes. *I don't think we're in Karari anymore, Ototo*...there's no lackadaisical prospecting for fossils here. When in *Kithangathini* (sorry, new locality name which I'll explain in a sec) you walk because you need to get from here to there. And *here* is never level for more than a meter and *there* is always some distance up or down a steep grade. If *there* happens to be downhill, getting back to *here* will involve serious leg strain. Ben Sila may not live at the highest point in this burg but he does live above his neighbors and everyplace else we go. The way home is always up and never easy. *Bleepin' ouch!* I've never been so sore.

Now, *Kithangathini*...This is actually where Ben lives. Not that I've been purposely neglectful with the specifics or don't care much for what anything is called; It's more like Ben's been keeping my helpings of info on a need to know basis. I didn't need to know I was going to Kithangathini when he instructed me to get to Nunguni. That's where the bus stop was and I innocently assumed that, long walk aside, this was going to be Nunguni all the way. Luckily *here* had only a few uphills and a whole lotta downhill to get from *there*. Nunguni, that is, which is obviously no longer the here and I'll need to limber up when I want to go back *there*. Got it? The gist is that I've been gradually zeroing in on an accurate concept of wherever the hell it is that I am. Now it is Kithangathini, as was revealed to me over the morning tea and French toast. The coffee board dude had mentioned something about Kithangathini, leading me to ask if it was a place we'd be going to.

"Ha ha," chortled the bean accountant, "You are *sitting* in Kithangathini!"

Smiling all dumb and the like I told him that I thought this was Nunguni. But it wasn't and we laughed some more and tomorrow

I'll learn that the dozen or so farms around us are properly called Pine Crest Acres.

I'm eating healthily here. Breakfasts consist of *chapatis*, which I've learned never to refuse, and French toast with plenty of Blue Band and treacle. We've got only dirt floors and an outhouse, but I doubt Nairobi's dandiest inns could whip up such impressively light, crisp, egg-battered bread. Lunches have included boiled arrowroot, potatoes and carrots stewed with tomatoes. Sounds simple, but jeez was it tasty. For dinner tonight there was *ugali*, the white cornmeal paste that's still a little tough to warm up to, and a sort of hot cole slaw - sans mayo, which is the downfall of cabbage anyhow. The slaw was cooked with tomatoes as well, emphasizing the universal magic of those squishy red love apples. Swell, hearty chow and my intestines are normal again. That's testament to the miserable effect the Chiromo and Nairobi's other slop chutes had on my personal septic system.

Today closed with a long draught of cool night air. Stars were fizzing where the clouds weren't obscuring the universe. The only significant sounds were the *good evenin*'s sung by bush babies and insects harmonizing to the murmurs around the fire. All new elements in the subtle, collective juju which has made me a night critter. The lovely, persuasive atmosphere of a world freed from the sun accompany the only hours when my heart can leave a stifling oven to exist throughout and beyond my wet plaster structure. The flesh is a seersucker suit for the soul and it rides up in the crotch. Night moments are the best moments for my core to seek connecting routes to another essence. The best essence is on a plane to western Canada by now. The night's also a good place to let go.

Christmas Sneeze and Pharisees

It's September here in the Southern Hemisphere. According to Serlingian Physics it must be February on my side of the equator and that explains why my nose has been running so much. The sniffles, the crisp Kalong morning air and the chickens have brought on thoughts of the holidays. September is the current Western advent of the Christmas Season, is it not?

It should always feel like Christmas – *honor it in my heart and try to keep it all the year*[7], *et cetera, et cetera.* When August passes the retail industry starts acting like it's in on that conviction, though the feeling isn't founded in the same hope for reciprocal humanity. *"It gets more and more commercialized,"* runs the annual gripe for many bastards who've failed to note the lessons of the Grinch. Christmas has probably been commerce driven ever since myrrh and frankincense[8] went out of vogue. So what? You only have to buy into that notion if your own convictions were store-bought in the first place. Folks have grumbled about the over-commercialized nature of Xmas for ages, so much that they have no other term to characterize it. Seventy five years ago, an animated Charlie Brown swung the term "commercialized" like a weepy war-club. Go back a few centuries to Hollywood's Golden Age and you'll find the same thing in *Miracle on 34th Street* or *It's a*

---

[7] Q. Magoo as E. Scrooge speaking C. Dickens' *A Christmas Carol*

[8] Both Biblical resins are derived from trees which grow in Koobi Fora. Myrrh comes from the *Commiphora* tree, which also lends its name to where we worked: Commi-phora, Koobi-Fora... get it?

Wonderful Life. Macys and Gimbelses wringing the last nickels out of veterans and grannies, Frank Capra smearing pithy emotion on camera lenses via the Wells-Fargo semen on his hands. Those celluloid grandpappies may have utilized the word "commercialized" as well, but I am no authority on that, having only seen about six nonconsecutive minutes of either flick. The holiday season has always had a taint of capitalism and its commercializing (not even searching for a synonym) ways and there hasn't been a sign of remorse since Coca-Cola gave us the Santa Claus version we all think of now.

Surely the materialism can't grow any more severe than back in 1990, when I believe I saw the light of Christmas' original meaning finally snuff. Gut feeling, can't exactly say why, but in that year the lingering glimmer of Jesus was ground out from the celebrations like juice under a stomped eyeball. Maybe it was pre-millennium tension or the excess and poor taste of the eighties had finally excised the American capacity to feel truly good inside. What's left now for the leviathan sellers of stuff is to keep pushing back the onset of Christmas shopping. Here it's simply September but shops back home are probably stocking tinsel and Snickers in green foil because smart consumers don't need the stress of buying holiday items at the last minute or because they need it for months on end. If you buy Halloween candy in late October you can bet that it's been sitting around since August and I'll wager it's only a few years before I'll be able to put fake blood and candy corn into Xmas Stockings.

There are people who still cherish the Christ saga and the observation of his birth as of prime importance during the Advent. Their views are in an ascension of loss in seas of gazes diverted towards neon lawn messiahs or bored into the woodgrain of pews during the unconvincing trips to Midnight Mass. Here in Kenya things are different. Many manic Christians, wailing at the dark indifference to God, fled like lovelorn mutts to recollect their religious sensibilities as missionaries in developing countries. In East Africa, the locals were wise enough to note that the incoming white ministers of faith in the Great Improbable were so screwed through their smooth brains that nothing of any sense could ever erupt from their spitty mouths. Thirty independent years of flailing economic progress has young

Kenyans suspecting that if God really does exist he's been having a ball fucking them over. And he was sending his comfortable white missionaries around to taunt them with hope and rob them of school fees. Granted, missionaries can't demand tithes from the absolutely destitute. But when they come across an older person with a longing for the eternal reward and five shillings in his fist, they'll get him to believe that four will get him there. *It's Christmas time; what can you give Baby Jesus so he'll let you into heaven?* The righteous denounce the retail stains on the season while the birth of their Savior has given them a tidy little saving-souls-for-profit scheme.

Christmas as usual, or something like it, goes on. Most Kenyans are Christian to the hilt though there's some measure of ancestor worship still in play. But the rest of the world is in on that too, keeping florists busy and granite workers employed. It's also part of why people still get to church on Sundays. Getting to heaven is still the objective but people also need reassurance that grandma is basking in God's light and sending down fresh baked cookies of guidance from on high. Ben and his fellow farmers are Mormon, something I learned by asking why he never drinks coffee. His tells me that his faith proscribes the ingestion of stimulants like caffeine. I can't say I know much about Mormons. They wear ties and backpacks and needle you on the subway, they build Post-Reichstag looking temples in Belmont, Massachusetts and every cute girl in my Arizona grade school had Brigham Young affiliations. That about exhausts my grasp of the Latter Day Saints but there can be no doubt they're aware of the caffeine in the tea they allow Ben to drink. So it could be suspected that the Mormon missionaries in Machakos are also in the pockets of the coffee industry, helping insure *all* the beans make it to the factory.

When I finally got a peak at the coffee mill it looked like something from America in 1910. Not that working conditions were abominable at the factory or that the laborers were ready to revolt and unionize – we've already covered what can happen when you don't bring all your beans to the warehouse. But the ramshackle shanties with half-built production lines smacked of mismanagement, squandered funds and corruption.

Loans and fees had been stolen by the recently ousted chairman of the Kithangathini Coffee Board. Ousted, but unlike the guys selling their own stuff off-market no mention of *conviction* followed his story. You can steal what belongs to everybody else with a measure of impunity but you can't freely sell what's yours. Sort of has an Oil Industry ring to it. So storage shacks were never constructed according to money allocations. Intended steel-roofed shacks haven't replaced rough wood buildings that are 'protected', as well as held together, by polythene tarps and empty burlap bags. There was even a huge, muddy pit on the grounds which should have been a fish pond for bolstering the protein intake of the farmers and their children. It's no more than an ugly sump now.

The board's new honchos are led by one of Ben's cousins. I hope it all works out. Perhaps Ben, who's been using his KFFS salary to increase the size of his farm, will benefit from having a relation at the top of the board. Nepotism, however, doesn't seem to fit Ben's style as a thoughtful, moral man. Moving up through his own hard effort seems to please him best. Maybe his integrity will find a conduit through his cousin and influence the way the board operates. Then again, with the way corruption runs through Kenya like a venereal disease, kinship may mean dick in Kithangathini. It seems as soon as Kenyans taste some power, however minor, they crave it above all else. The hopes of children, fraternal love, the golden rule or simply doing the right thing? *Not a fucking chance*. It's a screw everybody existence the moment one steps up to the pot and nobody just skims – they scoop and go deep until the ladle burns their paws. A cousin in charge may only mean that Ben Sila will get his sticking last.

It only takes a brief gander to realize the potential these hills have for giving their denizens comfortable or even prosperous lives. The earth is rosy-cheeked, bright-eyed and bushy tailed like I'm not used to seeing. The mineral rich, red earth and perpetually moist cool air make it coffee bush nirvana. A moderate outside investment could refurbish the factory; add some contraptions and some extra fertilizer and this hood would shift into high gear java producing. Most importantly, a little help is needed to tighten the reliability of the water supply. Ben is hoping to get four hundred bucks together for a pump to bring water from a stream upslope to his trees. The farmers already know how to grow coffee, but some updated gadgetry and backup supports against natural hardships are presently beyond the depths of their pockets. Think Santa will pack some agricultural gear into his sack soon? Does he even deliver to Mormons?

Rhinorrhea

The guest list at today's noon feast included John Muindi, vice-admiral of the Koobi Fora culinary crew. Since he'd been in command of the ketchup-on-spaghetti atrocity up at the Karari we'll nix the cooking praise and redub him as *Prince Among Nice Guys*. He and Joseph Kitila had popped over for a visit last morning. Tomas Muthoka lives around here as well and we've been expecting to see him any time now. It's been a real treat to see the guys - a Koobi Fora Field School First Week Reunion. Tomorrow we'll brunch at Kitila's and John has invited us to a second lunch, or first dinner, at his place today. Two lunches! No wonder Johnny was the only plump dude on the staff.

A new nocturnal conviction is that night now sucks in Kithangathini. The sniffles acquired in the end days on Turkana's eastern shore have committed to all out war on my breathing parts. I'm a cascade of clear snot, hot and cold running clamminess and unbearable itches – those, however, come from my fleas. A bubonic rat fucking itself in a sweaty wool sock filled with rancid oatmeal, fatally dehydrating through my face and deliriously wishing for malaria. A full-on infection would mean all these rolls of toilet paper won't be wasted on my nose alone. But I couldn't possibly get malaria now. Mosquitoes cover their mouths when I cough and my blood isn't liquid enough for swimming parasites. Everyone offers condolences but looks askance at the roll of potty wipe I clutch like a security blanket. My throat is a ricotta factory so I ought to knock the fresh, whole milk from the morning routine. I'm not huge on milk, but Ben boils it into our tea, straight from the udder of his amicable cow. How can I refuse the dairy when they've smothered me in nothing but supreme hospitality? Ben's been giving me some lemon stuff which is intended to cure me of clotting phlegm. *Lemon Oil? Bitter Lemon? Citron Whizzy?* A little tube of lemony something which imparts a feel-nice effect to those enduring the purgatorial precipitates of distressed throats and sinuses and why the fuck can't I remember the name of that elixir? I've tried so hard to pay attention to everything and now I recall fuck all about this morning. *Criminy.* Well, before I wander too far from the idea, that lemon whatever the hell you call it is the most effective symptom reliever I've ever come across. For about fifteen minutes. Then the magic vanishes as my airways get restocked with concentrated chowder.

Poor Ben seems puzzled as to why the remedy hasn't been effective; it works for him. But he's immunologically inured to the bugs of Kenya and his range of travel is akin to my Northeast rambles from Maine to Philly. The *Dassanetch* region where the Omo River penetrates Lake Turkana won't wreak havoc on his immune system just as a New Jersey malaise is no real threat to me. But if Ben ever took a two-month visit to North America he'd be laid waste by the first old bat to cough near him in Providence. Then I'd be the one perplexed at the inefficacy of Nyquil on his suffering.

All things considered, an awful cold isn't the worst that can happen on a first venture into Africa. Bilharzia, Dengue, malaria, polio, Ebola or even some as yet unnamed evil which could have arrived via bedbugs during the tryst with Jane that first week in Nairobi – crazy diseases exalt in dance all over Kenya and all I've got is this nasty cold. A bad, snotty, clotty, drippy cold. And fleas. A whole lotta fleas. Or one or two very, very busy fleas.

So fuck this cold, says I! Time to find the Viking in me and do whatever it takes – chew through iron or wipe my nose with rocks – to do whatever the hell it is Ben wants us to do. There were matters to attend to and matters meant leaving level ground and burning the glutes, searing the hams, slaughtering the calves, administering corporal punishment to the *tibialis anteriori* and making the quadriceps all hurty and junk. It's an aerobic landscape and I can incinerate calories humping down precipitous valleys and up inverted slopes just to reacquire them by having lunch at John Muindi's house. Mrs. Muindi out-sizzles her husband so we'd sucked up stew and chapati until our guts acquired stretch marks. Then there were photo ops with the hundred or so people in his family. Some of the children had a downright ball as the camera clicked and some were terrified of this pale anomaly to the point of tears. But it surely isn't a color thing - my little pasty cousins bawl and hide behind their parents whenever I show up at a cookout.

When all was said and done we hit the paths of imminent danger back home in the twilight. My Viking ass is weeping like a humid beer cozy and my nose is the region's leading mucal resource. Fatigue has let the piss and vinegar seep back in. I'll quit the histrionics about runny noses but I may just start sucking my thumb any goddamned minute now.

Which came first...the chicken? The egg? Who gives a shit? Did you realize that these genetically damaged birds snore? The rooster at the foot of the bed saws through its face like a fat trucker after the crystal meth wears off. What's the solution here? Turn it over on its side or bite its head off?

Adopted

Whining and crying. That crap is behind me now, the business of a yesterday nobody needs to remember. No more disquisitions hissed to myself in bed. Fevers still kink my eyebrows and nostrils will yet stiffen my shirtsleeves with snot. But I've never griped a peep to Ben or anyone else here and for that I am *mukamba* now. A man of Kithangathini *and* Kathangathini (I'll get to it...) An initiate of the *Wathungwa* clan as per decree of Benjamin Sila, Tomas Muthoka, Joseph Kitila, Martin Kiao, and other power brokers in this enclave. Bring on the malaise, baby, I've got local ancestors to protect me now

That was a real nice honor of the guys to bestow on me. Taking me in as one of their own even though I come from a place and lifestyle that's a far cry from theirs. The ways of living at home are degenerating at the same pace Ben's are progressing. I'm just a brat from a nation of bastards yet they've seen something about me that they like. Seems like too big a reward just for bending over those *karais* and washing dishes for a month in the deserts and forests. I realize that it was more than dinner plates. That part of it was just the willingness, as a member of a group, to just pitch in and help do anything in need of doing. To be someone who didn't see the tasks assigned to anybody else as beneath them. As a work ethic that will always gain you some respect from your comrades and make it easy to get some assistance when you find yourself in need of a hand. I've always reached for hands that were offered in friendship yet I feel like I'm getting more than I've been able to give. These men should get a fat cut from my tuition check because they really gave me a fat slice of the education here - even in terms of paleoanthropology. I'd picked up more from Muthoka, Casmus, Ben and others than in the combined teachings of Waybill, Burrows and Jomo.

Back to lunch. I love lunches in Kithangathini. And I now love them in *Kathangathini* – because that's where it was today. Hop over a hill, switch a vowel and you're feasting on Muthoka's veranda. Hell of a gorgeous setting. Like all the homes in this valley, Tom's and Joe's (neighbors *and* brothers, as I just found out) are made of adobe-style *matofali,* formed from the red earth of the area. The roofs are thatch but thoroughly watertight as I've yet to see a dewdrop on anybody's ceiling. Tomas' house is a little bigger than most. It's not quite the mudbrick palace of Kamoya Kimeu - the Leakey's ace fossil finder - visible near the crest of the valley's highest hill, yet it is pretty stunning. Straight off a Mediterranean postcard, it has a modest courtyard and stone benches overlooking slopes of leathery green trees and decorative coffee shrubs. Fruit trees flank the cozy villa while cascades of bougainvillea flush kelly and magenta over the walls and eaves. Heavens to Betsy, I love that plant. My domestic dream, apart from the one where I brush my teeth on a boat and not in a house, is to have a home engulfed in bougainvillea.

A lot of lunch happened to be liquid. We toasted our reunion with some of Muthoka's home brew, a sweet mash of sugar and water fermented by the microbes lodged in the spongy guts of a loufa fruit. Easy to make, as it was explained to me - put everything in a plastic jerrican and leave it near, but not over, a fire to get warm for a while. Let it sit for a couple of days and whammo! You got alcohol. Not bourbon, but not bad at all. Akin to the pineappley redeye I guzzled at Pegi's, this stuff put the giggles into you instantly. Thanks to my nasal affliction, I got away with accepting only one bowlful. The hills and the nose goblins were wiping me out and another helping would have hit me like an anvil swung in a camel. If health hadn't been the issue, I might have slurped through several tubs of the tasty fluid, deep into an Odede haze spent drooling on Ben's shoulder.

Muthoka and Kitila's aversion to dialog used to puzzle almost as much as it spooked me. Turns out not to be a simple matter of thoughtful reticence. The real key to their cool? The two of them are lightly-liquored smoothies who keep their stalwart serenity polished with a steady circulation of ganja. I nearly cackled out my least reverent raccoon laugh when I turned to see Muthoka deep hauling a fat roach. I bit my lip instead, converting it into a sneeze out of respect for Koobi Fora's elder guardian. He took it down all by himself, not even offering a toke to his kid brother. Then again, he didn't have to since a pudgy, thumb-thick joint was also incinerating at the end of Kitila's face. They both offered and I politely declined out of respect for Ben, for my withered immune system and for the fact that I am no longer good at marijuana. Add a little THC to the moonshine and I would have somehow found myself sliding headfirst down the slopes of Muthoka's backyard, giggling and barfing over my shirt.

Muthoka's English isn't as weak as he had us thinking during the field school. Opting not to use it, he takes in whatever the duller *wazungu* say and keeps an edge to himself. Once he felt we'd reached a proper bond this morning he opened up, showing me the official documentation on a new species of fossil bat found by and named for him. Then he went on to bursting out with stuff like:

"Man! *Mzee*! Men! Power!!!"

Hell yes, brother Tomas - Men and Power. That's what it was all about! *Me, man, sneeze in strength!* It was making sense. Clearly Tom was in the throes of a guy thing, but what the fuck? Our friendship was taking stride.

"Yes! *Mzee*! Absolutely right, Muthoka! *Groovy Sana*"

With that everything got quieter. The boys began to look at the ground a little as Ben cleared his throat and asked me what I was trying to say by '*groovy sana*'. I'd tossed it around so liberally throughout the field sessions and Ben finally felt my Kiswahili might need some assistance. *Oh Lordy*! The THC and the booze working us into a new stage. I gave it some reflection over my tea, bougainvillea splattering my skin in rosy shadow. I may have mused too long, but I was also tired and short on interesting things to say. And then I recalled what had brought on the deep rumination,

"Sorry, guys – got lost for a minute there. *Groovy* is what I say when things are great and *sana* is what you guys use for 'very'. *Groovy sana*: great very! I mean, very great!"

That set them at ease to know I wasn't shamefully dumb or intentionally insulting their tongue. Then I sneezed volcanically, a pyroclastic blast littering Muthoka's clean patio with clods of nasal pumice and hot streams of molten boogers.

"*Sawa*!!! Man! Power!!!" Tom howled, delighted by the event.

"Groovy," laughed Kitila.

"*Sawa! Sawa!!! Mzee!*" I shot back and conversation picked up all fresh and fluid. We rambled on about all sorts of neat things. Like Kitila's skill as an archer, able to shoot songbirds right between the eyes from a hundred meters off. The Akamba have a history in archery, once employing their deadeye distance aim against Maasai short range spears when the northern nomads began their incursion into traditional Bantu lands. I've always been fascinated with death by arrow, ever since I'd become a great slayer of grapefruits on the branch as a second grader in Yuma. *Twaaang! Swwwwipt!* If citrus could know fear, then my little bow and I gave them night terrors. Fucked up my share of prickly pear cactus back in the day, too. Tom had a bow and a quiver inside and brought them out. A medium-sized bow, handmade right down to the perfectly straight arrow shafts and their oiled, iron tip blades. Kitila explained the construction and technique to me, then notched an arrow on the string, drew back smoothly and launched the dart in a moderate arc towards a home across the valley. It was too far to see exactly, especially with moonshine bubbling through my veins and sinuses draining through my eyes, but it seemed like it sailed right through an unshuttered window. A moment later feminine shrieking began to bang echoes around the hills, followed by a little hubbub of people running into the house and right back out. Looked like they were chasing a person in a dress, waving frantically at a stick wagging off the back of her head. *Oh, what fun!* My sore jaws could no longer hold back the maddened chuckles. I snapped out of that daydream midway through Kitila explaining that the arrows were too precious to shoot for no good reason. But he did grab a thin, not too crooked, branch from the loufa tree and stripped it of its leaves. Then he notched an end with a pocket knife, demonstrated the proper stance and draw then launched the stick skyward. It wobbled around a lot and didn't kill anybody but I got the picture. He promised that if I were to return next summer he'd get some cheap arrows and teach me to shoot.

As things wound down, Kitila revealed another gift. Pulling out a guitar he began plucking and strumming out an afternoon lullaby. The flavor of the tune was like nothing I could recognize – it wasn't styled like anything from the continents on my side of the world, or any of the others for that matter. It didn't have a sound that would strike me as distinctly African either. Then again why should I think myself aware of all the sonic possibilities from a huge landmass filled with many very different peoples. The one thing I could put my finger on was that the music was enthralling, soothing me into a siesta in which I nearly failed to notice Muthoka as he presented me with a stick he'd begun carving. It was a three and a half foot, straight length of acacia. It had been stripped of the thin bark completely, with large, bare knots and branch bases sticking off in two rows on opposite sides of the limb. The naked, gnarled knobs lent it an unexpected supernatural quality; or it was at least arty. Something *avant garde* to glue to a base, stick in a gallery and listen to intellectuals sputter horseshit about it while eating cheese and lousy hummus. Muthoka explained that he had nothing else to offer but that he must give me something. I thought it was one of the coolest things I've ever received and it was extra wonderful because of the sentiment behind it. I unhitched my belt, slid the sheath of it and handed him my double-edged survival knife. Didn't make it myself, but Tomas Muthoka could whittle more wood with it or kill things as necessary. He clasped my hand and we all made a dozen affirmations of enduring brotherhood. Joseph Kitila kicked down an extra pack of Rooster unfiltered cigarettes to help me through my sinus troubles. In return I offered up my copper Zippo and the last of my lighter fluid. I'll get archery lessons if I ever get to return here and I promised to show Joe some Zippo tricks as well.

Ben, Muthoka and I hit the road. There were more people to meet; folks who'd sent Ben word that they wished to greet the American. Somewhere we lost Muthoka. Didn't even say "*Sawa! See ya later, Mzee!*" I just happened to turn and see him a good ways uphill, slipping silently, like an Arabica elf, into one of the local brew sheds. As it turns out *Kathangathini* - the hills, vales, dales, etc. where he and Kitila live – is the brewery district. Still shacks with corrugated aluminum roofs litter the hills like toasters in the rubble of a former appliance factory. Not really paying attention on the way here, I'd failed to notice these hills weren't as intensively farmed as the those in Kithangathini. In Ben's neck of the woods, agriculture and Christianity hold sway. Not a ton of drinking going on since all the toasters there are churches or water catchments. Neighborhood onomatopoeia. Fucking bizarre in that it all made perfect sense to me.

Tom and Joe live less than a mile from Ben. But that's a beeline measure and doesn't mean anything unless you have the gossamer sails of a butterfly and the anorexic bug body to go with it. Being foot-propelled and heavy-boned means at least four times that distance over oppressive terrain and aggressive gravity. To think I grieved over my aching ass over the last couple of days. After this day's bivouac, my failure to get immunized for polio ceased to be an issue. My fucking femurs are warped now anyway.

Ben was happy as a Lake Rudolph clam this evening as water flowed through the pipe to his shamba. Due to financial and organizational fuckups in the local water project the works ceased just shy of Ben's land and the adjacent school. So he ran out his own pipes to the village main with his own funds, providing flow to the school in the process. That was earlier this year. But when he'd returned from KFFS's first session, his pipes had gone dry. He's intimated that a farmer uphill may have rigged them to increase flow to his own shamba while cutting hydration to neighbors further down the line. The guy had a history with such despicabilities, yet Ben wished to stay charitable in speculation. There might have been a natural, wholly non-scandalous blockage. Aardvarks stealing the PVC for their dens maybe. Or pipe hamsters that'd now finally cleared out.

Today things finally were going just right. Water was flowing, filling his small holding tanks, and Sila floated around with a huge smile that couldn't be removed with a jack hammer. The event renewed his inspiration to finish a larger water tank, one to fill in reserve for any aridity he might face in the future. According to Ben, some farmers are inclined to monkey with the pipes when faced with drought. It increases their water pressure at the expense of the guy next door, yet it won't matter much if the water eventually stops anyway. That's when the guys with the reserve tanks have the last chuckle. That people regularly put the screws to each other here also lends support to Ben's first and magnanimously discarded hypothesis on the original cause of his dry pipes. Sila is an ant sharp enough to circumvent any of that bad business. He shrugs off the petty games of grasshopper dickheads, and builds water tanks for the rough times.

Tomorrow morning I'll straighten the sheets on this bed for the last time. This *motungwa* is about to leave his adoptive home and new family. The acceptance and honorary membership here was sweet - and I'm extra lucky for having come here precircumcised. Kenya has come to seem like home. I loved the work. I enjoyed KFFS, though not all of it; there were plenty of shitty altos in that choir. But I'll miss every last one who had me falling hard for them; who made me swim in a muck of love with visions of ivy-strangled picket fences, kids, Irish setters with cataracts and matching soft-tail Harley's. Once stateside, I'll see what I can do about washing Kalle out of my system with a slurry of tequila and bimbos. Bitter medicine is best choked down at home.

Just joking. There ain't enough sluts and booze to ever erase the shining daydream of my days here. I'll have memories of the bright grins of Ben, his wife and his kids to light up any dark stretches ahead.

The Minivans of Abaddon

With Ben Sila by my side, getting back to Nairobi meant a mere two hours of country bus perdition. How in Criminy's blazes the torture turned out so brief is beyond me. We must have caught the express. If anybody dares suggest that these two months amounted to a long vacation, I'll grab their scaly throats and bellow; *When I was in Kenya I rode to and fro on matatus...so up yours, Jack!* You get respect for that here, at least among my Eurocracker cousins. Well, no, that's not exactly true. White people here will merely look at you like you've lost your marbles for taking sub-public transportation in the first place. So obnoxious bragging about *matatus* would require some backstory in the States and that would really suck the poignancy out of my barks. Sigh. This is getting me nowhere. When I get back to Boston, I'll just have to carry a hatpin to poke jerks when they tease me.

Matatus are no day at the park. Not sure that was clear as I covered getting to Ben's village. This isn't just another complaint about a trifle. Gripes are fat men squeezing next to you on the subway, lazy and drunk *MBTA* trolley drivers and all manner of shitty foibles which constitute the daily commute at home. Here there aren't enough vehicles to carry people comfortably to work and drivers need every shilling they charge just to keep the brakes in near-working condition. Crammed, top heavy, misaligned and speeding vans are therefore a fact of life. Some things which comprise the stuff of everyday Kenya just can't be euphemized. *Matatu* riding is irreversibly ugly, no two ways about it.

Ideally these small buses are like the airport shuttle type, body wider and higher than the cab, but most are nothing more than minivans or little pickup trucks with ramshackle huts over their beds. They're very hard to miss. Pride in ownership is glaring as these jalopies get painted wilder and tackier than the Partridge Family bus. The garish barfs of color revolve around passionate slogans like *Chocolate Love* and *Total Madness* or more mystifying tags such as *Beauty Secret* and *Detroit Pistons*. I didn't think there were any Piston fans east of Cleveland.

Inside, seats and benches are shredded, smell of bad oranges, and the whole shebang rattles to frazzled sound systems cranked to 11 through speakers built for 2. Luggage, a whole fuckload of it, gets strapped on top, ambitiously held down by tattered rubber ribbons and sisal twine. Passengers sit, stand, get suspended in the human emulsion within or ride on top of the luggage to help the tie-downs in their improbable task. Touts take your money only after you've sat or found a way to wedge yourself up against the roof. When the machine is ready to roll, external passengers grab on to any hold outside the bus and dangle. You catch them shifting their bodies, and this is the most wondrously unnerving part of the ride for me, just like sailors on a racing catamaran to keep the metal beast from toppling over around corners.

White Kenyans, as has been noted, do not ride matatus. Not that Kenya is overflowing with indigenous honkies in the first place, but it is rife with Indians and they don't ride them either. Part of that has to be sage judgment, but elitism sneaks in there to boot. The non-African bourgeoisie use cars to go from there to here or they journey aboard regular, big commercial buses. But no Caucasoid brother had ever offered me a lift and while big buses will go from Nairobi to Machakos or Makueni, they won't take you into Nunguni. So at the start of my Kithangathini side trip, I had to get my way over to Nairobi's City Center. Where, by the way, you won't see pasty-white people either, but you will find Indians and Arabs running shops and cursing at everybody. That part of town, which feels less like the center of a city and more like the core of the earth, is a hornets' nest of shitware boutiques, thugs and airborne garbage. It's also where the Country Bus Station, such as it is, is located. Takes a little effort to find its location as well as a little help from locals who will point you back to it each time you've gone through but missed it. No help can be had from any Hindi you might ask because you'll be either ignored or told that it doesn't exist. But it does exist, in a tangle of sidewalks and roads with extra minivans hiding amongst the people. Since they're not out to board matatus, white folk do not populate City Center in any significant numbers. Walking around as the low-melanoma, hairy headed gent I am drew stumped stares. Women backed away as if I were a spitting lunatic, an intrepid Peace Corps douche, or Lucifer himself. Well they'd probably never even considered me as anything demonic. I just interpreted it that way because, hey, wouldn't it be cool to be Satan? The heat would be more trifling and I could just cruise to Nunguni in a cherry red Trans-Am.

I discovered the second Nunguni stage coach quick enough (I was an hour or so too late in finding the first). Not a bad looking van considering some of the mortally rusted clunkers heading elsewhere. As late as I was for the matatu I should have been on, I was early for this one. I waltzed through a deserted, peopleless cabin to slouch in the back left corner. *Window seat in the wide open rear, you lucky dog!* I stood the frame of my backpack between my knees the wide way, as there wasn't much room between my bench and the backrest ahead. A tout kept insisting that it go on the roof, but I politely let him know there was fat fucking chance of that happening. A foreigner's bag would be the first to "fall off" and it would probably happen before the bus got rolling. I boarded at noon on that sunny Monday. Almost immediately I felt like waiting for departure outside, to get out of that oven. The only breeze through the window was generated by people breathing into it. But I was stuck. Within a few minutes of taking a spot in the spacious transport there were six people with me on the red pleather seat built for the discomfort of four. So I sucked it up and waited. And waited. An hour went past and the van still hadn't gone anywhere. Obviously the scheduled matatu times they give at the Country Bus Station are not based on departure. The scheduled times suggest when vans will be on hand for boarding. Departure is based on however long it takes to cram the vehicle with passengers without totally cutting off oxygen to those in the middle. That meant I was ridiculously tardy trying for the morning matatu. Overly punctual for the afternoon one found me waiting the longest. My ass began to grow roots in the seat, all the while growing stiff as dozens of people came to my window or crawled over others inside to try selling me crap.

School notebooks and knotted leather strips and watches shoved in my face without even a rehearsed sale pitch. When the eighth fake Timex (who the heck makes knock-off Timexes?) came through the window, I just took it, put it on and thanked the dude. He stood outside smiling for a couple of seconds while I pretended to read a book. Then he rapped on the side of the van,

"Hey! Hey, my friend! One thousand shillings!"

Oh, a *twenty dollar* faux Timex...how could one go wrong? I apologized for assuming that it was a random gift and told him I didn't have a grand on me. Would he take a used notebook instead? Only mostly written in but slightly bent at the spine? He called me a crazy man but didn't spread the word, and the local sales force kept on me. The badgering was tedious but it killed time. As the matatu's engine finally started up an older gent decided he needed to come back and sit with us. No arguments came from my bench mates as the passengers ahead passed him over to us. Would have been in a very lonely minority to bitch so I kept my mouth shut, welcoming the *mzee* to our human knot with a vacant grin. Now there were seven, two of them children, which didn't offset the fact that I was taller, wider and probably fifty pounds heavier than any of the adults. *Fatty, fatty, two by four...* Narrowing the space I occupied was painfully limited by the pack frame now deeply implanted into both *adductor magnus* muscles. I tried to angle it off as much as possible, which wasn't much at all and I couldn't pull it up without my compadres picking up their asses and getting off me. I was doomed to lose circulation as the frame dug into my femurs and a young woman cozied in upon my right thigh.

Seven on my seat. Six on the seat ahead. Probably six more in the next. Three in the front passenger chair. A driver, maybe two. Another half dozen or more crouching or stooped over on their feet. It wasn't one of those kaleidoscope shuttle buses I'd mentioned earlier - a low end *matatu* is just a van. Ten, maybe twelve, people are supposed to be in a van at the same time. We had at least thirty jammed like wontons in a take-out box, not to mention the dudes swinging off the sides, rear and top. Shouldn't we all have been wearing clown suits?

There were no possible directions for any limb to move unless it was flesh squeezing into new districts of my body. The only parts at liberty to exercise were my neck and dozing head, which bobbed around for three-something hours. After driving for two we spun to a stop, snapping me out of a terrifying dream about riding in a matatu, and I saw a sign which read "Nunguni" as well as some other words. I needed to get out immediately, but the passengers jamming me in looked at me strangely the moment I began to shimmy up.

"*Nunguni*," I explained, pointing to the road sign.

Heads were wagging and the gal in my lap said,

"No."

No? No what? 'No, this isn't Nunguni' or 'No, you can't get out'? It didn't seem open to discussion. The anchovies were in charge of me now, whether they knew where the hell I was going or not. So off we rolled while I creaked my head around on a stiff neck to see if Ben was anywhere outside. The next stop had a Nunguni sign too. As did the next and the one after that and the one after that and the one after that. But each displayed a second name as well, different from the others. At all these stops one person would hop out and two or three would work their way into fissures in the crowd. And at each drop-off people would turn to me and silently swivel their heads. It was always no. How did they know where the fuck I was headed? Were they screwing with the stranger? Seeing if they could make him go way, way out of his way? Boy, if I wasn't on the splintered end of that crapstick, I'd think it was a decent prank to pull. Of course there might have been no practical joke at all with something more sinister afoot. The matatu was headed for Mt. Kilimanjaro where they'd strip, oil and scent me, then toss me off a precipice to appease the spirits of agriculture and mass transit. Maybe I was being taken by an unscrupulous syndicate to get sold into slavery. I'll bet that wouldn't be so bad. I'm pretty sturdy and have been known to take direction from time to time. Bet I'd be the best white slave ever, even better than Spartacus although you'd never catch me spooning up with Tony Curtis in the slave huts. Nor would I stab anybody in a slave fight just take his spot on a crucifix. Dying for days along a shadeless Roman boulevard for some bright-eyed pretty boy? Fuck that; stupidest thing I ever saw in a movie...

Well now, as I was screwed deeper at every moment, all I could do at each stop was wrench around a neck saturated with lactic acid, peering out the dusty window near me or looking through chinks in the bodies to see out others. All views were consistently Benless. Nunguni signs kept coming – the town must be huge, nearly bigger than all of Kenya itself – so there was yet a spit of hope. But I was banking more and more on riding that Judas' Cradle to the end of the line, spending the night paralyzed in a gully before doing it all over in reverse to Nairobi, then flying the hell back home.

But after a slow crawl up a final hill we rolled to a sign that read *Nunguni* and nothing else. The crate emptied as passengers motioned for me to disembark. *Ohhh, aha! All of us were going to Nunguni.* What do you know? While toppling over on the bench, because my support people had left, I heard a beautiful, smiley voice:

"Frank! Frank! Hello!"

Thank Jesus and up yours to the rest. Ben was at my window, come to save my lost little ass from certain and dismal discomfort on a long ride home.

The return matatu was slightly less severe. We got to that van late, but it isn't like they depart on schedule anyway. As previously noted, one has to be unbelievably off time to miss one's matatu. Getting from Ben's shamba to Nunguni (the town, not the spacious concept) meant over an hour of uphill walking or more if you encounter the aged father of a man who married Ben's brother's daughter. In a word, his *siatawa*. It's idiomatic – doesn't really have a parallel word in English, which is too bad since it takes my language a full, run-on sentence to explain the old gent. But thinking over it there isn't a good reason to have a word meaning the *"parent of another person wedded to a niece or nephew."* But here they're big on matripatristratofamiliolineal blah, blah... Moving on.

When you get caught up with *siatawas* you add forty-five minutes to your ambulatory ordeal while he adds the feeling that you're going to miss the bus and never see home again. We were ascending and the geezer slowed our march. Had heart trouble, he explained. Couldn't walk uphill and talk at the same time, yet desired to walk and talk with the two of us about money to tune up his heart and make it easier to do this all again next time around. There was the money thing again. The "*white = wealthy*" notion that not a few Kenyans I'd met also held. That's perfectly understandable as many of us Americans and Europeans perform ridiculous extravagances such as flying to Africa just to look at the things here. I'm almost guilty of that myself as it would've been far more fiscally responsible to have stayed home and learned fieldwork by desecrating a Wampanoag burial mound. But home is short on volcanoes and protohumans so I had to save and borrow in order to look at the things in Africa. I'm nearly tapped now at the end of the trip but I can also make money quickly at home. With that in mind I've been inclined to share what I have to the end and help where I can: a few shillings here, some candy and oranges there. The two kilos of beef[9] bought for Ben's family, though not appreciably expensive, pushed me right up against my financial safety net. And all that toilet paper my nose ate obliged replacement. The rest of my cash was maybe, *maybe*, enough to get another night at the Chiromo, a cab to the airport and a pack of smokes. Vittles and liquor nourishment would have to be at the benevolence of KLM Airlines so I'd be living lean for the next twenty-four. I had nothing for the siatawa but I still felt like helping the ancient nettle. Perhaps explaining that if talking uphill impeded his progress than he could just shut the hell up. Luckily, Ben skirted the money corner by prescribing *kitunguu sumu*, a little *poison onion*, which is to say *garlic*, for the knocks and pings in the siatawa's heart. The old chump was delighted with the advice, acting that way at least. He'd overplayed the gratitude, giving off an aura of mild anxiety, as it dawned on him that he had tamped on delicate turf. Apprehending that the hand-out innuendo took swipes at both Sila's dignity and my comfort as a friend running out of money he backed off.

The ETA for the bus stop itself had been screwed afoul but tardiness didn't mean missing the ride. On the other hand, it did

---

[9] chopped right off the dangling carcass of a beef animal in a butcher banda no less!

mean a matatu already crammed tight with Kenya's new breed of nomads – work commuters. No place to sit and standing would only work if I was a mere set of legs with a smidgen of torso. There was always riding on top with the luggage, but I'd had more than enough retard thrills for the year. However, Sila, ever so smoothly, talked people into standing themselves or getting skinnier so his new pal could sit. And they all agreed to do so with *smiles* on their faces. Once again, among the most hospitable people on Earth, I was sick feeling like an American who demanded service at the expense of others. What a douche! But as the largest douche bag on board, I thanked everyone humbly and took a seat with my back against the driver's cockpit. It was a splintery board on a metal storage bin, comfortable as a dollhouse hassock studded with scorpions. But it was a seat and I was grateful and completely ashamed to have it.

We must have caught the jet stream back since it took an hour less than it did to get out to Nunguni. It could also be attributed to not getting stopped by highway cops as often. Heading to Nunguni (the bus stop, not the nimbus of befuddlement) various members of the fuzz treated us to three fifteen minute delays. On the return we suffered lightly through a two-minute pullover. The Nairobi bound van obviously had a better deal worked out with the boys in very faded blue or just paid the requisite bribe without haggling. That's what the cops do on Kenya's highways - pull lots of vehicles over, threaten motorists on all sorts of quack violations until drivers kick down a little scratch to make them go away. One could debate the charge until the cops back down but that may never happen. From what I've gathered the cost of extortion isn't worth the loss of time and matatus are a hilarious example of that. Cops pull them over all the time, citing them mainly for violations of passenger limits which, if you haven't been paying attention, are right on the money. The police make people get out of the van until a legal amount remain within, then they accept payment of "fines" from the operators. Then they drive off as everybody crams back into the matatu and on it goes. Those were the fun moments en route to Nunguni (the actual hamlet, not the nebulous realm hinted at through the local signage). No such comedy going back, though we saw some matatus playing the game on the way. A lack of ethics among armed civil servants can be disheartening, especially when you're sitting in a miserable corner of a hot van filled with sweat vapors. You think you'll never get to where you're headed, that your bladder will rupture without a restroom and you wonder how a developing country will ever realize its potential if it can't even control corruption at the lower rungs of the civic ladder. Nothing but time to ponder and cast judgment during delays and the slow progress between them. You could piss yourself, wait for the urine to cool and soothe your legs while coming to the realization that cops are on the take because the payrolls aren't on the give. The government doesn't pay much and never on time. It doesn't feel obliged to fill squad cars with gas and I'll wager that sidearm ammunition is meagerly budgeted. So there's not much in a constable's job description that's truly worth the effort - except sitting on the hood of a car waiting for motorists to strong arm. They've got to feed families like everyone else. However, one hopes none of them ever get promoted. From what can be seen of the government, Kithangathini's java cooperative or even in the Museum administration corruption, at its most vile *fuck your fellow man* base, is a hard habit to shake. It's a funny thing, common in the States as well, that once somebody moves out of poverty the last thing they want is to be surrounded by poor people. Less funny is how the consuming greed of people on the way up helps ensure that the ranks of the poor never cease to swell.

The only real terror endured going back, ignoring my Kithangathini fleas which had tagged along, was having my right leg fall asleep into a violent dream. It was no ordinary circulatory disruption. It was a freak show. My right foot was planted right above the matatu's transmission, which churned out a mammoth, buzzing lullaby to that extremity. It was just run of the mill pins and needles at the onset. I'd wiggle my toes and pull in the arch to wake it up. It didn't and soon enough the foot was dead numb. Neural communiqués were sent south instructing the digits to keep at it, but it wasn't possible to tell if they were receiving the messages. I strained forward to see if I could spot some activity within the boot leather. Nothing. My tibia felt like it was poking into a spongy cobble of soapstone until it also morphed into damp, porous rock. The sensation, coupled with a lack thereof, kept scaling inexorably up my leg. As the calf lost contact with the central nervous system, panic took hold - I was going to lose all feeling on that side of my body. My head would loll, an eyelid would droop and I was gonna drool up a waterfall. At least the people who gave up their places to me would have new pity - *aww, it's okay for the mzungu prick to sit up front where we really should be... He's having a stroke.* I really needed the weirdness to end, closing my eyes to concentrate on moving the leg. I still couldn't sense any results but looked down again to discover that it was indeed in motion. It was bouncing. Up and down erratically and banging wildly against the knee of a lady off to the side who was struggling not to face me. She stared intently at a speaker dangling overhead not wishing to acknowledge a foreigner losing control of his limb all over hers. My knee was bashing up her thigh quite well and was she ever going to be sore in the morning. I stood desperately, to the amusement of bemused van-mates, and began stomping my leg with the trivial control remaining in my hip. I might have been stomping all over the poor woman's foot but sure as hell couldn't tell and she would have never let on, saving this nightmare tale for friends later on. When feeling came back it arrived angry. A wild, crazy pain which must be what it's like to get shot up with an automatic, rapid-fire staple gun.

The dead appendage debacle was almost the worst that had happened. My hiney muscles did get ground to the bone again, but I'd been weaned on that kind of agony on the ride out to Koobi Fora. But there was a fresh incident to add to my list of crimes against humanity; a brief moment when I'd dozed off just enough to have my neck go slack. A jarring bump in the road let my head career out of control to smash the man sitting at my left. Cocked him squarely in the mug with my rocky noggin. I could feel the goodwill of the commuters unraveling. They'd given me a seat and in return I'd spasmodically assaulted a lady and spastically head butted yet another innocent. Boy howdy, wasn't I just fucking up all over. One more transgression and somebody was probably going to say something unkind.

The next person to my front and left, and pretty darn close to kneeling in my lap, was a woman cradling an unusually clean baby. Spotless, except for a smidgen of gack at the corner of its mouth, like it had just gone through a carwash. It struck me as remarkable since the rest of us were kind of dusty and I always think of babies as muck magnets in general. And considering what ugly little freaks infants can be it always throws me off guard when one of them catches my eye to amuse me stupid with its antics and golly-goshable cuteness. I don't want to pansy up so let's just say me and the pup had some fun for a while. He was so interested in my shiny watch, determinedly trying to pull it off, he lost track of the meal he was having at mom's tap. He didn't seem to care if he was hungry or not, but he wasn't getting anywhere with the watch either. Unhitching it was beyond his non-criminally-seasoned mind. I considered showing him how it was done, but backed up on the idea, realizing that it could fall into the tangle of legs. That would mean losing it altogether or injuring another passenger in an attempt to retrieve it. So on it stayed and I jiggled my wrist to entertain the lad while I got to leer at a big dripping tit dangling a foot from my face. My, what a well polished and silky looking thing! What a huge, tubular nipple dribbling out the dairy! Ho boy, public transit fetish porn and cigarettes for a half buck per pack! Why the hell was I leaving Kenya?

But leaving had to be done and so I did. I'd given Ben a big bear hug when we parted at the museum, making him just a bit uncomfortable. But he smiled wide on the handshake as I promised to get back here someday, one way or another. I was getting uncomfortable too – goodbyes aren't my forte and my luck with matatus had me on edge about missing the plane. Something about being broke in Africa left me with the taste of wet newspaper in my mouth because that's what I'd be eating if I got stranded. While repacking my gear I found a slightly flattened pack of Sportsman cigarettes. It was a little rainbow arcing out of my duffel and for a mere shilling I got a pack of Roosters at the Chiromo bar. The hotel manager had taken a shine to me and promised to get me a cheap cab to the airport. I was going to go home. A changed man. A new beast in a bright, squishy spiritual realm. Returning to eat everything in the way of my destiny and to disinfect the stains of my past. And to get a shave. I left the Barbasol at Ma's in Rhode Island and this nappy auburn beard can really fucking itch. It needs to go.

Vroooom!

A negligible forty minute delay at Nairobi International and we took off to one of the most jarring, rattling and I don't know...*scuzzy?*...starts I've ever had on a jet. Initially I blamed the tarmac crannies of the Kenyan airstrip, but the bird continued to shudder during the ascent. It might've been a nasty, persistent East African crosswind, though that wouldn't account for the sustained, muffled shrieking noise. The kind you hear from movie planes when they're about to crash. Maybe there were banshees on the wings come to let the Irish sons know that God was cutting us from the squad. I was getting unhappier by the minute though the convulsing plane was obviously no worry for a Dutch flight attendant who'd trotted past twice with scissors in her hand. Hopes for cruising height to smooth the ride faded as well. Out the window, the lights of towns below looked so close that we could be dusting their crops. At least the radar-eluding trajectory suggested we were in for an eye-level blink at black pyramids as we passed through Egypt.

I relished the heck out of my second arrival in Holland. Firmly committed to the continued expansion of horizons, I lounged in a wholly different part of Schipol Airport. Repatriating myself to The Netherlands for hours, I moved now and again whenever I felt I'd absorbed all cultural insights the immediate walls, ceilings and carpets had to offer. It was a dizzying cyclone of culture shock. A whole freaking sixth of a day trying to suck on all that local flavor. Lordy.

I'd hoped to head into Amsterdam this time around but that would have meant facing the money ugliness. No significant money left beyond little coins from here and back there;

fractional guilders or partial shillings that weigh nearly nothing, so unsubstantial they'd been dented by lint in my pockets. I bottomed out by purchasing a newspaper which took $2.18 from me and offered up a remedial crossword puzzle. A warm, flat half-liter bucket of *Coke Light* squandered another $2.37. How I miss those days of fifteen-cent soda pops sold in genuine, rinsed out Fanta bottles. Oh Kenya! Where have ye gone? Nobody at this bland fucking airport shows even the slightest inclination at breastfeeding a brat for me.

The Dutch come across oddly. Half of them, rather the half of the half of them that are women, are quite beautiful. The rest are downright dopey looking. It's like God had once smoked some of his more interesting vegetation, threw his glasses in a drawer and started making Nederlanders out of white and yellow Play-Doh. Pasty folk, and though well-crusted even the thin ones are probably squishy when wet. Zwieback people. Except, as noted, a big handful of summarily attractive Dutch ladies who probably smell frightfully nice. They must get manufactured when the maryjane wears off and Jehovah puts the goggles back on. But they are a congenial squad of Europeans, crazy as that sounds. However, the friendly side is apparent only when you have to deal with them head on. Otherwise they amble about like free-programmed humanoid units that snap into a profusion of *Good Morning*'s when something blocks their path. Then it's right back to drone mode, expressionless, cold and dusty in the eyes. Dutch humans can be witnessed bantering and laughing amongst themselves, though it's hard to see why.

Having a sandwich would've been mint. But airport commissaries demand cash for that kind of happiness and I wasn't in the mood for some Pillsbury face to switch on and smile while I rooted for the cheapest pre-wrapped mayonnaise on rye. I can fast for a couple more hours yet. Then the plane will fly me home while I stuff my belly like a Carolina senator and get smashed on beer, *a la aeromaison.*

I had tried to pummel my brain to sleep on the Nairobi-Holland leg, but they couldn't deliver the Heinekens and Hennessey quick enough. Sobriety kept creeping back between rounds, my blood alcohol stuck at a level which had me awake and burning through evil thoughts: planes crashing and children of the rich choking on food. The last time I requested a brew, about four in the morning, the waitress either forgot or blew me off and never returned down my aisle. So I plotted against her. There is no forgiving that sort of insensitivity, especially when I am forced to sit still in a plane which nobody will let me fly. So I stewed in my place, smoking without blinking, staring at the stewardess nest, listening to scat jazz on the walkman, biding my time for her to walk by. A punch in the sternum and she'd be mine to drag to the lavatory and dye her naked with the magic blue water from the toilet. A cerulean tint of blame to bear as she faithfully honored passenger requests for the remainder of the flight. I wouldn't get the chance though. Gave myself away, I think, laughing much too audibly beneath the Ella Fitzgerald blowing into my ears. No stewardess chanced by my seat until the cabin filled with sunlight.

Warranty Restrictions

A glance at the bilingual wristwatch read *la una y trece de la tarde*. Okay, only the day of the week is in Spanish – *Dom, Lun, Mar, Mie, etc.* – while for time it merely points to little triangles on the dial. I do feel *muy suave* when muttering to myself in Spanish. Shortly after lunchtime, for those who can afford food, a Northwest Boeing 747-400A was ready to snuggle under my bucket and carry me home. It felt like the crazy stories were ending and I started to really think about Africa. What I did. What other people did. And what it all means and where I fit into all that.

If I wasn't fully absorbed by the moments, if I didn't love what was happening around me all the time, I might be just returning from a vacation. Boredom is the ultimate misery for me. The horrible and the hardships are as charging to me as the good or the glorious; it's a fifty-fifty deal. It has to work that way every time even if it means ransacking a world of pleasant things just to pull a little rottenness out for balance. All yang and no yin makes Jack miss a lot of points.

It had been an eight week love story. Not between me and some soft, feminine creature to make breakfast for every day. Two months in Kenya brought me to a world I'd only half imagined was in the cards. Up until July 18th, when I stepped on that fat red plane in Boston, paleoanthropology might've never been more than a reading phase I was going through. Killing credit hours until I'd gotten me a baccalaureate diploma for lining a sock drawer with over-and-done-with achievements.

But it wasn't another infinite daydream. It was a couple of months surveying ecologies, rubbing volcanic tuff sediment in my fingers, and fingering the petrified transmutations of ancient teeth from the dirt. Staring at the bones of things which had fought so hard to live one more day that the battle would eventually change them; taking a million years, give or take, but inexorably molding a new vision of themselves. One thing which carried a certain arrangement of bones would erect into a new creature with too much time on its hands to pay attention to its future. I'd gotten two million years all to myself. Glad I got to Africa before I turned thirty, as wasting my piece of life would amount to just another evolutionary dead end.

The peace and promise uncovered in the sediments around Lake Turkana fucked me up good. I mean real good. All the cluttered ideas held about myself were whipped from the few platforms of my mind with hard foundations. Shedding illusion like sun roasted skin and seeing things as clean and crystalline as the desert's morning landscape. With no other way of describing it, I'd say I had finally arrived home after twenty-six years of never being there. But I tend to harbor the harshest cynicism for myself – growing up through army-brat transience, divorce flavored adolescence and ever cartwheeling off from commitments - I've already got an inkling that I won't be at this home for long.

Paleontology was in my blood before I could even say the word, a term I'd finally spit out in first grade's "*What I Wanna Be When I Get Big*" sessions. My teacher Mrs. Kemper didn't even know what a paleontologist was, suggested the term I was looking for was *archaeologist* and that I must have made the other one up. At six I'd been proud to know such a ten-dollar word, felt I was gaining an edge in vocabulary, especially in the science department, and then my teacher kicked the stool out from under my feet. There were many more words I didn't know at the time. Such as *cunt*. What I would've given for a term like that to describe my frustration over her accusation. Well, sludge under the bridge, no?

It was dinosaurs, naturally, that I wanted to look for back then. But it wasn't a simple fascination with fleshed out monsters in picture books about legitimate dragons. I was stoked by all the weirdness, the fantastic details of things past and present, which amounted to both the variability in organisms and the anatomical threads which connected us all. I grooved on an understanding of the differences between the Saurischians (lizard-hipped dinosaurs) and the Ornithischians (bird-hipped), always trying to guess from pictures of living dinosaurs what sort of bones were in their pelves. Got pretty good at it for a grade-schooler, except when it came to Pterosaurs; dinosaurs which behaved like birds and which were, funny enough, neither. Still not sure if I've ever seen the fossilized hips of a pteranodon. I was a big-headed, mildly egotistical, primary bastard totally turned on by the geologic longevity, from lobe-finned seafood 350 million years ago to the present muddy-bottom meanderings, of coelacanths. Fucking lungfish! Flippin' proto-legs! My Sunday School teachers had their work cut out when I started drawing coelacanths into my biblical coloring books.

Somehow paleontology had faded, obscured by half a dozen newer dreams of the grand works I might do with my life, from renowned genetic engineer to drugged-up alcoholic dead by twenty-five, I couldn't anchor myself with a single ambition until I rediscovered digging up prehistory while doing English at Boston University. It began with an elective in Etruscan-Villanovan archaeology with Prof. Murray McClellan, a bearded Scotch elf who painted archaeology with broad strokes of dusty drudgery spattered vibrantly with tales of drinking liquor in hot places where exotic women live. Holy crap, it never dawned on me that the excavating life could earn you a degree and get you paid in money - with travel to boot! How awful dumb of me not to notice. Fuck, I must have been leaning harder towards that soused corpse career than I'd been aware. But in fairness to myself I hadn't thought a thing about *ological* stuff in ages. Yet there it was all over again. A few snoops through various courses and whammo: *biological anthropology*. Or paleoanthropology when the people biology gets substantially old. Which is also to say *paleontology*; of humans, not dinosaurs and with only a fraction of the scientific rigor, though we're expecting that to improve.

Full circle in a way, with fresh ideas to crack through my cranium and bathe my brain with crisp air after a decade of musty neglect. At last a way out of my misguided, safe-haven major...*See ya later English Fucking Lit!* No more of your Elizabethan pap ribaldry, Renaissance smegma, Enlightenment philosodoodoo, rancid Victorian pith, Early 20th Century American pig fucking or rape repeated to death and blandalized by Black American women writers. Screw it all. Fuck Chaucer. Fuck Fitzgerald and Hemingway. Fuck Hardy. I bet I wouldn't have minded fucking Mary Shelley, but fuck Hobbes, up yours Toni Morrison, Yeats, Ben Johnson and above all fuck you William Shakespeare. Jesus Christ, what on earth are we still doing reading that shit? Worse still, why are we trying to dissect the same crates of stale words over and over again? Sonnets and plays; zipadee fucking doodah. Is there nothing else to teach or read? Didn't anybody else, aforementioned aside, pen some stuff since then? My Bard-slander failed with every cute English major I chose to cozy up to. *Oh, but he's still so relevant...his themes are so timeless.*

Goddammit, everybody who has ever written anything is just as relevant and all themes are timeless because the core spirit of humanity never changes. Mankind is corrupt, fairy tales are charming fillers for autumn entertainment, men and women go at each other's throats for love, people will always be shadowed by their misdeeds and if you throw some salacious innuendos into the dialog your audience will pay attention for another fifteen minutes. So they dress Macbeth in Armani suits or *Waffen* jack boots, set the story in the Forties or Nineties or One Million BC but use the exact same five hundred year-tired dialog. Isn't that something? Mmmmmmmmmmphh, fuck! I blame Hollywood and all its dipshit actors with the cult conviction that if they can pull off Shakespeare with a convincing British accent they'll have achieved perfection in their craft. Tinseltown can't grasp that the best drama comes from Irish and Black Americans, or from Russia, and each year that it has trouble whipping up one more Holocaust tear-jerking uplifter it's going to dump some Shakespeare into the cineplexes and validate all those tread-worn college curriculums. Since I'm no longer watching it's goodbye to all you turtlenecked, cardiganned, brown-shoed jizzlobbing professional lit wangs. Shitheels all with your fucking Frisco bathhouse mustaches and smarmy, sour, revomited themes on Herman Fucking Melville. Adios, you sniveling witches with hemp-fed organic yeast infections that learned me right into hating Edgar Allan Poe. Go to hell, please. I should have looked harder at the catalogs and found courses that read Miller or even Chester Himes just for the thrills. Or gone Spanish, though I probably would have gotten stuck with the pith and drudge of Gabriel Garcia Marquez or Carlos Fuentes instead of the filigreed erections of Jose Lezama Lima. Nice, lazy eloquence is what instructors prefer to teach. Repetitive discourses from daffodil beds rather than guided tours through cataclysmic orgies or minefields under hailstorms. It helped to run out of money and leave college, as it allowed me to wander cheap bookstores and discover the kaleidoscopic vivisections of Reinaldo Arenas. Swimming through the hallucinogenic rhapsodies of that Cuban has kind of spoiled me on fiction. It's made book hunting disappointing since, but even second tears through *Otra Vez El Mar* and *El Asalto* still incite ecstasy in reading. So once again, to organized reading: Fuck off, please; it's time to dig.

A couple of years later to the now in East Africa, where hominid paleontology first began to explode, I felt born again. The famous bone books and tales of "heart stopping" hominid hunts were back home in boxes. I was out there in the heat loving the burning air and praying for record temperatures. I scanned the earth for blue, black, green, and brown pieces of mineralized bone with my jaw ajar ready to grin up stupid the moment I came across a piece of monkey tooth. But behind the slappy enthusiasm I had to keep a sobered awareness of all that was around me in the fossil fields. The understanding of something that's almost human doesn't emanate solely from its fossil; it comes with a grasp of what lies in the rubble surrounding it. Clues to what it ate, how it moved, what chased it and who it died with were scattered in the gravels all around it. My face was calloused from grazing in the dirt; the morphological detail of just about any old thing absorbed me instantly. A prospecting group lost me one morning as I dawdled over some fat fossils we'd passed. Broken chunks of an ancient elephant's femur and tibia. Not only were they huge, but the realization that they were becoming exposed after two millions years of burial was simply hypnotic.

Area 130 of the Karari is no place to get separated from the people who know the landscape. Being lost amid miles of waterless rock is only good for abbreviating your life story but I might never get another opportunity to die alone among gravel hummocks. Hills just high enough to block easy views of the horizon and most just low enough to look the same as all the rest. *Area 104* happens to be worse as a rocky labyrinth, and there another small fossil party left me picking at a huge *suid* jaw jutting face-high from an exposure. Somebody else could play with the hominoid teeth that day. I couldn't toss away chances to know everything while they were raining in my lap. The rest of the group must have shared that view as nobody came back to look for me. After quite a bit of time scraping, dusting and talking to the fossil I had to scramble to the top of my pig's hill and listen for voices. That failed as the group's chatter echoed all around me. So I just lit up cigarettes, played with the hilltop fish teeth and waited for heads to bob through the gullies. A couple of hours later and we were united once more.

Chances...were raining in my lap. Jesus, sappy prose still burps up from a squirrely mindset which began in the days when I first tried to write. Lots of 19th Century literature under the belt of an unguided teen. It took disenchantment with BU's English program and its admiration for doilied turds to make me quit thinking in English and start looking for better stuff to read. Still need to fully exorcise the inclination towards crap poeticizing in my scribbles.

The field school and the trips up to and back from the Koobi Fora spit...Crikey that was some torture. Short of being Palestinian in an Israeli jailhouse, one might never expect to be less comfortable again in life (unless one took a matatu to the Hebron clink). There's no pavement for half the journey's length and it's often hard to tell if the trucks are actually on any kind of road. Sometimes you can tell for sure that you're rolling on the edge of a steep escarpment. A hundred meter drop off, into rocks and trees, is hard to miss when it's barely feet from the lorry's tires and you're seated cliffside in the open air on a seatbelt-free plywood bench. Orthopedically luxuriant rides are out of the question as even the most powerful lorry shock-absorbers, anointed by God himself, would be slaughtered less than two hours past the end of the asphalt at Rumuruti but the roadtrips and spinal misalignment was electrifying. Why the hell would anyone pass on feeling life's bumps just to wither in armchairs, feigning excitement over a pompous and dull prick, like Seamus Heaney, whose bold new translation just sucked all the action, gore and *poetry* out of *Beowulf?* Damn, those hot Shakespeare loving chicks must have scarred me deep...

Give me Grevy's zebras, damp Nyahururu, hot rocks at Jarigole, and so forth. Burn the fucking classics and bring me back to the moment I first saw elephants in the Maralal suburbs. Ten of them spread in a line among the low trees, lumbering along and flapping their ears, unnerving for their numbers, sizes and proximity to our convoy. It was also a bit dream-like in that I heard all the excited whispers from out group but no sound at all seemed to penetrate an invisible barrier about twenty feet from our trucks. Not a crunch or rustle from beneath the massive feet of the pachyderms. How the hell will I ever recapture that? Not many books can offer you a story and at the same time put its dirt under your fingernails and warp its sounds through your ears.

And with that the story ends. There will always be more detail to fill in as my head will be stuck in Kenya for years to come. But as plane entered New England airspace it was time to fill out my Customs questionnaire and think about how quickly I'll adjust back to life without tents. I'm thinking a trip to Dunkies for a barrel of iced coffee then a swing by Taco Bell for a dozen hard shells. That'll be a fine start. Maybe I'll run over to the clubs in the Alley the night after tomorrow and see if this *man-back-from-the-wild* look gets me anywhere with women. Or at least with the woman who manages the club office - she liked me quite well a little scruffy the night before I left the states. If not, it'll be a shave and some benzoyl peroxide then off to Wordsworth's to ask the little red-haired girl if there's anything I need to read.

Hatima

Glossary of Terms

Acheulean – Stone tool industry named for prehistoric site at St. Acheul, France. A wicked long running tradition (in the ballpark of a million years) Acheulean tools are generally associated with *Homo erectus*.

Activity Facies – A level in an archaeological excavation which shows evidence of human, well, activity. Fire pits, the detritus from stone tool production, processed animal parts, bongs, etc.

Aharyaraga – *"Love born from habit, affection produced by long cohabitation"* The field school had a collection of books dumped by departing students. I found a copy of the Kama Sutra. It had no pictures so it was far less funny than I'd always heard.

Base Pair – The "rungs" on the DNA "ladder", base pairs are the molecular building blocks of DNA where the chemicals *adenine*, *thymine*, *cytosine*, and *guanine* are joined in pairs by weak hydrogen bonds. In DNA adenine always pairs with thymine and cytosine with guanine. In RNA thymine is replaced by *uracil* to bond with adenine.

Biface – A stone tool which has been chipped or flaked on two sides to produce a sharper edge. *Trifaces*, *quadrifaces*, etc. are evidence of extraterrestrial intervention. As such they are not mentioned in the literature as the government confiscates all *polyfaces* to New Mexico so the aliens can repair their star cruisers.

Bioclastic – rocks formed with an organic component. Limestones, formed by accumulation of the carbonate remains of marine life, or sandstones loaded with clam shells are common bioclasts. Wee-wee mudstones from Paleolithic toilets are the coolest bioclasts, although none have yet been identified.

Biostratigraphy – An ordering of fossil assemblages in space and time. It can be used to create relative time scales. Geologic sediments can be indirectly dated based on occurrences of fossils of known ages or fossils can be placed in a chronology according to morphological features relative to other fossils which have securely dated. Or one always hopes.

BP – "Before Present". Also written as "**bp**", it replaces **B.C.** as a dandy way to avoid pissing off the heathens.

Bovid – a member of the family which includes cows, antelopes, my ex-fiancée's mother and sheep. Ruminants with four-chambered stomachs, the bovidae are four-toed ungulates (walking on the hooved central pair of each foot) with permanent hollow horns attached to bony protrusions.

Burin – A chisel-like tool used to shape other stuff into other things. Like using a stone burin to make an antler burin for making bone burins for cleaning fingernails.

Bwana – (*KiSwahili*) Man, Sir, Mr., *El Capitán* and the like.

Cercopithecine – "tailed ape", refers to members of the Cercopithecoidae, or Old World monkeys having origins in Africa and Asia.

Chai – Just the word for "tea" in Arabic. Or Urdu or Hindi or possibly Farsi. Definitely used in Kiswahili. Doesn't necessarily mean a fashionably spiced & overpriced beverage marketed by coffee house cornholers, although one can score a fine *masala chai* from any of the filthy little Indian slop chutes in Nairobi.

Changaa – (*KiSwahili*) moonshine.

Chapati – Indian origin. Unleavened flatbread made from whole wheat flour, cooked on a skillet or something hot and flat which doesn't include baking. Greasy, crispy, chewy, awesome.

Dassanetch – One of Kenya's northern-most tribes, with origins in Ethiopia.

Dawa – "Medicine". Also the name of Kenya's most famous cocktail, and who can argue the difference?

Dimorphic – Having two distinct forms or structures. We're generally concerned with sexual dimorphism here – not so much in the obvious differences of the dirty parts, rather hominoid species which show pronounced size variation between females and males.

Equid – A member of the horse family, Equidae - zebras, horses, donkeys and extinct relatives. Or anything that reminds you of a horse. Like Sarah Jessica Parker.

Gabbra – Nomadic herders of Northern Kenya & Ethiopia. They don't have smile muscles and carry semi-automatic weapons.

Gene – a sequence of DNA bases which code for a particular protein via translation by RNA. Molecules which can make you swim faster than Shamu or turn you uglier than hair on an ice cream cone.

Gerenuk – *Litocranius walleri*. A slender antelope with long legs and long neck. They sport somewhat cartoonish ears making the head look like a boomerang on a chopstick. The bastard spawn of giraffes and greyhounds, I guess you just gotta see one.

Great Rift Valley – A geologic feature which runs from Syria (in Asia) to Mozambique (in southern Africa). A product of sinking and tearing along tectonic plates it is particularly spectacular in East Africa.

Hand Axe – A large, flaked biface characteristic of the Acheulean industry. Probably the multi-tool of the Paleolithic Age it could have been used for digging, breaking apart animal carcasses, writing and calculus.

Harambee - Kenya's motto. Means "pulling all together at once".

Hatima - End

Hominids – Let's start the confusion! These are living or extinct creatures of the family *Hominidae* which includes *Homo*, *Australopithecus*, *Ardipithecus*, *Paranthropus*, and probably *Sahelenthropus, Kenyanthropus and Orrorin*. Essentially, we're speaking upright hominoids here, although uprightyness might go way back before these varmints.

Hominin – Oh boy. We used to call 'em *hominids* but now people are thinking people and apes are so closely related that they have to stress that by coming up with some extra confusing **taxons**. The Hominoidae family got busted up by kicking out the Orangutans into the unpopular *Ponginae* subfamily. They were redheaded stepchildren anyway. So the *Hominidae* (humans and ancestors) became the *Homininae* (same thing but chimps and gorillas are now on board) which was further split into the **tribes** *Panini* (chimps and sandwiches), *Gorillini* (gorillas and associated pastas) and the *Hominini* which are the same thing as hominids. You still with me?

No? Well, for the purposes of almost-expedient reading I've stuck largely with the convention of referring to the bipedal apes (Australopithecines, Paranthropines, Homos) as **hominids** which was what we were calling them in 1994.

Hominoids –Members of the *Hominoidae*, a *superfamily* which includes hominids and apes.

Homo ergaster – A species name used by some paleoanths when referring to certain fossils of early African Homo erectus. There is some measure of exclusionism to the name, suggesting that *ergaster* is a more likely direct ancestor of Homo sapiens than the rest of the *Homo erectus* species. You've got researchers kind of saying, "These fossils may look just like your *erectus* crap, but ours are way better – up yours!" The name means "Working Man"

Homo georgicus – Recently suggested name for the hominid fossils from Dmanisi, Georgia (Eastern Europe). Initially thought to be early *H. erectus*, these comrades seem primitive enough to warrant a new name and evolutionary placement between *H. habilis* and *H. erectus*.

Homo habilis – "Handy Man". The more you look into it, the more you begin to think *habilis* isn't all that distinct a species. Some of the fossils look like *Australopithecus africanus*, though slightly less apey, and some look like *H. erectus*, only smaller and somewhat more primitive. And still others look like mashed up skulls of little use, isolated elbows, stray chunks of jaws or scattered teeth.

International Omo Expedition – (1967 – 1976) A joint French-American-Kenyan project for exploring the southern Omo River and Lake Turkana basin in Ethiopia. The Kenyan Leakey team found some hominid jaws around Lake Turkana and split from the IOE to form the Koobi Fora Research Project in

1968. Ever since then fossils from Ethiopia and Kenya have had no relationship whatsoever…

Johanson, Don – Famous as a discoverer of the *Australopithecus afarensis* fossil, "Lucy", and for desecrating tribal burial grounds in Ethiopia. Believe it or not, swaggering loudmouths of his type are beneficial to the field, helping to maintain the public's interest in human origins.

Jumanne – (KiSwahili) Tuesday. I don't know what the other six days are called.

^{40}**K/**^{40}**Ar** – **Potassium / Argon** - A dating method for establishing the age of rocks based on the decay of a radioactive Potassium isotope into Argon.

KANU – Kenya African National Union. Ruling political party in Kenya from independence in 1963 through 2002. Other parties have always been welcome in the government as long as they keep their traps shut and always vote KANU.

Karai – a basin or big bowl. We used them to wash stuff and to sift through dirt and for battering French Toast.

Khalarata – (Sanskrit) "degrading love, to satiate one's basest instincts" I really thought the *Kama Sutra* was supposed to be a picture book. See *Aharyaraga.*

Koobi Fora – "place of the *Commiphora* tree" in the *Gabbra* language

Lacustrine – pertaining to lakes, mainly referring to lake sediments in this book.

Laga - A seasonal river. Or "sand river" as we call them since they spend more time as sand than anything else. Not sure if it's a Swahili term, from a language of a northern Kenyan tribe or just something the school made up.

Lake Rudolph – Former, colonial, name of Lake Turkana. It was named for Crown Prince Rudolph of Austria by its European "discoverer" Count Samuel Teleki at the end of the 19th Century. It's the world's biggest alkaline lake as well as the largest desert lake. It has some nice beaches but no snack bars.

Lucy – Possibly the most famous hominid, she was an *Australopithecus afarensis* discovered in 1974 by Donald Johanson and Tom Gray at Hadar in Ethiopia. The fossil has been dated to about 3.2 Myr and her 40% complete skeleton (including leg and pelvis parts) show clear evidence of an upright posture.

Myr– Million years (Before Present). Also **My** and **Mya** (the "a" for "ago")

Maa – Language of the Maasai and Samburu

Malaya – One heck of a generously accommodating woman....

Mandazi – Beignet, doughboy, perhaps even a hush puppy. A fried wedge or lump of dough made from cornmeal and/or flour.

Matako - bum

Matiti – breasts. Also a pair of small hills which serve as landmarks astride the final stretch of road to Koobi Fora

Matofali – bricks (sing. *Tofali*)

Microstratigraphy – Examination of the fine details of a sedimentary section – laminating layers of silt or sand, small fossil-bearing strata, snail poop and so forth.

Miraa – an East African plant, *Catha edulis*, whose leaves and stems are chewed as a stimulant. Also known as *qat* or *khat* in and probably a bunch of other terms which sound cool and funny to Kenyan teenagers

Mke (Kiswahili) – wife, woman

Mnyvo – (Kiswahili) booze

Moran – (*Maa* language) "Warrior"

Mzee – (KiSwahili) man, old fart, respected male, parent, ancestor.

Mzoga - carcass

Mzungu – (KiSwahili) white person; pl. **wazungu**

KNM – Kenya National Museums. Fossils discovered in the Lake Turkana region recieve museum "ascension" numbers such as *KNM-ER 1813* (ER for East Rudolf, the lake's former name)

or *KNM-WT 15000* (WT – West Turkana, for fossils found on the west side of the lake after it became Lake Turkana in 1975)

Ni Sawa Hasa – (Kiswahili) Slogan from Kenya's *Sportsman* cigarettes. It means "It is so Good". Sort of a double entendre, especially if one has seen the ads, suggesting that they're not only enjoyable but that they are also good for you. Just for chuckles I ran the phrase through an online Swahili translator and got this gem instead: "I am exactly a eunuch"

Nyama Choma – (KiSwahili) Grilled or roasted meat. While absolutely awesome on the frontier, never ever eat Nyama Choma in Nairobi.

Obligate Drinker – requiring a regular supply of water. They need to drink frequently whereas other animals can maintain hydration via the moisture in their food.

Packie – (coll. Rhode Island) a *likka staw...*

Panga – (KiSwahili) machete

Pyroclastic – refers to the hot sediment barf of volcanoes – pumice, ash, bits of rock.

Rhizolith – fossilized impression of a plant root

S.A.S.E. – *Standard African Site Enumeration* grid system for organizing archaeological sites. Ex. GbJj1. Developed by Dr. Charles Nelson.

Sawa – (KiSwahili) "so", "yes", "the same", "ok"

Shamba – (KiSwahili) farm

Stringer, Chris – British paleontologist who's hell bent on proving that Neandertals have no ancestral relationship to us whatsoever. Archenemy of **Milford Wolpoff**.

Stromatolite – A fossil formed by the mounding of successive layers of microbial mats and trapped sediments.

Sukumu Wiki – Literally "push the week", it's stewed dish of all the scraps of vegetables and or meats remaining from previous meals. Kinda like a Kenyan minestrone. Travelers are more likely to encounter it as a side in eateries where it will be a simpler dish of seasoned, stewed greens such as collards.

Telson – the terminal segment of an arthropod; if I used it somewhere I probably meant a scorpion's stinger.

Tephra – the pyroclastic material blasted out of a volcano. Ash, Scoria, Cinders, Pumices and the like.

Tribe – Apart from the common usage, in biology a *tribe* is a subdivision of Family or Subfamily in phylogenic nomenclature. Like so – **Kingdom**, *Animalia*; **Phylum**, *Chordata*; **Subphylum**, *Vertebrata*; **Class**, *Mammalia*; **Order**, *Artiodactyla*; **Family**, *Bovidae*; **Tribe**, *Bovini* (cows and close cow cousins)

Tuff – A sedimentary rock layer formed by pyroclastic materials (*tephra*) *ejected* from a volcano, as opposed to the dense, hard igneous rocks formed by magma (lava) flows.

Ugali – Inarguably undelicious cornmeal paste that's a staple in Kenyan diets. It's just bland as all get out, since nobody seems to ever add any salt to it.

Walker, Alan – British anatomist, paleoanthropologist, primatologist apparently held in low regard by some Kenyan field workers. While looking into the veracity of an ugly Alan Walker tale, as told to me by a Kenyan friend, one researcher put it like so, *"Well...Alan is not a very nice person"*

Wolpoff, Milford – A leading proponent of the Multiregional hypothesis of human evolution. Also known as the Regional Continuity Model it holds that beginning with *Homo erectus* departing from Africa modern humanity developed across Eurasia and Africa. Regional characteristics of modern populations appeared and *Homo sapiens* evolved *throughout* the Old World via gene flow of neighboring populations. It contrasts with the *Out of Africa / African Eve* model which posits that *H. sapiens* evolved only in Africa before leaving to replace more primitive populations everywhere else. This "replacement" idea is championed by the likes of Christopher Stringer, and most British researchers who hate the idea of their genes having been mingled with more recent savages.